THE LABOR ARBITRATION PROCESS

THE LABOR ARBITRATION PROCESS

R.W. FLEMING

HD5481
.F59

80137

UNIVERSITY OF ILLINOIS PRESS URBANA 1965

To my mother,

whose warmth and courage
inspire all who know her.

Acknowledgments

I am indebted to the Walter E. Meyer Research Institute of Law, Inc., for the grant which made this volume possible. It financed released time from my teaching duties at the College of Law, University of Illinois, the full-time assistance of Leah Lee, without whose able and conscientious help the book would not have been possible, and the part-time assistance of law students, including Judy Jackson and Alice Cannon.

The analysis, judgments, and conclusions are, of course, my own responsibility.

Those of us who have grown up with the arbitration process have a special responsibility for it. In a dynamic society, we must not expect that labor arbitration will remain the same. The industrial world is changing, and the continued success of labor arbitration almost certainly depends on its ability to respond to new needs. This book represents the effort of one academician, with considerable practical experience, to think out some of the problems of the time.

OCTOBER, 1965   R. W. *Fleming*

Contents

Chapter 1

HISTORY AND GROWTH

From the vantage point of 1964 the American experience with labor arbitration seems to be clearly divisible into three periods. The first extends from 1865, when the iron puddlers of Pittsburgh arbitrated wages in the first recorded arbitration proceeding,[1] to the outset of World War II in 1941; the second from 1941 to the *Lincoln Mills* decision in 1957;[2] and the third from *Lincoln Mills* to the present. There are great differences in these periods — indeed, the word "arbitration" even lacks a common meaning. But there are also great similarities, and the arbitration machinery of today has deep roots in the past. Common themes run throughout all three periods, e.g., outside pressure for arbitration in the "emergency" situations, and private efforts to develop a continuing mechanism for settling day-to-day disputes. Related philosophical and practical differences, such as whether arbitration is to be adjudicatory or mediatory in nature, likewise show up in every period. Beyond these generalities, true perspective comes only with a more detailed examination of each of the periods.

THE PERIOD 1865 TO 1941

"Arbitration," in the early discussions, meant what we would now call "negotiation" rather than a third-party decision-making process. This is not surprising when one recalls that it was 1886 before the first enduring national labor federation (the American Federation of Labor) was formed, and it was 1935 before companies were legally required to recognize unions for purposes of collective bargaining. Initially, it was a struggle to persuade companies even to recognize unions, let alone enter into detailed trade agreements involving impartial arbitration in the decision-making sense.

The first mention of arbitration in American labor history seems to date to a clause in the constitution of the Journeymen Cabinet-Makers of Philadelphia in 1829.[3] The earliest recorded arbitration, as men-

---

[1] *Results of Arbitration Cases Involving Wages and Hours, 1865 to 1929*, 29 Mo. LABOR REV. 14, 16 (1929).

[2] Textile Workers Union v. Lincoln Mills, 353 U.S. 448 (1957).

[3] WITTE, HISTORICAL SURVEY OF LABOR ARBITRATION 5 (1952). Examples of nineteenth-century beginnings of arbitration not included in this account may be found in *Id*. at 3–16.

tioned above, involved the iron puddlers of Pittsburgh in 1865. Clearly a collective agreement was arrived at through negotiations between conference committees representing the parties, without any outside assistance. Other arbitrations were reported in the early 1870's in the Pittsburgh iron trade, the boot and shoe industry in Massachusetts, and in the anthracite coal fields. Boards of arbitration were often modeled after the bipartite British example and only occasionally did the agreement provide for utilization of an outsider in the event the parties could not agree. Attention was generally focused on wage rates.[4]

The first known case in which an outside umpire was employed took place in 1871. The Committee of the Anthracite Board of Trade and the Committee of the Workingmen's Benevolent Association agreed to settle their disputes over "questions on interference with the works, and discharging men for their connection with the Workingmen's Benevolent Association" by referring the matter to Judge William Elwell of Bloomsburg, Pennsylvania.[5] The result was apparently satisfactory, but in 1874, when the Ohio coal operators and the coal miners' union submitted their dispute to another judge for decision, one company refused to accept the result and a strike occurred throughout the valley. Ultimately, the operators all conformed to the desires of the dissenting company rather than to the arbitrator's award.[6]

As a general proposition, arbitration prior to the turn of the century, and even during the early 1900's, was thought of as a substitute for the strike in bringing about agreement over basic issues like wages. Norman J. Ware has said of this period: "The experience of the Crispins [International Grand Lodge of the Knights of St. Crispin] was common to the trade unions of the sixties and especially of the depressed seventies, and the idea that arbitration should replace strikes was general. The National Labor Union and the Industrial Congress took the same position. It was, in fact, almost a truism of the period that strikes were dangerous and ineffective, did more harm than good, and should be supplanted by peaceful and intelligent methods for the settlement of industrial disputes." [7]

Despite labor's interest during this period, arbitration schemes of-

---

[4] *Ibid.*
[5] *Ibid.*
[6] *Id.* at 11–12. A somewhat differing account appears in WARE, THE LABOR MOVEMENT IN THE UNITED STATES, 1860–1895 33 (1929).
[7] *Id.* at 19–20.

ten met with failure and disappointment. A Philadelphia agreement designed to make strikes and lockouts unnecessary failed in 1885 because of the occurrence of illegal strikes.[8] Jay Gould refused to submit the Southwestern Railroad dispute of 1886 to arbitration.[9] In other instances, established arbitration boards stopped functioning as a result of decisions which were unsatisfactory to the parties.[10] On the other hand, a streetcar strike was avoided in Detroit in 1891 by an agreement to arbitrate. The leader of the Detroit union, W. D. Mahon, later served as president of the Amalgamated Association of Street Railway Employees for many years, during which time a majority of all agreements entered into by the union contained agreements to arbitrate.[11]

Interest in arbitration was furthered in the 1890's through the work of the Congress of Industrial Conciliation and Arbitration, which was composed of a group of leaders from industry, labor, and government who were interested in promoting industrial harmony.[12] Their initial conference was held in Chicago in 1894, and a second meeting took place in 1901. The proceedings of the conference were published and distributed widely.

Along with these private efforts came pressure on state legislatures to establish boards of arbitration. By 1901 seventeen states had enacted such laws. Their function was primarily one of mediation rather than arbitration as we now know it.[13]

In 1902 Theodore Roosevelt forced the parties to arbitrate the five-month-old anthracite strike.[14] A United States Strike Commission, appointed by the President, handed down its award in March of 1903. Among other things, it called for the establishment of a Board of Conciliation to resolve disputes that arose between the operators and miners over application of the Commission's award or which grew

---

[8] *Id.* at 203.

[9] *Id.* at 145–48.

[10] WITTE, *op. cit. supra* note 3, at 14.

[11] Mahon, according to 4 ARB. J. (n.s.) 267 (1949). This source quotes him as having said, "strikes were never intended to settle anything except which side is the strongest. Arbitration should always be among the chief goals of unionism. There isn't a labor dispute that cannot be settled by arbitration."

[12] *Id.* at 15–16.

[13] *Id.* at 7–8. Modern state laws also make provision for arbitration. All but four states had some provision in their laws for arbitration of labor disputes in 1943. *Id.* at 59, citing KALTENBORN, GOVERNMENTAL ADJUSTMENT OF LABOR DISPUTES 171–201 (1943).

[14] Fisher, *Anthracite*, in HOW COLLECTIVE BARGAINING WORKS 280, 291 (Millis ed. 1942).

in any way out of the relations between employer and employee. Disputes which could not be resolved by a majority vote of the six-man bipartite Board were to be submitted to an impartial umpire for final and binding decision. As modified, an industry-wide arbitration system has continued since that time.

The coal operators rejected at the outset the Commission's idea that the Board should serve as an industry-wide bargaining agency respecting new agreements. The authority of the Board has been restricted to interpretation of the industry-wide agreement and local agreements and preservation of the established practices at each colliery. Since accord within the Board has usually not been possible, its function is to hold hearings, collect evidence, and submit the dispute to the umpire.[15] He does not attend the hearings, does not live in the anthracite region, and receives the testimony and briefs by mail. He is expected to fulfill an exclusively judicial function and to give as literal an interpretation of the agreement as possible. He may, however, render substantive decisions where the terms of the contract are vague, ambiguous, or conflicting. Such decisions are important for they become binding precedents. Thus, anthracite experience with grievance arbitration of a strictly adjudicatory nature has been sufficiently satisfactory to keep it going although the idea was originally imposed by outside forces.

Another of the "critical" industries, the railroads, in the last quarter of the nineteenth century felt public pressure for the establishment of arbitration machinery. The great railway strikes of the 1870's and 1880's brought about the introduction into Congress of bills providing for conciliation and arbitration. The first law, the Arbitration Act of 1888, was ineffective,[16] and was replaced by the Erdman Act in 1898. This too worked badly during the early years because the carriers were opposed to intervention. By 1906, however, the unions had grown stronger and in the period 1906 to 1913 sixty-one controversies were settled, six by arbitration, without a single important strike over operation of the trains.[17]

In 1913 the Newlands Act, creating a Board of Mediation and Conciliation with four full-time members, was passed when a deadlock developed over the composition of arbitration boards under the Erdman Act. This Board worked successfully until 1916, when the

---

[15] *Id.* at 710–12.
[16] MILLIS & MONTGOMERY, ORGANIZED LABOR 730–31 (1945).
[17] *Id.* at 731.

employees, who were dissatisfied with some previous awards, refused to submit their demands for an eight-hour day to arbitration. A nationwide strike was averted only by passage of the Adamson Act two days before the strike was to take place.[18]

Congress came close to passing a compulsory arbitration law for the railroads in 1920, but finally settled for decisions which were not enforceable.[19] In 1926 further changes were made, including the establishment of a five-man Board of Mediation similar to the one provided under the terms of the Newlands Act. A distinction was made between disputes arising out of interpretation and application of the agreement and those having to do with changes in rates of pay, rules, or working conditions. For a time this act worked rather well, but the Depression of the 1930's brought about an accumulation of unsettled disputes and grievances which caused further amendments in 1934.[20] As amended in 1934, the Railway Labor Act has remained substantially the same to the present time.

While the coal and railroad industries were feeling governmental pressure to devise a mechanism for avoiding strikes, certain of the less critical industries, like newspapers and apparel, were experimenting with private plans.

The advantages of arbitration in the newspaper business were seen as early as 1847.[21] In 1901 the adoption of the typesetting machine created great anxiety among printers who feared permanent job displacement. Many strikes and lockouts followed. Progressive publishers realized that they had to have some sort of safeguard against strikes, boycotts, and other interferences with publication if their businesses were to prosper. A history of the period reports:

. . . stoppages not only were irritating but involved an irreparable loss in money and prestige. A newspaper is unlike most other commodities. It has to be produced daily and sold daily, or it is worthless. Moreover, a newspaper plant was no longer a small, inexpensive enterprise, but a business in which thousands or hundred of thousands of dollars were invested. Consequently it was to the interest of both publisher and employee to effect some sort of an agreement which would guarantee the proprietor against strikes and boycotts on the one hand and protect printers against lockouts and sudden reductions in pay on the other. Thus in 1899 and 1900 we find various branches of the American Newspaper Publishers' Association dis-

---

[18] *Id.* at 732–34.
[19] *Id.* at 734–35.
[20] *Id.* at 738–40.
[21] MacKinnon, *Arbitration in the Newspaper Business*, 3 ARB. J. 323 (1939).

cussing the practicability of local and national arbitration, with just such a purpose in view.[22]

A tentative agreement between the publishers and the Typographical Union was reached in 1901 under which all disputes affecting wage scales would be submitted to an arbitration board consisting of one representative of each contending party with a third impartial member to be chosen by the other two.[23] At the same time the parties set about establishing a permanent arbitration mechanism. A local board, patterned on the above lines, was set up to decide all disputes within its jurisdiction. If the judgment rendered was unsatisfactory, an appeal could be taken to the national board, consisting of the labor commissioner of the publishers and the president of the international union. If they failed to agree, a disinterested person was to be selected to preside, and a majority decision would be binding on both sides.[24]

The success of the above plan caused it to spread throughout the printing industry. An interesting sidelight is that the parties rejected the idea of one or more full-time chairmen of the arbitration boards because of a desire to keep the costs as low as possible and also to obtain more flexibility. On this score, the chairman of the Special Standing Committee of the American Newspaper Publishers' Association said, "it has appeared that the fairest decisions could be rendered by attempting to utilize as chairmen residents of the locality where the arbitrating parties reside, in order to give proper weights to the purely local considerations of the dispute."[25] It will be remembered that this conclusion is exactly the opposite from the one reached by the parties to the anthracite agreement, who wished their umpire to be entirely disassociated from the local scene.

It was the apparel industries — clothing, millinery, hosiery, etc. — which proved to be the great testing laboratory for private labor arbitration. Clothing, which led the way, is an industry which is subject to constant change and accompanying turmoil. Frequent style changes, a piecework system of payment, the widespread prevalence of subcontracting, and the problem of runaway shops bespeak the need for some stabilizing mechanism. In so volatile an industry,

---

[22] Weiss, *History of Arbitration in American Newspaper Publishing Industry,* 17 Mo. LABOR REV. 15–16 (1923).
[23] *Id.* at 17–18.
[24] *Id.* at 19.
[25] MacKinnon, *supra* note 21, at 328.

moreover, a remote, detached system of adjudication would hardly do. The critical time factor and the reliance on piecework production place a premium on expeditious and harmonious settlement of differences.

Thus, when 50,000 workers in the New York cloak and suit industry struck in 1910, Louis D. Brandeis was the principal architect of a protocol of peace which provided for a permanent machinery for conciliation and arbitration.[26] Disputes which could not be settled by union-management shop committees were to go to a Board of Grievances composed of five members from each side. If a settlement could not be reached in the Board of Grievances the matter had to be taken to a Board of Arbitration before a strike or lockout could be called. The Board of Arbitration consisted of three members, one representative of each of the parties and a neutral who served without pay. The decision of the Board of Arbitration was to be final, and Brandeis was to serve as chairman of the Board.

The tension which followed the 1910 strike was so great that both parties found it difficult to abjure their self-interests in favor of the peaceful objectives of the Protocol. Since Brandeis felt that success depended primarily on conciliation and mediation, he resisted calling a meeting of the Board of Arbitration and tried to encourage settlements at the steward and Board of Grievance levels. Grievances nevertheless continued to accumulate and Brandeis finally had to call a meeting of the Board of Arbitration in March of 1911. One result of the meeting of 1911 was a strengthening of the Board of Grievances.[27] This had the effect of encouraging negotiated settlements, contrary to what was probably the original intent of the workers who participated in the signing of the Protocol. A strong faction in the union continued to favor outright arbitration and in 1914 the Protocol was converted to that end. The new committee consisted of two representatives of the employers, two of the union, and an outside full-time impartial chairman.[28] Even this change was not sufficient to keep the Protocol alive and a massive lockout-strike in the spring of 1916 brought it to an end.

Before its collapse, however, the Protocol idea was copied in other

---

[26] Signed by the International Ladies' Garment Workers Union and the New York Cloak and Suit Manufacturers Association. SLICHTER, HEALY, & LIVERNASH, THE IMPACT OF COLLECTIVE BARGAINING ON MANAGEMENT 744 (1960).

[27] MASON, BRANDEIS, A FREE MAN'S LIFE 301-2 (1946).

[28] Id. at 87.

branches of the clothing industry in Chicago, New York, Boston, and Philadelphia. In most of these cases the machinery collapsed after a few years,[29] but the Protocol of Peace left an enduring mark on much of American industry. Benjamin Stolberg summarized its effect this way: "In spite of its failure at the time, the Protocol of Peace was one of the most important charters in American industrial relations. It laid the groundwork for the present vast and effective system of arbitration in all the needle trades, covering over 700,000 workers. Its ideological influence on American industry as a whole proved to be immense. In many ways it foreshadowed such contemporary institutions as the National Labor Relations Board, the Railway Mediation Board and even the War Labor Board of both World Wars." [30]

After World War I the impartial machinery was revived in the New York cloak and suit industry and ultimately in the balance of the apparel industry.[31] Meanwhile, the Hart, Schaffner & Marx agreement, signed in Chicago in 1911, proved to be both successful and enduring. It too followed a long and bitter strike, and was modeled after the Protocol of Peace in New York, though with some quite different provisions.[32] An arbitration committee of three was to hand down binding decisions on grievances. Clarence Darrow was the original union representative and Carl Meyer was chosen by the employer. Unable to agree on a third member, they functioned for some time as a board of two. By 1912 they were so swamped with problems that an intervening Trade Board was established, with appeal permitted to the Board of Arbitration. The Trade Board delegated the first handling of cases to deputies. The plan worked very well. Eighty-four per cent of the cases were settled by the deputies, 15 per cent by the Trade Board, and only 1 per cent had to be brought to the Board of Arbitration.[33]

Much of the success of the Hart, Schaffner & Marx system has been attributed to Sidney Hillman, then a rising young labor leader, and to some of the great chairmen who were finally selected to head

---

[29] WITTE, *op. cit. supra* note 3, at 24.

[30] STOLBERG, TAILOR'S PROGRESS 91 (1944).

[31] In most of the other cases mentioned in the text accompanying note 29 new arbitration machinery was created after some lapse. Witte, *op. cit. supra* note 3, at 24–25.

[32] JOSEPHSON, SIDNEY HILLMAN, STATESMAN OF AMERICAN LABOR 62 (1952).

[33] SEIDMAN, THE NEEDLE TRADES 256 (1942).

the Board of Arbitration.[34] It was Hillman who, as he sponsored similar plans in other areas of the country, stressed the need for an impartial chairman familiar with the industry.[35] And it was William M. Leiserson, one of the towering figures in American labor-management history, who proved to be one of the great chairmen in the developmental days. Dr. Leiserson endeavored to bring about settlements by mediation. Whenever it was possible, he referred the case back to the parties for further discussion by a joint committee which he appointed. Even when mediation failed and Leiserson was forced to hand down a decision, he sought guidance from the parties. Usually he would clear his decision first with a small committee of union and management representatives in order to avoid implications which he might not see in making the award, but which might become troublesome precedents. He also discussed the contents of his decisions at union and management conferences in order to hammer out general acceptance of the principles he helped to form.[36]

The millinery industry followed much the same pattern as clothing. Arbitration machinery was first established in 1915 between the New York industry and the United Hatters, Cap and Millinery Workers Union. By and large it was successful, but some in the union opposed it because to work well the machinery required that the employers be as well organized as the union. This, they feared, would strengthen the manufacturers to the union's disadvantage. The agreement was thus allowed to lapse in 1923, but it was re-established in 1932.[37]

Arbitration came to the full-fashioned hosiery industry only in 1929, but its success since then is unquestioned. In the late 1920's

---

[34] JOSEPHSON, op. cit. supra note 32, at 65. In somewhat broader terms, William M. Leiserson wrote that industry is very largely indebted to Williams for "laying the foundations of this system of industrial law and developing the necessary judicial machinery." He continued that Williams' technique, which he described as being that of a court of equity rather than a court of law, must ever be an essential part of any successful system of industrial arbitration. Leiserson, Constitutional Government in American Industries, 12 AM. ECON. REV. (Supp. 1922, at 56, 65, & n. 8).

[35] Straus, Hickey-Freeman Company and the Amalgamated (CIO), in CAUSES OF INDUSTRIAL PEACE UNDER COLLECTIVE BARGAINING 121–23 (Golden & Parker eds. 1955).

[36] Id. at 124. For further discussion of Leiserson's use of mediation techniques, see Kleiler, William Morris Leiserson, IND. REL. RES. A. 98–100 (1957).

[37] ROBINSON, SPOTLIGHT ON A UNION 235–36 (1948).

unionized manufacturers were finding it more and more difficult to compete with non-union manufacturers, and union hosiery workers were having a difficult time finding and keeping jobs. In a joint meeting in the spring of 1929, unionized operators and union leaders agreed upon a system of arbitration employing a single impartial chairman.[38] Under the agreement all problems which arose during the life of the contract and which could not be settled by negotiation were to be submitted to a permanent impartial chairman for final and binding settlement.[39] The privilege of bringing a case before the impartial chairman was and is reserved to the Full-Fashioned Hosiery Manufacturers of America, Inc., and the American Federation of Hosiery Workers. The parties are thus given a greater opportunity for settlement than might otherwise be true, but they may, as we shall see in a later chapter, be faced with the problem of the right of the individual to control his own grievance.[40]

Under the hosiery agreement the impartial chairman was not given the power to change the terms of the existing agreement, nor might he change the general wage level or decide terms of new agreements. He could, however, interpret contract clauses, fix individual rates in line with established levels of wages, and determine issues which arose in the life of the contract but were not covered by its terms.[41]

From the outset the parties to the hosiery agreement rejected the anthracite model of an impersonal adjudicatory machinery in favor of an informal, friendly atmosphere which places the chairman in the role of conciliator, mediator, friend, counselor, and, only as a last resort, arbitrator.[42] Among a number of distinguished impartial umpires, the one said to have contributed most to the success of the hosiery system is Dr. George W. Taylor, who served as impartial chairman from 1931 to 1941.[43] During this period and ever afterwards, Dr. Taylor emphasized the mediation function of the impartial chairman. Moreover, since it has been customary for the chair-

---

[38] KENNEDY, EFFECTIVE LABOR ARBITRATION, THE IMPARTIAL CHAMPIONSHIP OF THE FULL-FASHIONED HOSIERY INDUSTRY 20–22 (1948).

[39] Id. at 1.

[40] Id. at 46.

[41] Id. at 34.

[42] Id. at 50–51.

[43] Id. at 27–29. Succeeding impartial chairmen have been: W. E. Simkin, 1941–1943; Thomas Kennedy, spring, 1943–December, 1943; Dr. W. R. Buckwalter, 1943–1945; G. Allan Dash, Jr., 1945–. Id. at 29–30.

man to hand down a written decision which becomes a precedent for later decisions, Dr. Taylor established many of the principles — dealing with such important subjects as management's rights, uninterrupted production, the use of property and the union's rights of protest and appeal, retroactibility, control of jobs, discharges, layoffs, and promotion — which were to guide the parties thereafter.[44]

While these private efforts to develop arbitration and conciliation machinery were taking place, there were accompanying efforts to establish governmental agencies. The work of the state legislatures has already been described, and in 1913 a United States Conciliation Service was established as a part of the Department of Labor. While the Service was basically an agency for mediation, it could suggest arbitration, and it would name or help select an arbitrator.[45]

As they typically do during periods of war, unions grew in strength, but work stoppages were regarded as against the public interest. The government's influence over labor-management affairs was increased accordingly, and the use of arbitration was encouraged. To supplement the Conciliation Service, more than a dozen new labor dispute adjustment agencies were established, the most important of which was the National War Labor Board. It had authority to intervene in any labor dispute which affected war production and which was not within the jurisdiction of a special adjustment agency.[46]

Immediately after World War I, President Wilson called a Labor-Management Conference with the idea in mind of agreeing upon a national peacetime labor policy. The first conference of labor, management, and public representatives, meeting in October, 1919, broke up without agreement over the question of labor's right to collective bargaining. A second conference of representatives only of the public reached agreement on the question of collective bargaining, but their recommendations had little effect.[47] A quarter of a century later another President would call a similar conference following World War II. It too would fail in reaching an over-all agreement, but the differences in views of labor and management

---

[44] *Id.* at 90.
[45] MILLIS & MONTGOMERY, *op. cit. supra* note 16 at 727.
[46] *Results of Arbitration Cases Involving Wages and Hours*, 1865 to 1929, 29 Mo. LABOR REV. 14, 17 (1929).
[47] MILLIS & MONTGOMERY, *op. cit. supra* note 16, at 146.

representatives, as compared with their counterparts in 1919, would be revealing. More will be said on that subject later.

While governmental efforts to achieve agreement at the national level failed, continuing progress was made in more limited private areas. Commercial, as distinguished from labor, arbitration was becoming increasingly popular in business circles. The Arbitration Society of America was formed in 1922 and the American Arbitration Association in 1926. The example of the use of arbitration in commercial affairs doubtless served to popularize the method, particularly among lawyers and businessmen.[48] The Actors' Equity Association had already been interested in arbitration for some time when the American Arbitration Association was formed. In New York, where such cases were likely to arise, court dockets were crowded and it might be years before a case would come to trial. By that time the actor and his witnesses might be scattered all over, while the manager and his witnesses and records might be readily available. This caused the union to turn to arbitration, and it asked the American Arbitration Association to handle its cases.[49]

The liaison between the AAA and Actors' Equity proved so successful that the Association was soon performing a similar service for the Dramatists' Guild, the Authors' League, and later the Screen Actors' Guild and the American Federation of Radio Artists. In the course of establishing arbitration machinery in the amusement industry, the AAA rejected the idea that arbitration could or should be combined with conciliation efforts and strove to make it a strictly adjudicatory process.[50]

A limiting factor on the growth of arbitration during this period was, of course, the relatively small size of the labor movement. Just before the 1929 disaster union membership was estimated at only about 3.4 million. This figure represented a decline of more than a million and a half since World War I, and this period was the first time that the unions had failed to gain in a time of prosperity. Also "the main concentrations of the estimated 3.4 million members of the American labor movement were found in a relatively small number of industries and areas — the anthracite mines of Pennsylvania;

---

[48] WITTE, *op. cit. supra* note 3, at 38–39.

[49] Gilmore, *Arbitration in the Entertainment Field*, 2 ARB. J. 24, 25–26 (1938). At the time of the writing of the Gilmore article, the principle of arbitration was spreading throughout the entertainment field. *Id.* at 28.

[50] *The First Year of the Voluntary Industrial Arbitration Tribunal*, 3 ARB. J. 126–27 (1939).

the clothing markets of New York, Chicago, and a few other large cities; the shoe towns of Massachusetts; the major railroad centers; and the building construction and printing industries of some of the large metropolitan areas." [51] Unionism was virtually nonexistent in the large-scale manufacturing sectors of the economy.

The passage of the Wagner Act in 1935 changed the picture greatly. The question of union recognition, about which there had always been so much dispute, was now settled (though it would be 1937 before the Supreme Court would sustain the constitutionality of the Wagner Act in the *Jones and Laughlin* case).[52] Henceforth, national policy favored collective bargaining. By 1939 union membership was estimated at over 8 million and by the end of World War II it would double.[53] Hundreds of new contracts, some of them hastily drawn, were entered into. The immediate result was to raise questions of interpretation and application and, upon becoming deadlocked, the parties often turned to arbitration.[54] Although there are no reliable estimates as to the use of arbitration prior to 1940, it is estimated that fewer than 8 to 10 per cent of the agreements in effect during the 1930's provided for arbitration as the final step in the grievance procedure.[55] By 1941 the United States Conciliation Service found such clauses in 62 per cent of the 1,200 agreements which were in its files.[56]

In response to the greatly increased demand for labor arbitration, the AAA established in 1937 its Voluntary Industrial Tribunal, which has functioned ever since. The Association maintained a panel of labor arbitrators available to the parties.[57] Rules were gradually promulgated and model arbitration clauses for inclusion in collective bargaining contracts were also recommended.

The trend toward widespread use of arbitration was further accentuated in 1937 when the giant General Motors Corporation signed an agreement with the Auto Workers Union which included in its grievance procedure as a final step the reference of disputes to an

---

[51] Derber, *Growth and Expansion*, in LABOR AND THE NEW DEAL 5 (1957).

[52] NLRB v. Jones & Laughlin Steel Co. 301 U.S. 1 (1937).

[53] *Supra* note 51, at 3.

[54] Parker, *The Industrial Arbitration Tribunal Completes Its Second Year*, 4 ARB. J. 24, 25 (1940).

[55] SLICHTER, HEALY, & LIVERNASH, *op. cit. supra* note 26, at 739.

[56] Steelman, *The Work of the U.S. Conciliation Service in Wartime Labor Disputes*, 9 LAW & CONTEMP. PROB. 461, 466 (1942).

[57] KELLOR, ARBITRATION AND THE LEGAL PROFESSION 36 (1952); KELLOR, AMERICAN ARBITRATION 85 (1948).

impartial umpire upon mutual consent of the parties.[58] Since this grievance procedure did not work well, by 1938 both the Corporation and the Union were studying ways of instituting a permanent umpire system. Speaking to GM Council members in June of 1940, Walter Reuther, then head of the General Motors Department of the union, said: "You cannot strike General Motors plants on individual grievances. One plant going down will affect the 60 other plants. You have to work out something to handle individual grievances. . . . I don't want to tie up 90,000 workers because one worker was laid off for two months. That is a case for the umpire." [59] In taking his stand, Mr. Reuther cited the experience of the Clothing Workers, and argued that "they have made more gains with an impartial umpire, more gains without a strike than any other group of workers in America." [60]

While Mr. Reuther was exhorting his colleagues to consider arbitration, the Corporation was also studying systems in other industries. The views of Charles P. Neill, formerly umpire in the anthracite industry, appear to have been influential. Discussions were also held with George W. Taylor, then the umpire in the hosiery industry, and Harry A. Millis, who occupied a similar role in the men's clothing industry.[61]

The General Motors-UAW "Office of the Umpire" was created on June 24, 1940, and has remained substantially unchanged ever since. The umpire has no power to mediate and is regarded as strictly an adjudicator.

General Motors and the UAW unquestionably pioneered in bringing arbitration to the great mass production industries. By the time their system was in operation only a short time remained before the United States would become officially embroiled in World War II — an event which would leave a profound mark upon industrial relations practices in the United States.

THE PERIOD 1941-57

Once the nation was at war, industrial disputes could no longer be tolerated. Accordingly, labor and management accepted President

---

[58] See Alexander, *Impartial Umpireships: The General Motors-UAW Experience*, in NATIONAL ACADEMY OF ARBITRATORS, ARBITRATION AND THE LAW, PROCEEDINGS OF THE 12TH ANNUAL MEETING 108 (McKelvey ed. 1959).

[59] *Id.* at 114.

[60] *Ibid.*

[61] *Id.* at 116.

Roosevelt's request for a no-strike, no-lockout agreement and a tri-partite War Labor Board was established. Executive Order 9017, which was the original source of the Board's authority, provided that the Board would assume jurisdiction of "labor disputes which might interrupt work which contributes to the effective prosecution of the war," and that it would "finally determine the dispute" through "mediation, voluntary arbitration, or arbitration under rules provided by the Board." [62] The Order did not apply to "labor disputes for which procedures for adjustment or settlement are otherwise pro-vided until those procedures have been exhausted." [63]

Throughout the war the War Labor Board vigorously supported the utilization of existing voluntary arbitration procedures and pro-moted the inclusion of arbitration in those contracts which did not already contain it.[64] Under the Stabilization Act of 1942 [65] free col-lective bargaining was limited by the requirement that the govern-ment approve wage and related matters. This Act made it impossible for the Board to give *carte blanche* approval to arbitration awards which affected wages, but the Board nevertheless strove to work out an accommodation. Writing about the War Labor Board's support for the inclusion of arbitration clauses in collective bargaining con-tracts, the Board's General Counsel said in 1945:

This widespread adoption, before the war, of arbitration clauses in griev-ance procedures demonstrates the felt need for an industrial jurisprudence adapted to the needs of modern industrial organization and practice and proves that important segments of American industry and labor have tested and found practicable this method of making collective bargaining agree-ments work. The onset of war and the establishment of the no-strike, no-lockout agreement increased the urgency of the need for these procedures. From the first, the Board urged and encouraged the voluntary inclusion of a grievance arbitration clause in collective bargaining agreements, and where the issue was in dispute, it has not hesitated to order it.[66]

One of the cases in which the Board ordered the parties to include a provision for an impartial umpire in their contract involved the Chrysler Corporation and the UAW. Fifteen years after the order was issued in 1943, the man who had become the impartial umpire

---

[62] 7 FED. REG. 237 (1942).

[63] *Ibid.*

[64] Freidin & Ulman, *Arbitration and the War Labor Board,* 58 HARV. L. REV. 309 (1945).

[65] 56 STAT. 765 (1942), 50 U.S.C. §§ 961–71 (Supp. III, 1943).

[66] Freidin & Ulman, *supra* note 64, at 344.

described the experience to the members of the National Academy of Arbitrators.[67] By and large, the system had worked well. Previously, since 1939, the parties had had a bipartite appeal board which met in appellate-like sessions, unattended by witnesses. Company and union members of this board came from plants or locals other than those immediately involved in the dispute, and thus had some degree of objectivity. When the parties adopted an umpire system in response to the Board's directive they retained much of this structure. They agreed that

the impartial chairman was . . . to be called upon to determine only a limited number of cases, and was not to function as part of the normal collective bargaining process; the facts, issues and arguments in all cases were to be first fully investigated, disclosed, and discussed by the parties' appeal board representatives, meeting without the chairman; the parties themselves were to attempt to dispose of cases without calling upon the chairman; cases requiring determination by the chairman were to be presented to him in appellate proceedings without the presence of witnesses or others; decisions by the impartial chairman were to be in strict accordance with the provisions of the parties' Agreements, and were to serve as guides to the parties in their bargaining in other situations.[68]

From 1943 to 1957 the number of employees covered by the above contract ranged from 80,000 to 140,000, but the average number of decisions issued annually by the umpire was less than twenty-three.[69]

The remaining giant of the auto industry, Ford, also adopted an umpire system during the war years, though without being directed to do so by the War Labor Board. Unlike either the General Motors or Chrysler apparatus, that system swung heavily in the direction of utilizing the impartial umpire as a mediator, wise and trusted counselor, and sometime decision-maker. Perhaps this simply reflected the genius of Harry Shulman, who helped the parties work out the system and then became the first umpire. Since he has passed from the scene the system seems to have lost some of its free-wheeling characteristics, but the case load remains high. The current umpire, Harry Platt, spoke in 1958 about the comparative umpire systems in the auto industry in these terms:

. . . it would hardly be right to judge the effectiveness or worth of an arbitration system or the health of a labor-management relationship by the

---

[67] Wolff, Crane & Cole, *The Chrysler-UAW Umpire System*, in NATIONAL ACADEMY OF ARBITRATORS, THE ARBITRATOR AND THE PARTIES, PROCEEDINGS OF THE 11TH ANNUAL MEETING 111 (McKelvey ed. 1958).
[68] *Id.* at 115.   [69] *Id.* at 117.

number of cases decided each year by the umpire. At Ford, for example, where labor relations are at least as good as at Chrysler, the umpires handed down about 6500 decisions in the same 15 years [1943–1958] or an average of close to 435 a year. At Ford, workers have much freer access to the umpire than workers in the other large automobile companies. And though some may look upon this with gloom, there are others who sincerely regard it as an important advantage both to the union leadership and the company. There has been a good deal of speculation as to the reasons for the vast difference in the volume of umpire cases in the Big Three automobile companies. Some people have suggested that this may be due, in part at least, to the rigid pre-arbitration union screening procedures that exist in the other companies but not at Ford; others attribute it to the manner in which the parties investigate and prepare their cases before they come to arbitration; and still others believe it may be due to differences of philosophy and content of umpire decisions. But there *is* an additional reason many have overlooked. Chrysler and General Motors, for example, have *always* had a relatively small umpire case load, while Ford has *always* had a relatively large umpire case load. This does not mean that there is a greater dissatisfaction at Ford than at the other companies or necessarily greater worker confidence in the effectiveness of one arbitration system than in the others. What it means is that today's case loads are partly the result of traditions.[70]

The importance of the War Labor Board's attitude toward grievance arbitration is underlined if one looks again at the state of union organization in 1941. The passage of the Wagner Act in 1935, and the ruling that it was constitutional in 1937, caused many corporations, like General Motors, U.S. Rubber, Jones and Laughlin, and General Electric, to accept collective bargaining. But others, like the "Little Steel" companies, Ford, Goodyear, Westinghouse, Swift, and others, did not sign agreements until 1941.[71] The decision of the United States Supreme Court in the *H. J. Heinz* case, requiring collective agreements to be put in the form of signed written contracts, caused a change in attitude in many quarters.[72]

Just before the passage of the Wagner Act, union membership stood at approximately 3 million members. By 1939 there were 8 to 9 million members, and by 1945 the figure had increased to between 13 and 14 million. Ten years later, in 1955, the figure stood around 16 to 17 million.[73] The number of collective bargaining contracts naturally increased greatly. So did the disposition of the parties,

---

[70] *Id.* at 142.
[71] *Supra* note 51, at 12.
[72] H. J. Heinz Co. v. NLRB, 311 U.S. 514 (1941).
[73] *Supra* note 51, at 3.

either voluntarily or at the instance of the War Labor Board, to include grievance arbitration clauses. By 1944, the Bureau of Labor Statistics reported finding arbitration in 73 per cent of the agreements in its file. The figure increased to 83 per cent in 1949, and to 89 per cent in 1952.[74]

The War Labor Board ceased to exist shortly after the war ended in 1945. Had grievance arbitration been proven unsatisfactory, one might have expected that it would be dropped from the many contracts that had adopted its use during the war. As the above statistics show, this did not happen. But there is even better evidence that the principle of grievance arbitration had been widely accepted. In July of 1945 Senator Arthur H. Vandenberg of Michigan suggested, in a letter to the Secretary of Labor, that a Labor-Management Conference be held "to lay the groundwork for peace with justice on the home front." [75] This idea had already been under discussion between President Truman and the Secretary of Labor, and the Vandenberg letter served to crystallize the desirability of such a meeting. Accordingly, the Conference was convened in Washington in October of 1945. Six committees devoted themselves to six different subject areas. They were able to agree on only three of them, and separate reports had to be issued on the others. Of the desirability of grievance arbitration, however, they had no doubts. A twelve-man committee, equally divided between labor and management, studied "the extent to which industrial disputes can be minimized by provisions incorporated in collective bargaining agreements." Portions of the unanimous report read as follows:

I. Collective-bargaining agreements should contain provisions that grievances and disputes involving the interpretation or application of the terms of the agreement are to be settled without resort to strikes, lock-outs or other interruptions to normal operations by an effective grievance procedure with arbitration as its final step.

. . . . .

IV. The parties should provide by mutual agreement for the final determination of any unsettled grievances or disputes involving the interpretation or application of the agreement by an impartial chairman, umpire, arbitrator, or board. In this connection the agreement should provide —

---

[74] Moore & Nix, *Arbitration Provisions in Collective Agreements, 1952*, 76 Mo. LABOR REV. 261–66 (1953).

[75] *Labor Organizations and Conferences*, 62 Mo. LABOR REV. 37 (1946).

(a) A definite and mutually agreed upon method of selecting the impartial chairman, umpire, arbitrator, or board;

(b) That the impartial chairman, umpire, arbitrator, or board should have no power to add to, subtract from, change or modify any provision of the agreement but should be authorized only to interpret the existing provisions of the agreement and apply them to the specific facts of the grievance or dispute;

(c) That reference of a grievance or dispute to an impartial chairman, umpire, arbitrator, or board should be reserved as the final step in the procedure and should not be resorted to unless the settlement procedures of the earlier steps have been exhausted.

(d) That the decisions of the impartial chairman, umpire, arbitrator, or board should be accepted by both parties as final and binding.

(e) That the cost of such impartial chairman, umpire, arbitrator or board should be shared equally by both parties.

. . . .

VI. When an agreement contains a renewal clause and a change or modification or reopening of the agreement is requested by either party, or where the existing agreement is about to be terminated, ample time prior to the termination of the agreement should be provided for the negotiation of a new or modified agreement. If such negotiations should fail, the parties should make early use of conciliation, mediation, and where mutually agreed to, arbitration.

VII. Nothing in this report is intended in any way to recommend compulsory arbitration, that is, arbitration not voluntarily agreed to by the parties.[76]

In retrospect it is clear that World War II did three things insofar as voluntary arbitration is concerned. First of all, it encouraged widespread adoption of arbitration techniques. Second, it sharpened the distinction between arbitration over "rights" and "interests." Henceforth, it would be clear that the commitment of the parties was to grievance arbitration, not to arbitration of the terms of a new agreement or to substantive issues not covered by the contract. Finally, the War Labor Board served as a training ground for the men who subsequently served as arbitrators. This cadre has ever since constituted the hard core of the arbitration profession. Without the understanding which they brought to the job it is possible that grievance arbitration would have been less readily accepted.

After 1945 grievance arbitration was firmly established. The debate was no longer *whether* an arbitration clause should be included in the contract, but was concerned solely with mechanics. Should

---

[76] *Id.* at 41–42.

pressure be put on the government to provide a free arbitration service? (There was precedent for this in the railroad industry.) Was it better to have a permanent umpire, *ad hoc* appointees, or a rotating panel? Should the arbitration board be tripartite, or should a single impartial individual be asked to make the decision? How formal should the proceedings be? Should the parties be represented by lawyers, or train their own people to present the cases? Were the parties willing to have the arbitrator attempt to settle the case, or did they want him to remain aloof and detached? To what extent should the courts be involved in deciding what kinds of cases the parties had in fact agreed to arbitrate? How great should the remedy power of the arbitrator be? Was he to be a policeman in the industry, or only a decision-maker in questions on which the parties differed, with the proper remedy being left to their further negotiation?

Some of these questions were answered; others were not. After experimenting with free arbitration services for a brief period, the Federal Mediation and Conciliation Service abandoned the practice on the advice of labor and management.[77] Thereafter it would maintain a panel of arbitrators from which names could be supplied to the parties, but arrangements would be made directly by the parties and they would pay the bill. As to the other questions, most of them remained items of preference without any fixed pattern emerging.

This was the formal structure of grievance arbitration as it emerged from the war. What remained was to breathe life into the structure so that the dynamics of the process became clear.

To the uninitiated, grievance arbitration looks like a simple and logical terminal point for deciding contractual disputes on which the parties cannot agree. There are, in fact, many reasons for going to arbitration which have little or nothing to do with the merits of the dispute. The grievance procedure is not, and cannot be, isolated from the bargaining relationship between the parties to the contract. A good example is the familiar phenomenon of multiple grievances being slated for arbitration during the period of contract negotiations, but being withdrawn as soon as a contract is agreed upon. Bargaining pressure is simply being exerted through the grievance channel.

There are many other institutional problems which must be taken into account. No impartial machinery which is always limited to the

---

[77] See ch. 2, p. 51.

same two parties can survive if one side always wins. In bringing cases the parties take this into consideration. Being a political organization is an additional problem for the union. Too rigid screening of grievances can alienate needed local support. It may be better to blame an adverse decision on an arbitrator than to assert that the grievance is wholly without merit. Newly elected officers may take cases to arbitration to fulfill campaign promises, or just to gain experience for the future. In an otherwise peaceful and quiet plant an occasional arbitration may inject some color and excitement to whet the interest of committeemen. On the management side, the company may prefer to back rather than reverse an erring foreman. Or a clash in views may exist between the operating and industrial relations divisions, with the latter preferring to have the arbitrator push the company in the direction they deem desirable or inevitable.

In short, the years between 1941 and 1957 made clear that grievance arbitration was not only a device for settling differences of opinion over the meaning and interpretation of contracts. It was also related to bargaining strategy, to human relations within the plant, and to organizational imperatives within the management and union structures. It was not, however, much concerned with the law, and that is what distinguishes the next period — after 1957. True, a number of states, like New York, had arbitration statutes, but for the most part they were not of much significance in the area of labor arbitration. After 1957 that situation changed, and it is to those years that we must now look.

THE PERIOD 1957 TO THE PRESENT

When the Taft-Hartley Act was passed in 1947 the now famous section 301 was added to the law. Subsection (a) read: "Suits for violation of contracts between an employer and a labor organization representing employees in an industry affecting commerce as defined in this Act, or between any such labor organizations, may be brought in any district court of the United States having jurisdiction of the parties, without respect to the amount in controversy or without regard to the citizenship of the parties." [78]

For some years after section 301 was added to the law a furious debate raged as to whether it was intended to be substantive or

---

[78] Labor-Management Relations Act § 301(a), 61 STAT. 156 (1947), 29 U.S.C. § 185(a), (1958).

procedural.[79] If it was purely procedural it would simply give federal courts jurisdiction in controversies involving labor organizations in interstate commerce without regard to the amount in controversy or diversity of citizenship. In this event the section would not be a source of substantive law, i.e., it would neither supply federal law to answer questions which might be raised, nor would it direct the federal courts to rely on state law for answers. If, on the other hand, the section was intended to be substantive, the federal courts would have to find a source of law for deciding such questions as might arise.

In June of 1957, the United States Supreme Court resolved the dispute over the meaning of section 301 in the *Lincoln Mills* case.[80] In that case the union sought to enforce an agreement to arbitrate which was included in the collective bargaining agreement. At common law agreements to arbitrate future disputes were not generally enforceable. For the court to hold with the union would require a ruling that 301 was both a substantive section and a source of federal law from which it could be determined that agreements to arbitrate were meant to be enforceable. A majority of the court ruled with the union on both counts. After first pointing out that most of the lower courts had ruled in favor of a substantive interpretation of section 301, the court went on to declare that "the agreement to arbitrate grievance disputes is the *quid pro quo* for an agreement not to strike. Viewed in this light, the legislation does more than confer jurisdiction in the federal courts over labor organizations. It expresses a federal policy that federal courts should enforce these agreements on behalf of or against labor organizations and that industrial peace can be best obtained only in that way." [81]

Having found that section 301 was substantive the court had to locate a source of substantive law. This it did in the following words:

The question then is, what is the substantive law to be applied in suits under § 301(a)? We conclude that the substantive law to apply in suits under § 301(a) is federal law, which the courts must fashion from the policy of our national labor laws. . . . The Labor Management Relations Act ex-

---

[79] See Cox, *Some Aspects of the Labor Management Relations Act, 1947 (II)*, 61 HARV. L. REV. 274, 303 (1948); Mendelsohn, *Enforceability of Arbitration Agreements Under Taft-Hartley Section 301*, 66 YALE L.J. 167 (1956); Wollett & Wellington, *Federalism and Breach of the Labor Agreement*, 7 STAN. L. REV. 445 (1955); Note, *Section 301(a) of the Taft-Hartley Act: A Constitutional Problem of Federal Jurisdiction*, 57 YALE L.J. 630 (1948).

[80] Textile Workers Union v. Lincoln Mills, 353 U.S. 448 (1957).

[81] *Id.* at 455

pressly furnishes some substantive law. It points out what the parties may or may not do in certain situations. Other problems will lie in the penumbra of express statutory mandates. Some will lack express statutory sanction but will be solved by looking at the policy of the legislation and fashioning a remedy that will effectuate that policy. The range of judicial inventiveness will be determined by the nature of the problem. . . . Federal interpretation of the federal law will govern, not state law. . . . But state law, if compatibile with the purpose of § 301, may be resorted to in order to find the rule that will best effectuate the federal policy. . . . Any state law applied, however, will be absorbed as federal law and will not be an independent source of private rights.[82]

Lincoln Mills posed one other somewhat more modest problem for the court. The Norris-LaGuardia Act prohibits federal courts from issuing injunctions in labor disputes. Read literally, a contractual dispute could be said to be a labor dispute in which the federal court is without power to enjoin the parties to comply with the contract. The court brushed this off by stating that "the failure to arbitrate was not part and parcel of the abuses against which the Act was aimed."[83] It saw no reason to restrict 301(a) to damage suits.

After *Lincoln Mills* Pandora's box was open. If one could enforce an agreement to arbitrate under section 301, surely the ensuing award could be similarly enforced. The circuit courts promptly agreed.[84] This led some observers to predict that the Norris-LaGuardia Act would no longer bar the issuance of an injunction in federal court in the event a union struck in violation of the collective bargaining contract. In *Sinclair Refining Co. v. Atkinson,* however, the court refused to go this far.[85] Nevertheless, lower courts have enforced arbitration awards which enjoin unions from continuing to strike in violation of the contract.[86]

Three years after *Lincoln Mills,* in June of 1960, the Supreme Court decided three Steelworker cases, popularly known as the *Trilogy.*[87] Arbitrability, i.e., the question of whether the contract required the parties to arbitrate a given issue, had been trouble-

---

[82] *Id.* at 456–57.

[83] *Id.* at 458.

[84] Textile Workers v. Cone Mills Corp., 268 F.2d 920 (4th Cir.), *cert. denied,* 361 U.S. 886 (1959); A. L. Kornman Co. v. Amalgamated Clothing Workers, 264 F.2d 733 (6th Cir.), *cert. denied,* 361 U.S. 819 (1959).

[85] Sinclair Ref. Co. v. Atkinson, 370 U.S. 195 (1962).

[86] New Orleans S. S. Ass'n v. General Longshore Workers, 49 L.R.R.M. 2941 (E. D. La. 1962); Ruppert v. Egelhofer, 3 N.Y.2d 576, 148 N.E.2d 129, 170 N.Y.S.2d 785 (1958).

[87] United Steelworkers of America v. Warrior & Gulf Nav. Co., 363 U.S. 574

some, for despite the contractual commitment to arbitrate, one party (usually the company) might refuse to submit a given issue on the ground that the contract did not require it to do so. In some states, like New York, a state statute made the agreement to arbitrate enforceable and an attempt might then be made to persuade the court to order the recalcitrant party to proceed with arbitration. Theoretically, the court would then be asked to decide simply the question of whether the issue was, or was not, one which the parties had agreed to arbitrate. In the course of doing so, however, many courts looked into the merits of the question. The *Trilogy* put a stop to this. Said the court:

In the absence of any express provision excluding a particular grievance from arbitration, we think only the most forceful evidence of a purpose to exclude the claim from arbitration can prevail, particularly where, as here, the exclusion clause is vague and the arbitration clause quite broad. Since any attempt by a court to infer such a purpose necessarily comprehends the merits, the court should view with suspicion an attempt to persuade it to become entangled in the construction of the substantive provisions of a labor agreement, even through the back door of interpreting the arbitration clause, when the alternative is to utilize the services of an arbitrator.[88]

Elsewhere in the same opinion Mr. Justice Douglas waxed almost ecstatic about the function of the arbitrator. In a paragraph which caused many arbitrators to purchase new mirrors, Justice Douglas said:

The labor arbitrator is usually chosen because of the parties' confidence in his knowledge of the common law of the shop and their trust in his personal judgment to bring to bear considerations which are not expressed in the contract as criteria for judgment. The parties expect that his judgment of a particular grievance will reflect not only what the contract says but, insofar as the collective bargaining agreement permits, such factors as the effect upon productivity of a particular result, its consequence to the morale of the shop, his judgment whether tensions will be heightened or diminished. For the parties' objective in using the arbitration process is primarily to further their common goal of uninterrupted production under the agreement, to make the agreement serve their specialized needs. The ablest judge cannot be expected to bring the same experience and competence to bear upon the determination of a grievance, because he cannot be similarly informed.[89]

(1960); United Steelworkers of America v. Enterprise Wheel & Car Corp. 363 U.S. 593 (1960); United Steelworkers of America v. American Mfg. Co., 363 U.S. 564 (1960).

[88] United Steelworkers of America v. Warrior & Gulf Nav. Co., *supra* note 87, at 584–85.

[89] *Id.* at 582.

In another of the *Trilogy* cases, the court gave strong support to the power of arbitrators to create remedies. After noting that "the question of interpretation of the collective bargaining agreement is a question for the arbitrator," and "the courts have no business overruling him because their interpretation of the contract is different from his," the court said:

When an arbitrator is commissioned to interpret and apply the collective bargaining agreement, he is to bring his informed judgment to bear in order to reach a fair solution of a problem. This is especially true when it comes to formulating remedies. There the need is for flexibility in meeting a wide variety of situations. The draftsmen may never have thought of what specific remedy should be awarded to meet a particular contingency. Nevertheless, an arbitrator is confined to interpretation and application of the collective bargaining agreement; he does not sit to dispense his own brand of industrial justice. He may of course look for guidance from many sources, yet his award is legitimate only so long as it draws its essence from the collective bargaining agreement. When the arbitrator's words manifest an infidelity to this obligation, courts have no choice but to refuse enforcement of the award.[90]

The effect of the *Trilogy* was to enhance greatly the power and prestige of the arbitration process. But this was not the end. In a series of subsequent decisions the Supreme Court broadened the jurisdiction of arbitrators by adding matters traditionally brought before the National Labor Relations Board. *Smith v. Evening News Ass'n* involved a situation in which the collective bargaining agreement contained a clause where the company agreed not to discriminate against individuals because of union activities.[91] Smith, alleging violation of this provision of the contract, brought suit against the company. The Supreme Court decided that the matter fell within section 301 of the Taft-Hartley Act, that individuals could bring suits under that section (which had theretofore not been clear), and that exclusive jurisdiction was not vested in the National Labor Relations Board despite the rule of the *Garmon* case [92] and the fact that the charge stated a perfectly clear unfair labor practice.

In January of 1964 the court added to the possibilities of overlap between arbitration and the National Labor Relations Board by deciding, in *Carey v. Westinghouse Elec. Corp.*, that work assignment disputes are subject to arbitration as well as NLRB proceedings.[93]

---

[90] United Steelworkers of America v. Enterprise Wheel & Car Corp., *supra* note 87, at 597.

[91] Smith v. Evening News Ass'n, 371 U.S. 195 (1962).

[92] San Diego Bldg. Trades Council v. Garmon, 359 U.S. 236 (1959).

[93] 375 U.S. 261 (1964).

This and other similar developments have not upset the Board, for it is already overburdened with other business. There is some difference among the members as to just how far the Board should go in refusing jurisdiction where matters have already been subjected to arbitration, but there is no doubt that the Board is generally friendly to arbitration.[94] The arbitration of disputes in which more than one union has an interest is, of course, a very complicated matter. It may, and in some cases already has, brought about further interaction with the courts by causing arbitrators to invoke interpleader procedures.[95]

Finally, in early 1964 the Supreme Court decided *Humphrey v. Moore*,[96] which is discussed elsewhere in this volume in some detail.[97] It clarified certain questions, such as the capacity of a union to represent conflicting interests among its members, but it also suggested that there is an implied contractual obligation on the part of the union to represent its members fairly. The possibility thus appears that individual grievants may demand access to the arbitration machinery for adjudication of grievances which the union is alleged to be unfairly refusing to process.

One would naturally expect some apprehension, particularly on the part of companies, at the prospect of such broad powers in the hands of arbitrators. In 1962 Professor Smith surveyed some fifty lawyers, mostly representing management, to see how their clients were reacting. He reported that there was no uniform pattern, but that the large companies seemed undisturbed. Smaller companies, however, were very often seriously concerned.[98]

In April of 1964 Benjamin C. Sigal, General Counsel of the International Union of Electrical, Radio and Machine Workers, AFL-

---

[94] For speeches by Board members on this subject see McCulloch, *Arbitration and/or the N.L.R.B.*, in NATIONAL ACADEMY OF ARBITRATORS, LABOR ARBITRATION AND INDUSTRIAL CHANGE, PROCEEDINGS OF THE 16TH ANNUAL MEETING 175 (Kahn ed. 1963); McCulloch, *Concurrent Jurisdictions of the NLRB, Arbitrators*, 56 LAB. REL. REP. 11 (1964); 56 LAB. REL. REP. 290 (1964) (Board Member Brown address to Teamster conference summarized).

[95] E. Jones, *An Arbitral Answer to a Judicial Dilemma: The Carey Decision and Trilateral Arbitration of Jurisdictional Disputes*, 11 U.C.L.A.L. REV. 327 (1964). E. Jones, *Autobiography of a Decision: The Function of Innovation in Labor Arbitration, and the* National Steel *Orders of Joinder and Interpleader*, 10 U.C.L.A.L. REV. 987 (1963).

[96] 375 U.S. 335 (1964).

[97] See ch. 5, pp. 117–20.

[98] Smith, *The Question of "Arbitrability"— The Roles of the Arbitrator, the Court and the Parties*, 16 Sw. L.J. 1, 23 (1962).

CIO, reported on a somewhat similar survey which he had made. In fifteen important and widely different industries he examined contracts negotiated since the *Trilogy* to see the extent to which there had been changes in the contract clauses on arbitration, management rights, and prohibition of strikes. The industries which he examined included steel, auto, electrical manufacturing, airframe, meat packing, food processing, longshore and warehousing, paper, rubber, leather goods, glass, agricultural machinery, textiles, garment manufacturing, and non-ferrous metal. From the survey he reached the following conclusions:

With the exception of only one industry there have been *no significant* changes in the arbitration, management rights, and no-strike clauses in these industries.

There have been significant changes in the arbitration clause in the principal contracts in the electrical manufacturing industry, executed in *late 1963*, namely those of General Electric Co. and Westinghouse Electric Corporation. The arbitration clauses, originally negotiated in 1955, and renewed without change about 4 months after the trilogy, have been revised to incorporate the idea that only those grievances may go to arbitration which are expressly made arbitrable. There was a very conscious effort on the part of the employers involved to nullify the trilogy.[99]

There is other evidence that companies and unions have not been frightened away from arbitration by the sweeping court decisions. The two principal appointing agencies, the Federal Mediation and Conciliation Service and the American Arbitration Association, report the following growth figures in the last few years:[100]

FMCS			AAA		
Year	Appointments	Percentage Increase	Year	Appointments	Percentage Increase
1956	1099				
1957	1270	15.5			
1958	1755	38			
1959	1756	0	1959	2816	
1960	2039	16	1960	3231	14
1961	2231	9.4	1961	3492	8
1962	2555	14.5	1962	3842	10
1963	2757	8	1963	4074	6

[99] Sigal, *Impact of Steelworkers Decisions on Arbitrability*, 56 LAB. REL. REP. 20, 23 (1964).
[100] *Id.* at 21.

Court decisions have not, then, changed the fact that grievance arbitration is basically a private system of jurisprudence. They have, however, profoundly affected the rules of the game. Contractual agreements to arbitrate, as well as awards, are no longer gentlemen's agreements, but are enforceable by order of the court. Entirely new areas, heretofore the province of the National Labor Relations Board, have been opened to arbitration. Most important of all, the new rules are all federal rules, many of which remain to be created by the "judicial inventiveness" of which Justice Douglas spoke.

Historians will doubtless say that grievance arbitration in the United States began to undergo subtle changes after 1957, not just because of the major court rulings which have been mentioned, but because in other court cases concepts were developed which later spilled over into the arbitration arena.[101]

All this emphasis upon the law must not be allowed to hide the fact that the bargaining context, from which arbitration cannot be entirely separated, has changed greatly in recent years. Throughout the period since World War II, with seeming acceleration of late, technology has displaced people. In the traditional union stronghold of manufacturing, employment in the 1950's remained substantially stationary while production went up about 43 per cent. Until a recent 1964 report from the Bureau of Labor Statistics marked a 1962 upswing, union membership had shown a drop of almost half a million since 1960.[102] The strike weapon no longer functioned in some industries for plants could be kept operating by supervisory personnel. Unions necessarily sought to exploit the possibility of using arbitration to gain advantages which might not otherwise be possible.

One other wholly new use for arbitration has emerged in the period between 1957 and the present. On January 17, 1962, President Kennedy signed Executive Order 10988 which was designed to encourage recognition of and bargaining with unions in the federal service.[103] Under the order a union which represents the majority of the employees in an appropriate unit is entitled to exclusive recognition. Because disputes may arise as to what is the appropriate unit, or over whether the union does represent a majority of the em-

---

[101] Fleming, *Some Observations on Contract Grievances Before Courts and Arbitrators*, 15 STAN. L. REV. 595, 612 (1963).

[102] 54 LAB. REL. REP. 393 (1963). Although a decline was registered for the years 1960–62, a slight gain was recorded for the year 1962 alone. 56 LAB. REL. REP. 108 (1964).

[103] 27 FED. REG. 551 (1962).

ployees, arbitrators, drawn from the panel maintained by the Federal Mediation and Conciliation Service, may be nominated by the Secretary of Labor to resolve those questions. By the end of 1963 there had been no cases involving the question of majority status, but there had been twenty decisions on appropriate units.[104]

SUMMARY AND CONCLUSIONS

The word "arbitration," as used at the turn of the century, usually meant what we would now call "negotiation." Since the basic problem of unions was then one of recognition, their primary concern was one of sitting down with the company to discuss contract terms. The limited umpire systems which existed grew out of great strikes, though the systems were intended to deal with continuing problems.

From the very first some parties preferred a third party decision process which came to be labeled the "judicial" type. In these systems the umpire had no authority or encouragement to mediate settlements. However, there were parties who by choice traveled in the opposite direction. Why one idea rather than the other was selected probably has no better explanation than that which can be found in the preferences of the individuals involved. Over the years, however, the movement has seemed to be toward acceptance of the "judicial" type of arbitration.[105]

Once the Wagner Act was passed and held constitutional the number of collective bargaining contracts began to increase rapidly. The fact that many of them were inexpertly drawn promoted the cause of impartial interpretations. Fragmentary statistics indicate that grievance arbitration was growing rapidly at the time World War II came along. The war gave it an enormous boost because the War Labor Board, already saddled with an unbearable load in terms of "interest" disputes, both encouraged and directed the use of voluntary arbitration to resolve grievances. By the end of the war grievance arbitration was not only widely used, it was widely accepted. This was proven when President Truman's Labor-Management Conference of 1945 unanimously agreed on the desirability of such clauses in collective bargaining contracts.

An outgrowth of the heavy reliance on arbitration in the years

---

[104] Labor Management Services Administration, U.S. Dep't of Labor, FEDERAL EMPLOYEE UNIT ARBITRATION 2 (June 1964).

[105] Killingsworth & Wallen, *Constraint and Variety in Arbitration Systems*, in NATIONAL ACADEMY OF ARBITRATORS, PERSPECTIVES AND PROBLEMS, PROCEEDINGS OF THE 17TH ANNUAL MEETING 56 (Kahn ed. 1964).

immediately after World War II was the founding of a professional association, called the National Academy of Arbitrators, to which most of the experienced arbitrators belong.[106]

In 1957 the Supreme Court of the United States issued the first of a series of decisions on arbitration which would thereafter change the rules of the game. Prior thereto arbitration was a system of almost wholly private jurisprudence. Now, though the well-established and experienced systems go along much as they always did, there is a developing federal law which marks the boundary lines. At the same time the public policy which favors arbitration is being used by the courts to expand the field so that arbitrators are being asked to decide questions which did not previously come before them.

As of 1964, "arbitration" in the industrial context clearly means grievance arbitration. With rare exceptions, such as the railroad rules dispute which Congress ordered submitted to compulsory arbitrations in 1963, it is voluntary and applies only to the meaning and interpretation of collective bargaining agreements.

No one doubts that grievance arbitration is here to stay. But there are many complaints about its cost, the increasing time-lag, alleged irrelevant formalities, the lack of competent new arbitrators, the undue impingement on or respect for management rights (depending on who is doing the complaining), and the ever troublesome question of individual versus union rights in the grievance. The balance of this volume is devoted to an exploration of those problems.

---

[106] McKelvey, *Preface* to NATIONAL ACADEMY OF ARBITRATORS, THE PROFESSION OF LABOR ARBITRATION, SELECTED PAPERS FROM THE FIRST SEVEN ANNUAL MEETINGS (McKelvey ed. 1957).

Chapter 2

THE COST PROBLEM

The cost of arbitration has been a subject of great concern in recent years. It is said that one of the original virtues of arbitration, i.e., economy, has disappeared, and that small companies and unions now find the process financially burdensome or even out of range.

To some extent complaints about arbitration costs reflect general discontent with rising prices. They are, in this sense, the counterpart of familiar laments about everything from higher rents to the price of the movies. Nevertheless, it cannot be assumed that this is all there is to the problem, and that it should be ignored.

Much of the criticism with respect to costs has been directed at the rise in arbitrators' fees. Whatever the merits of that criticism, knowledgeable students of arbitration recognize immediately that arbitrators' fees are only a part of the problem. There are many factors which contribute to the cost of an arbitration. How well the parties screen grievances will, for instance, determine how many arbitrations they will have. The way in which arbitration is employed — does it simply replace the strike, or does it provide the union with new service opportunities which the cost of a strike would prohibit — will have much to say about total costs. The kinds of issues which are arbitrated — are they relatively clear-cut discharge and discipline questions, or are they complicated subcontracting problems — will necessarily affect costs. And, of course, the straight service fees charged by court reporters, counsel for the parties, and arbitrators will be the most visible of all costs.

Before one can intelligently discuss costs in arbitration he must look at the context within which arbitration occurs. Let us look first then at what might be called the "institutional" aspects of the problem.

INSTITUTIONAL ASPECTS OF COST

Throughout the literature there are references to arbitration as the substitute for the strike. Indeed, it is apparent that the decisions of the Supreme Court which have so greatly enhanced labor arbitration in recent years are in large part based on the theory that the arbitration clause is the *quid pro quo* for the no-strike clause.[1]

It is true that the availability of arbitration makes it possible to contest unilateral decisions without resort to the strike. But to equate the cost of arbitration with the cost of a strike is to overlook the fact that arbitration, once installed, takes on a logic of its own which is quite different from that of the strike. The strike is useful as an ultimate weapon, not for the purpose of settling routine differences of opinion. When X alleges that the company paid him 50¢ less per hour than he was entitled to while working for two hours on a higher rated job, he has a grievance, but the union does not have a strike issue. When Y is suspended for one day as a result of reporting for work late he may feel that the penalty is unjust and the union may wish to contest it, but no one seriously thinks of having a strike over the issue. When Z, who has served the union long and faithfully as a steward, is passed over on a promotion to which he thinks his seniority entitles him, the union may be delighted to take the case to arbitration though it would not consider striking over the issue. Examples of this kind could be repeated ad infinitum. They illustrate why arbitration is much more than a substitute for the strike, and why neither company nor union people normally think of arbitration costs in terms of what a strike would cost.

A modern corollary to this more realistic view of arbitration is the fact that the function of the strike is itself changing. In some industries, like chemicals and oil, lengthy strikes have demonstrated that supervisory personnel can keep a plant going at capacity indefinitely despite the complete and continued absence of production workers. In such cases arbitration furnishes the union with a procedure for which there is *no* substitute. One could argue that arbitration is then more valuable than the strike to the union, yet no union would seriously consider the cost of a strike the proper cost of an arbitration. Thus in any comparison of costs we need to abandon the rhetoric which suggests that the cost of an arbitration is reasonable simply because it is a small fraction of what a strike would cost. Whatever value there is in thinking of arbitration as the strike substitute does not apply in the cost area except for rare and unusual situations.

There is another comparison which is equally invalid. It is the

---

[1] Textile Workers Union v. Lincoln Mills, 353 U.S. 448 (1957).

nostalgic wish for an earlier day in which it is alleged that labor and management could turn to some public-minded individual in the community for a quick, informal, and economical disposition of their differences. Like television's version of the old West, there is grave doubt that such a period ever existed. Certainly repeated efforts by the appointing agencies and the National Academy of Arbitrators to persuade companies and unions to accept as arbitrators men who have known competence in the industrial relations field, but who are without actual arbitration experience, have been largely unsuccessful.[2] And these efforts have failed at the very time in which the accepted professional arbitrators, who charge higher fees than could be expected from new men, are turning away cases because they do not have time to do them.

Some of the reluctance of the parties to accept new arbitrators may be traceable to the emergence of new and more difficult issues. One can document this in a loose sense by looking through the labor arbitration volumes published by the Bureau of National Affairs. Volume 1, covering the period 1944 to 1946, includes no cases involving subcontracting, transfer of jobs out of the unit, racial discrimination, or integration of seniority lists. Volume 24, published in the year 1955, offers cases on all of the above issues. Volume 38, containing 1962 decisions, includes all of the things mentioned above but also adds decisions on the appropriate unit, plant removals, supplementary unemployment benefits, technological displacement allowances, and damages for failure to do assigned work. The sample may be unscientific but it accords with known bargaining history, since some of the issues in the later volumes were the result of fairly recent bargaining.

Aside from the increased complexity of cases, there is another factor which has changed the outlook of arbitration and made it more costly. That factor is the law. Prior to the *Lincoln Mills* decision in 1957, the law played a relatively small role in the whole arbitration process. Since then it has burgeoned. Agreements to arbitrate are now clearly enforceable in either state or federal courts.[3] Courts retain the right to determine what is arbitrable, but in doing so they

---

[2] D. Jones & R. Smith, *Management and Labor Appraisals and Criticisms of the Arbitration Process: A Report with Comments*, 62 MICH. L. REV. 1115, 1136 (1964).

[3] *Supra* note 1.

must not look into the merits of the dispute, and they must keep in mind that public policy favors arbitration.[4] The remedy power of the arbitrator is very broad and it need not be found in specific terms in the contract.[5] If the contract does not contain an arbitration clause, a breach of contract suit may be brought by the individual, the union, or the company in state or federal court.[6] The fact that the cause of the dispute may constitute an unfair labor practice does not give the National Labor Relations Board exclusive jurisdiction, or prevent the arbitrator from acting on the issue.[7] What constitutes an appropriate unit for purposes of union recognition may be taken to arbitration even though it might also go to the NLRB.[8] A second union, affected by but not involved in a dispute between the first union and a common company, may find itself faced with an interpleader so that the issue can be resolved in a single proceeding.[9] Even though the contract does not contain a clause which requires the union to represent all the employees fairly, there is an implied statutory obligation which may be ground for action.[10] A strike in violation of a no-strike clause will not be enjoinable in federal courts because of the Norris-LaGuardia Act, but a restraining order from an arbitrator will most likely be enforced.[11] These are but a few of the important principles which have emerged from the courts in recent years. From the company standpoint they are being read to mean that more and more issues may be brought to arbitration, and that the arbitrator will have very broad authority in dealing with those issues. From the union standpoint they mean, among other things, that jurisdictional disputes may be brought to arbitration, that individual members may now more easily claim unfair treatment in the handling of grievances, and that strikes in violation of the contract may be subject to restraint after all.

Inevitably lawyers are called upon more frequently than before to advise companies and unions in the processing and arbitrating of

---

[4] United Steelworkers of America v. Warrior & Gulf Nav. Co., 363 U.S. 574 (1960).

[5] United Steelworkers of America v. American Mfg. Co., 363 U.S. 564 (1960).

[6] Smith v. Evening News Ass'n, 371 U.S. 195 (1962).

[7] *Supra* note 6.

[8] Carey v. Westinghouse Elec. Corp., 375 U.S. 261 (1964).

[9] E. Jones, *An Arbitral Answer to a Judicial Dilemma: The Carey Decision and Trilateral Arbitration of Jurisdictional Disputes*, 11 U.C.L.A.L. REV. 327 (1964).

[10] Humphrey v. Moore, 375 U.S. 335 (1964).

[11] Fleming, *Arbitrators and the Remedy Power*, 48 VA. L. REV. 1199 (1962).

grievances. The need for professional advice naturally boosts the total cost of arbitration.

Finally, it must be recognized that the mechanics of the grievance procedure give companies and unions a somewhat different perspective toward arbitration. In the normal case the company retains the initiative while the union can complain that the action which the company has taken is in violation of the contract. If the company prevails in the arbitration its right to do what it has already done will simply be sustained. Thus there is some encouragement to the union to challenge company actions which it has only a small chance of upsetting. If the union should be successful in the arbitration it may have gained a substantial advantage, while if it loses it will be no worse off than it was before. For the most part this is an acceptable state of affairs for both sides, because the company can usually live with an adverse decision even though it may feel strongly that it is an incorrect interpretation of the contract. On the other hand, there are cases which touch extremely sensitive management nerves. In those cases the risk of loss must be minimized and cost is of minor importance to the company. It not only can, but from its point of view must, prepare its defense in depth. This means reliance on technical defenses, court actions, full-scale hearings with lawyers, reporters, briefs, and all sorts of outside aids. Regardless of its wishes the union may be forced into a very expensive procedure in such a case and it may complain bitterly. Yet it is perfectly possible for the company in such a case to be in complete good faith, doing its best to protect against an attack which it may regard as ruinous.

For the reasons indicated above, along with a difference in available resources, cost is often of considerably less importance to the company than to the union. There is, however, an aspect of the cost problem with which the union is less concerned than is the company. The union is political in nature. It initiates grievances. Whether to process a grievance to arbitration is a decision which it can make. Careful screening will reduce the number of cases which will go to arbitration and thus reduce costs to the local. But careful screening may also alienate faithful members who feel, rightly or wrongly, that they have a valid grievance. In such a situation the union may not wish to take the responsibility for saying that a grievance is without merit. The financial cost of having an arbitrator say "no" may be less burdensome than the political cost of having the union officer say "no" to his faithful member. On occasion, particularly when there is turmoil within the local union, admittedly spurious grievances go to arbitration. This may be very annoying to the company. Aside from the out-of-pocket costs, valuable time of supervisors and executives is tied up in the proceeding.

As we turn to a consideration of direct costs in arbitration then, the gap between the talk on the subject of costs and the reality must be kept in mind.

SERVICE ASPECTS OF COST

The obvious out-of-pocket costs of an arbitration center upon the arbitrator, counsel for the parties, and the court reporter. We have information which may be enlightening on those items, but it ought to be noted at the outset that there are other direct costs which are not included in our calculations. At least five other items can be listed immediately. They are:

1. Both company and union representatives must spend time in preparing the grievance for arbitration and in presenting the case. No cost calculations have been undertaken in this connection.

2. Many contracts provide pay for time lost by union officers or committeemen in attending an arbitration hearing. If the company does not pay this item the union usually does. In any event, it is a cost of arbitration which is not included in our calculations.

3. If the hearing is held in a hotel conference room for which a charge is made, this will add to the total costs.

4. If a service agency, like the American Arbitration Association, is used there will be a modest service fee to add to the other costs.

5. If the arbitrator's award involves back pay or other cost items, this will be added to the total cost of the case.

Despite the above omissions, there is some logic to concentration on the fees of arbitrators, counsel, and court reporters. Insofar as costs are of concern to companies and unions, they are familiar with, and can calculate, the money which will be involved in items 1 through 5 above. This may vary widely in individual cases. Some of the items are relatively small and do not compare with the larger items which are involved in direct fees.

ARBITRATORS' FEES

Let us start with the arbitrators. The criticism is that fees are increasing to the point where arbitration is becoming too costly. The only way to know how much fees have increased is to find a base point and then make a comparison. There are, of course, conceptual difficulties in making any such comparison. If it is true, as was suggested earlier, that new and more difficult issues are being tried today than was true some years ago one might be adding apples and oranges in simply picking a random sample of cases. To avoid that problem we selected only discharge cases on the theory that a discharge case would be much the same whether heard in 1945, 1955, or 1965. With the consent of the Federal Mediation and Conciliation Service we then dipped into their files for 100 discharge cases decided in 1951-52 (the first year in which complete files were available), 100 cases decided in 1956-57, and a third 100 cases decided in 1962-63. With this information we were able to make certain comparisons which are set forth in the following charts.[12]

Charts I and II show per diem rates and total fees of arbitrators. Chart I indicates that in 1951-52 over half of the arbitrators were charging less than $100 per day. Practically all of the others were listed at an even $100. In a relatively few cases the rate was a bit higher than $100.

CHART I. *Arbitrator's per diem hearing rates* [a]

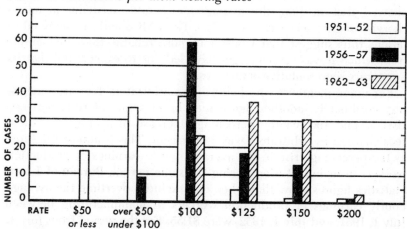

a Selected years, 1951–63. Discharge cases. All information taken from Federal Mediation and Conciliation Service files. Each year's sample included 98 cases.

In contrast, in 1956-57 less than 10 per cent of the arbitrators charged less than $100 per day. Approximately 58 per cent had a per diem rate of $100, almost 18 per cent charged $125, and 14 per cent

---

[12] Fleming, *The Labor Arbitration Process: 1943–1963*, in NATIONAL ACADEMY OF ARBITRATORS, PERSPECTIVES AND PROBLEMS, PROCEEDINGS OF THE 17TH ANNUAL MEETING 33 (Kahn ed. 1964).

charged $150. In 1962-63 the rate had moved up so that no one charged less than $100, 24 per cent were charging a flat $100, 38 per cent had a fee of $125, and 30 per cent worked for $150 a day.

If one calculates the average rate for the respective periods he finds that it was $84 for 1951-52, $110 in 1956-57, and $129 in 1962-63. Since our sample included only discharge cases a question could be raised as to whether it is representative of all cases. Subsequent tabulations run by the Federal Mediation and Conciliation Service on *all* cases during certain years indicate that discharge cases are more representative than one might have expected. In 1962 the average per diem fee in all cases having their origin in FMCS appointments was $120.45, as compared with a $129 average for discharge cases. Since many of the professional arbitrators who belong to the National Academy of Arbitrators are too busy to take cases through FMCS appointment it is not possible to tell, from the above figures, how their average fees would compare with the ones that have been given. Fortunately, however, the Academy released parts of a survey which it had made prior to its 1964 annual meeting. That survey showed that in 1962 the average daily rate Academy members charged in grievance cases was $126. The FMCS and Academy tabulations thus suggest that Chart I is more reliable than the sample from which it was drawn might have led one to expect, and that its figures are representative of all cases.

For union members who believe that arbitrators' fees are increasing inordinately, another figure may be of some interest. Between 1951-52 and 1962-63 the percentage increase in average per diem fees charged by arbitrators was 54 per cent. This is almost the same as the percentage rise in the average hourly earnings of production workers in manufacturing during the same period. Bureau of Labor Statistics figures show that when one excludes overtime the average hourly earnings of production workers in manufacturing between July 1, 1951, and July 1, 1952, were $1.55. For the period from July 1, 1962, to July 1, 1963, the same average jumped to $2.34. The difference is 79¢, and this, rounded to the nearest percentage, is 51 per cent more than workers were receiving in 1951-52.

Chart II shows total fees for arbitrators in each of the three periods. What it does not show, but what one can derive from it by calculating averages, is that average total fees have not risen by the same percentage as have per diem fees. The average total fee in 1951 was $277, while the comparable figure in 1962 was $402. The percentage difference is 46 per cent, as contrasted with a 54 per cent rise in per diem fees. The average fee in *all* Federal Mediation and Conciliation Service cases for 1962, incidentally, was a little less than our figure for discharge cases only. It was $375.

CHART II. *Arbitrator's total fees* [a]

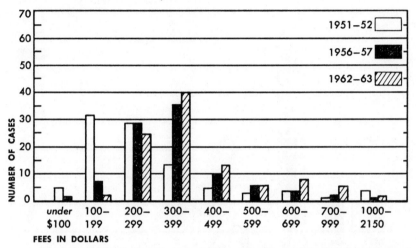

[a] Selected years, 1951–63. Discharge cases. All information taken from Federal Mediation and Conciliation Service files. Each year's sample included 98 cases.

The fact that the total fee did not rise as fast as the per diem fee would suggest that arbitrators cut back on study days at the same time that they raised per diem fees. Since this appears to be inconsistent with the study day chart which follows, a logical explanation may be that the arbitrators with the higher per diem fees charged fewer study days.

Per diem fees of arbitrators are not particularly revealing unless one knows the number of hearing and study days which are required in a typical case. To get this information we relied on the same sample of discharge cases drawn from the Federal Mediation and Conciliation Service files. Chart III shows that there has been very little change in the number of hearing days from 1951 to 1963. There is an insignificant variation in the number of hearings which took less than one day. There are a few more cases in 1956 and 1963 than in 1951 which took more than one day to hear, but on the other hand there were more cases in 1951 which took a day and a half to hear. If the two are balanced together one suspects that differences are easily accounted for by the nature of the sample. Once again subsequent FMCS tabulations for *all* cases in 1962 make it appear that the discharge hearing is very comparable in length to all cases, the figure for which is 1.15 days.

CHART III. *Length of hearing* [a]

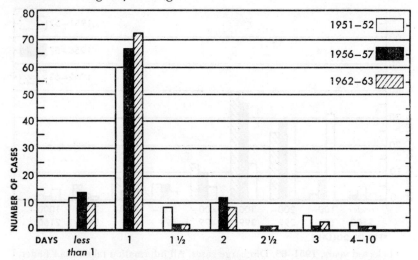

[a] Selected years, 1951–63. Discharge cases. All information taken from Federal Mediation and Conciliation Service files. Each year's sample included 98 cases.

If arbitrators are padding their fees this would be more likely to appear on study days than hearing days, for the former are not readily ascertainable by the parties. Our sample of study days is shown on Chart IV. It shows that there has been some upward movement since 1951. In that year about 20 per cent of the cases were decided in less than a day of study time, while in 1956 the figure was 9 per cent, and in 1963 it was only 8 per cent. The number of cases in all three periods requiring one day of study remained relatively the same. In those cases requiring more than one day, but less than two, 1951 and 1963 are not far apart, but 1956 climbed above both. The number of cases, however, is not significant and may well be accounted for by the small size of the sample. Cases requiring two days of study have shown a steady upward trend from 1951 to 1963, although once again the movement is slight. The remaining data simply demonstrates that few cases require more than two days of study. The FMCS tabulation for *all* cases in 1962 showed average study days of 1.84. Our tabulation for discharge cases in 1962-63 was about an average of 1.75 study days.

Conclusions from this data are tentative, but they would seem to indicate that there is a drift away from less than a day of study for the decision in any case, and that there is a slight upward drift in the number of days, up to two, which are charged for preparing the decision. Beyond two days there is no discernible trend.

CHART IV. *Study days charged* [a]

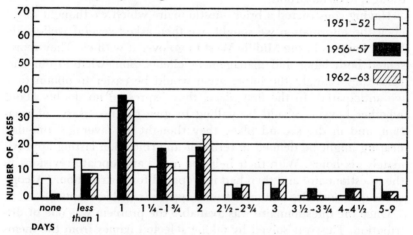

[a] Selected years, 1951–63. Discharge cases. All information taken from Federal Mediation and Conciliation Service files. Each year's sample included 98 cases.

LAWYERS' FEES

The best sources of arbitration statistics are the files of the two major appointing agencies, the American Arbitration Association and the Federal Mediation and Conciliation Service. Unfortunately, in neither case do the files contain any information about fees which lawyers charge their labor and management clients. Nor were we able to locate any useful information in the hands of the bar associations. We therefore undertook our own survey. The accuracy of the results can be debated, hence we offer them only after a full explanation of how they were obtained.

We were not interested in identifying particular practitioners, but we did want to know whether counsel represented companies or unions, and the geographic area of his practice. Our theory in both of these situations was, of course, that there might be a differential based on the kind of client and/or the area of the country in which services were rendered. We also wanted to know whether most lawyers represented their clients on a retainer basis, whether they charged an hourly fee, or whether there was some other type of fee arrangement. Ultimately we wanted to find out how much a lawyer received from his client for an "average" one-day arbitration hearing, including advance preparation and post-hearing briefs. This was the most difficult information to obtain simply because defining "average" was thought to be hazardous.

Having constructed a brief questionnaire which we thought might elicit the information we sought, we then asked several well-established lawyers in the Middle West to go over it with us. They represented both labor and management clients. Somewhat to our surprise they thought the information would be easier to obtain than we anticipated. In the first place, they expressed no doubts about whether lawyers would be willing to give the necessary information, and in the second place they thought an "average" one-day hearing might be defined in terms of an arbitration lasting approximately six hours. With their help we made appropriate revisions in the questionnaire and then had it prepared for distribution. (A copy of the questionnaire is attached as an appendix to this chapter.)

Once the questionnaire was available the problem was one of distribution. This was solved by taking selected names from the membership list of the Labor Law Section of the American Bar Association. With the help of professional arbitrators in most of the major industrial states a list of 400 lawyers was drawn from this roster. It was intended to include only active practitioners, fairly well divided between lawyers who represented management and those who represented labor, and not to include house counsel.

The questionnaire was distributed to the 400 lawyers with a brief form letter, indicating the nature of the research, promising anonymity, and asking for their cooperation. From the 400 lawyers, 175 usable replies were received. This represents 44 per cent of the original sample. Approximately a dozen questionnaire respondents stated that total fees vary too much to give a fair answer. Others had difficulty with our definition of an "average" hearing because it does not accord with their experience. Still others do not use an hourly rate and found it difficult to translate the retainer into hours of work. In large firms where hourly rates are used the rates differ according to whether a senior or junior man works on the case. In that situation we asked them to furnish us with an average hourly rate which would take into consideration differing hourly rates.

Many of the responses pointed out a further limitation on our data. The difficulty in defining a typical case is compounded by the fact that fees vary with the financial condition of the client, the success of the individual case, the nature and complexity of the issue, the importance of the case, and the estimated inconvenience to the attorney in handling the case.

Interestingly enough, our respondents showed considerable interest in the survey, despite their reservations about its validity, and many of them returned the forms on their own letterheads (rather than in our anonymous stamped envelopes) and asked for a copy of the results.

One final caveat needs to be entered before some of the results of the survey are given. Though we had 175 "usable" replies from our 400 questionnaires, the totals on any given question do not always equal 175 because not every question was answered on what was otherwise a "usable" return. Moreover, about twice as many company as union lawyers responded, thereby giving us a larger sample on the management side.

To no one's surprise, the first clear conclusion which one can draw from the survey is that management lawyers are better paid than are union lawyers. Hourly charges by union counsel showed up as follows:

UNION LAWYERS' HOURLY RATES

Fee	Number Charging	Per Cent
$12.50 to $15.00	3	6
$20.00 to $24.00	16	32
$25.00 to $29.00	19	38
$30.00 to $34.00	6	12
$35.00 to $39.00	5	10
$40.00 to $45.00	1	2
	50	100

The average fee of the union lawyer is $25 per hour. The median fee is in the $25 range, and the largest number of union lawyers charge in the range of $25 to $29 per hour. (Two lawyers indicated that they represent both companies and unions, and they are therefore included in both lists.)

The fee structure for company attorneys looks quite different. It shows:

COMPANY LAWYERS' HOURLY RATES

Fee	Number Charging	Per Cent
$15.00	1	1
$20.00 to $24.00	5	4
$25.00 to $29.00	21	18
$30.00 to $34.00	25	22
$35.00 to $39.00	28	25
$40.00 to $49.00	19	17
$50.00 and up	15	13
	114	100

The average fee of the company lawyer is $36 per hour. The median fee is in the range of $35 to $39, and the largest number of lawyers also charge fees in this range. Nearly a third of the company lawyers charge more than $40 per hour, the highest reported fee being $75 per hour.

Though fees do not show any apparent regional differences, they do vary with the size of cities. Fees are naturally higher in the big cities, but in all of the cities there are fees which cover the entire range, and many lawyers practice over an entire region though they have offices in a big city. For purposes of definition we labeled as "small" a city having less than half a million people, a "medium" city as one which had between 500,000 and 1,000,000 people, and a "large" city as any over one million. The large cities are Detroit, Chicago, New York, Los Angeles, and Philadelphia. The medium cities are San Francisco, Boston, Houston, Dallas, Washington, D.C., Cleveland, Baltimore, St. Paul–Minneapolis, Milwaukee, and Pittsburgh. The small cities include Miami, Louisville, Portland, Salt Lake City, Tampa, Indianapolis, and Newark.

Because of the difference between union and management lawyers' fees the two must be shown separately, even within the city charts.

The disparity in rate is not large among union lawyers. The average hourly rate in the small city is $23, for medium cities it is $24, and for the large cities it goes to $28.

UNION LAWYERS' HOURLY RATES BY CITY SIZE

Size of City	Under $25	$25–$29	$30–$45	Number of Lawyers
Small (Under 500,000)	9	5	3	17
Medium (500,000 to 1,000,000)	8	7	3	18
Large (Over 1,000,000)	2	7	6	15
	19	19	12	50

For company lawyers the city picture is as follows:

COMPANY LAWYERS' HOURLY RATES BY CITY SIZE

Size of City	Under $30	$30–$34	$35–$39	$40 and Up	Number of Lawyers
Small (Under 500,000)	13	13	5	6	37
Medium (500,000 to 1,000,000)	12	4	11	9	36
Large (Over 1,000,000)	2	8	12	19	41
	27	25	28	34	114

Two-thirds of the small city company lawyers charge less than $35 per hour, while three-fourths of the large city lawyers charge over that amount. Close to half of the large city lawyers charge upwards of $40. The small city company attorney averages $31 per hour, the medium city lawyer averages $34 per hour, and the large city company attorney averages $40 per hour. Even the small city company lawyer earns a bit more on the average than the large city union lawyer.

The problem of total fees for an "average" one-day hearing was a little harder to pin down, for reasons already explained. Using our definition of an average one-day hearing addressed to a single issue and consuming approximately six hours, lawyers gave us information which led to some total fee calculations. Collateral information showed that company attorneys spent somewhat more time than did union attorneys in preparing the case which, along with the higher hourly charges by company counsel, accounts for the higher total charges. The typical company attorney apparently spends about eleven hours in preparing for his "average" case, while the union lawyer spends about seven hours on the same case.

Just over half of the company attorneys indicated that they do some work on retainers which are calculated to produce the same income as would hourly charges for the same amount of work. More than two-thirds of the union lawyers indicated that they have retainers, and in about one-fourth of these cases the retainer is calculated at a level below the income which an hourly rate would produce.

Post-hearing briefs are also included in total charges. Many lawyers, representing both companies and unions, indicate their belief that post-hearing briefs are unnecessary, yet almost three-quarters of the respondents regularly submit such briefs. Company lawyers said that they spend an average of eight hours in preparing post-hearing briefs, while union lawyers said they spend seven hours. Practically all company attorneys charge for post-hearing briefs, but 16 per cent of the union lawyers said that they do not.

The total fee picture, including preparation of the case, presentation of the evidence at the hearing, and preparation of a post-hearing brief, shows the following:

UNION LAWYERS' TOTAL FEES

Amount	Number Charging	Per Cent
Under $200	18	31
$200–$299	10	17
$300–$399	12	20
$400–$499	10	17
$500–$599	4	7
$600–$749	2	3
$750–$1,000	3	5
	59	100

From these figures it is clear that almost one-third of the union lawyers charge less than $200 for the average case. The average total fee for the union lawyers is $315.

Although the average company lawyer earns more than $700 in total fees from an average one-day hearing, there is no great uniformity in charges. The median is just under $600, and from $200

COMPANY LAWYERS' TOTAL FEES

Amount	Number Charging	Per Cent
Under $200	8	7
$200–$299	11	9
$300–$399	17	15
$400–$499	11	9
$500–$599	12	10
$600–$749	15	13
$750–$1,000	27	23
$1,000 and over	16	14
	117	100

to the category of over $1,000 the distribution is fairly even until one reaches the category of $750–$1,000, where the grouping is significantly larger. The highest reported fee for a union attorney was $1,000, while the highest fee for a company attorney was $2,500. Nearly one-third of the union attorneys reported charging less than $200 per case, while more than one-third of the company attorneys received more than $750 per case.

A breakdown of total fees by size of cities shows the following comparison for union and company lawyers:

TOTAL FEES FOR AVERAGE ONE-DAY HEARING

Size of City	Average Union Lawyer	Average Company Lawyer
Small (Under 500,000)	$273	$491
Medium (500,000 to 1,000,000)	$297	$639
Large (Over 1,000,000)	$382	$890

The average company lawyer in the large city makes 39 per cent more than his counterpart in the medium-sized city, and 81 per cent more than his colleague in the small city. The range on the union side is much smaller. The big city union lawyer gets 29 per cent more than his counterpart in the medium-sized city, and 40 per cent more than the small city attorney.

The difficulty of working with averages shows up if one goes back over the figures involving lawyers. The company attorney says that he spends an average of eleven hours preparing for a case. By definition the case itself takes another six hours. He then spends eight hours in preparing a post-hearing brief. His total hours would then equal twenty-five, and the average hourly fee would give a total fee of $900, yet our average fee for the management lawyer comes out just over $700. The same disparity shows up in connection with union lawyers. The union lawyer says that he spends an average of seven hours of advance preparation. Added to this is six hours of case hearing, and another seven hours of post-hearing brief preparation. The total is twenty hours, the average hourly fee is $25, and the total fee should then be $500 — but our previous statistics show that it is $315. This distortion arises out of piling averages on averages. There are also other contributing factors, such as the fact that in about one-quarter of the cases counsel do not prepare briefs, thus eliminating a substantial number of hours which have been included in the above computations.

It is likely that the total fee figures given by the respondents in answer to Question 10 on the questionnaire are accurate, because they are readily obtainable from the lawyers' account books.

THE COST OF COURT REPORTERS

A transcript is not required in arbitration hearings, and is not provided in the majority of the cases. An American Arbitration Association study in 1954 found that out of 1,183 cases a transcript was provided in about 23 per cent of the cases. In a more recent survey of about 100 discharge cases, the AAA found that there were transcripts in one-third of the cases.

Our information with respect to charges by court reporters comes from a selected sample of court reporters who belong to the National Shorthand Reporters' Association in the larger cities, and from lawyers who were asked to tell us, along with information about their own fees, what transcripts cost their clients. The reports from lawyers would indicate that the cost of the transcript is somewhat less than the figure one would obtain by computing costs on the basis of the rates supplied by reporters. The discrepancy may be accounted for by the intimation which occasionally appeared that where there is a rate range reporters may charge a little less for arbitration than for court work, and by the use of "averages."

Rates for reporters usually include three items: (1) an attendance fee which is generally billed at an hourly rate, (2) a per page charge for reproduction of the testimony, with a higher rate for the original copy than for the carbons, and (3) travel expenses for the reporter.

A court reporter can apparently take about fifty pages per hour in the course of a hearing. Travel expenses would, of course, vary with the location. As to the other items, this is what we found in a survey of six cities:

COURT REPORTERS' FEES

City	Price, Original and One Carbon	Second Carbon	Attendance Fee
City 1 (Southwest)	$1.40	.40	none
City 2 (Southwest)	$1.55	.30	$9.50 per hour
City 3 (West Coast)	$1.37	.25	Not available
City 4 (Middle West)	$1.30	.40	$6.00 per hour
City 5 (Middle West)	$1.25	.25	$6.00 per hour
City 6 (East—not New York)	$1.25	.25	$5.00 per hour

Our average one-day hearing was defined as six hours, but the reporter is not transcribing testimony all of this time. The total cost of a transcript seems to run between $200 and $300, with each side paying one-half of the expense. The range of the total bill varies with the number of copies which the parties obtain. Sometimes each side obtains a copy but one of these copies is then sent to the arbitrator, along with the brief, and he is asked to return it when the case is decided. On a 200-page transcript, which might represent something like four hours of fairly steady reporting, a third copy of the transcript would cost the parties between $50 and $80, depending on the rates in the particular city.

TOTAL SERVICE FEE COSTS OF ARBITRATION

From the previous information it is possible to put together a schedule which will show what purport to be average service fee costs to a union and to a company for a one-day arbitration case. This does not represent the total cost because it does not include the following items, and perhaps others which might apply in a particular case: (1) travel expenses for the arbitrator, (2) travel expenses for counsel, (3) travel expenses for the court reporter, (4) lost time paid for committeemen attending the hearing, (5) conference room expense, (6) preparation time by company and union representatives other than counsel, (7) service fee for agency under whose auspices the hearing is conducted, (8) and any damages which the company may have to pay as the result of the decision. Of these items only travel and lost time paid are likely to add up to much.

Looking solely at the fees of arbitrators, lawyers, and court reporters the cost of an average one-day hearing emerges as follows:

	Cost to the Union	Cost to the Company
Arbitrator's fee ($400)[a]	$200	$200
Lawyer's fee	315	700
Court reporter's fee ($250)	125	125
Total	$640	$1,025

[a] Average fee per case for all FMCS cases in 1963.

In comparing lawyers' charges to companies and unions it will be remembered that hourly charges by company lawyers are more than in the case of union counsel, but that they also reported working more hours in preparing the case and in writing post-hearing briefs.

POSSIBLE ALTERNATIVES TO ARBITRATION

If arbitration is indeed becoming too costly consideration must be given to other alternatives.

One of the alternatives, of course, is to abolish arbitration and return to the strike and the lockout. But this is not a real alternative. As has already been pointed out, arbitration serves a much broader purpose than mere replacement of the strike, and in any event the strike is no longer feasible in many industries. Whatever dissatisfaction there may be with arbitration there is no evidence that the parties are giving any serious consideration to abandoning it in favor of the strike.[13]

Another possible alternative is to seek free arbitration through the state or federal governments. There was a time, starting in the late

---

[13] *Supra* note 2, at 1116.

1930's and extending into the middle 1940's, when the United States Conciliation Service (predecessor to the Federal Mediation and Conciliation Service) offered free arbitration. Staff members supplied the service. The practice was abandoned in 1947 after the passage of the Taft-Hartley Act, and was replaced by the present system under which the Service furnishes the parties with the names of private arbitrators. In the last few years of free arbitration the Service instituted a requirement that those applying for free service must be recommended as being in need by a local representative of the Service. This requirement was apparently bitterly resisted by local union representatives. In 1945 the President's Labor-Management Conference recommended that free services be abandoned partly because of the undesirability of having the government choose among applicants for free service, and also because there was thought to be an inconsistency between mediation and arbitration functions when performed by the same staff members.

A few states provide a limited amount of free arbitration,[14] with New York doubtless being the most active among them. Even in New York, however, the amount of free service is declining by deliberate choice of the state agency. Little or nothing is done to make known the availability of the free service, while attention is called to the Board's list of private arbitrators who are paid by the parties for their services. In 1955 about 95 per cent of the arbitration conducted under the auspices of the New York Board was free, but in 1962 the figure had declined to 45 per cent and there was hope that the figure would drop still further. One concern which some of the Board members have felt is that if free arbitration is too readily available it will be used by the parties as a routine part of their grievance procedure and will thus have an undesirable effect upon bargaining.

Under the New York system there is a screening process through which free arbitration is made available. In the first place, both parties must ask for it and if either party prefers a private arbitrator the Board will not assign a staff arbitrator. Even if both parties make the request it is not always granted. In general the Board apparently tries to provide free service only where one of the parties is unable to pay and where the issue is not critical to the future relationship of the parties. Opinions by staff arbitrators are usually not published.

---

[14] *Supra* note 2, at 1146.

The best known and most extensive of all governmental services in the arbitration field are those carried on under the Railway Labor Act. Arbitration boards are tripartite and the government pays the neutral arbitrator, supplies the hearing site, furnishes the court reporter, and absorbs administrative costs. The parties supply their own board members and pay counsel to prepare cases for them.

At one time the Railway Labor Act arbitration procedures seemed to be working well, but in recent years they have bogged down. In 1961 an independent study group, working under the auspices of the Committee for Economic Development, recommended that the Railway Labor Act be amended so that the parties could set up their own arbitration machinery. Said the study group:

. . . there seems little reason for the public to subsidize grievance arbitration on the railroads. It may be noted that the airlines, whose operations fall generally within the provisions of the Railway Labor Act, have been encouraged under the Act to develop their own grievance machinery and have done so. There is no good reason why the railroads and their unions should not also be required to set up machinery of their own making. If experience in other industries is any guide, this would lead to a swifter and more responsive grievance procedure. It would thereby serve the public interest and place the burden for their own affairs on the parties.[15]

Finally, there is the possibility of labor courts, modeled after those found in Western Europe. While the pattern found in those countries is not completely uniform, most of them appear to be tripartite, and heavy reliance is placed upon settlements reached through conciliation. Jurisdiction is usually based upon the collective contract, but in France the court hears only individual complaints, growing out of employment and apprenticeship contracts.[16] In many of the countries private arbitration is available alongside the labor court system. More information is needed than is presently available before a judgment can be made as to the usefulness of a labor court system adapted to the American needs. The case load in the Scandinavian countries has recently run only 40

---

[15] Labor Study Group, Comm. for Economic Development, THE PUBLIC INTEREST IN NATIONAL LABOR POLICY 105 (1961).

[16] BRAUN, LABOR DISPUTES AND THEIR SETTLEMENT 306 (1955); GALENSON, THE DANISH SYSTEM OF LABOR RELATIONS 210 (1952); GALENSON, LABOR IN NORWAY 238 (1949); McPherson, *Basic Issues in German Labor Court Structure*, 5 LAB. L.J. 439 (1954).

to 100 cases a year.[17] Obviously this would be but a trickle of the current American case load.

CONCLUSIONS

Much of the difficulty in sensibly discussing arbitration costs arises out of a failure, or an unwillingness, to distinguish between the deluxe and the economy models. For instance:

1. It is possible in most cases to hold arbitration hearings in company conference rooms. This is frequently done, and there is no reason to think that it in any way prejudices the hearing. Why do the parties so frequently rent a hotel room?

2. A majority of cases are heard without court reporters being present even though the parties (General Motors, for example) could well afford a transcript. Have the parties really given careful consideration to whether they need a reporter?

3. Despite increased legal implications in the arbitration area, the bulk of the cases still involve old stand-bys like discipline and discharge, seniority, and job classification. Our sample of discharge cases heard before FMCS arbitrators showed lawyers present only a small percentage of the time.[18] Are lawyers necessary if the parties are willing to give their own representatives training in presenting routine cases?

4. There is an admitted need for new arbitrators, and there are available candidates, but the parties have been very slow in accepting them. New arbitrators are in less demand than the professionals and therefore charge smaller fees. If, as we shall argue in chapter 4, there is a high degree of predictability in the outcome of the routine arbitration case no matter who hears it, why do the parties not show a greater willingness to use lower-priced arbitrators?

5. Part of the arbitrator's total fee (perhaps the most substantial part) is attributable to the expectation of the parties that there will be a written opinion. A decision, sans opinion, would be considerably more economical. The American Arbitration Association suggested this to its clientele and got almost no response. Do the parties really need opinions as much as they think they do?

The economy-deluxe choice is admittedly complicated by the fact

---

[17] McPherson, *Labor Courts in Western Europe*, 18 ILL. BUS. REV. 6 (1961).
[18] *Supra* note 12.

that the two parties to the proceeding—the company and the union — may prefer different models. And a union which tries to economize while the company goes first class is always left wondering whether it exercised a false economy, or whether it would have lost the case on the merits in any event. The only answer to this problem is a recognition by both parties that they have a stake in a mutually acceptable arbitration system. If the union is indeed hard pressed financially the company which deliberately runs up the expense of an arbitration proceeding is undermining the process. Such a decision ought at least to be made with full recognition of its consequences.

Discounting the occasional abuses which will take place under any system, arbitrators' fees have not increased by an inordinate amount; that is, they do not appear to have increased disproportionately to such standards as average hourly wages in manufacturing. This being so, one wonders whether most of the complaints about rising costs in arbitration do not in fact have their origin in other — although related — factors.

Is it possible that the taste of the parties has changed over the years, and that they are no longer satisfied with the stripped-down arbitration model? Do they now want some of the frills which were once considered unnecessary, just as they now want air conditioning despite the fact that it was long considered unessential?

Is the increased resort to arbitration, shown by all the statistics, running up total costs to the point where the parties think the unit cost is much greater though it may not be?

Is the fact that the context of bargaining now places a much greater emphasis on job security than it once did, and thereby raises some very difficult issues in arbitration, causing more time and effort to be devoted to cases than they once required, thus distorting the total picture?

Is the increased time-lag between the final step in the grievance procedure and an arbitration decision, which is discussed in chapter 3, creating a climate of criticism of the arbitration process which spills over into unhappiness about costs?

In capsule form the cost problem reduces itself to this: Costs are increasing, and there are doubtless situations in which this fact imposes an onerous burden on the parties. Nevertheless, there are perfectly clear devices open to the parties for reducing costs. In all except the most extreme cases these steps, if taken, will prove effective. First, however, the parties must reach a mutual conviction that they want to do something about costs. To date they have not done so.

Fee Questionnaire

1. I practice in and around the city of _____.

2. My clients are primarily: _____ Companies _____ Unions.

3. My labor arbitration work is done: _____ On Retainer _____ On fee _____ Both.

4. My usual hourly fee for labor arbitration work, including adjustment for time spent by associates if necessary, is _____.

5. On retainer I do _____ substantial _____ some _____ little _____ none of my arbitration work. (Estimated per cent, if possible: _____)

6. When I work on retainer, it is calculated or estimated as follows:
   a. _____ To approximate my usual hourly fee.
   b. To be _____ per cent less than my usual hourly fee.
   c. _____ As a minimum payment to be consumed at the hourly rate as work is performed, with excess hours billed at the usual hourly rate.
   d. _____ Other (Please explain.) _____

7. For an average one-day one-grievance arbitration, lasting approximately six hours, I estimate that we spend _____ hours in preparing the case, including research and interviews, preparation of hearing and pre-hearing statements, exhibits, etc.

8. I usually file a post-hearing brief. _____ Yes _____ No

9. I estimate that it takes _____ hours to prepare a post-hearing brief following a one-day one-grievance arbitration lasting approximately six hours. I usually charge for the preparation of a post-hearing brief. _____ Yes _____ No

10. I would estimate my *average total fee* for a one-day one-grievance arbitration lasting approximately six hours at _____ dollars.

11. I usually bill my clients for time spent in travel. ____ Yes ____ No
    a. Travel time is billed at my usual hourly rate. ____ Yes ____ No
    b. Travel time is billed on a different basis. (Please explain) _____

12. My clients pay my travel expenses in addition to my fee. ——— Yes ——— No

13. I ——— encourage ——— insist on ——— discourage the use of transcripts by my labor arbitration clients.

14. My clients' transcript cost for the average six-hour one-day one-grievance hearing is about ——— dollars. This average cost includes, usually, ——— half ——— all the attendance fee *and* one one and one-half copies (splitting the arbitrator's copy) ——— two copies of the transcript.

15. In multiple grievance cases is it your opinion that the cost per grievance is ——— appreciably less, ——— a bit less, or ——— about the same?

16. In general, are the grievances, in your opinion, as effectively screened by parties when several are presented at once as in single grievance cases? ——— Yes ——— No

Chapter 3

PROBLEMS OF TIME-LAG AND FORMALITY

Along with costs, alleged excessive formality (sometimes called "legalisms") and time-lag share most of the criticism which is directed at the arbitration process. The nature of the time-lag charge is self-evident, i.e., that a process once known for its speedy resolution of disputed matters now moves at a ponderous pace. The formality criticism is more complicated since it includes a bundle of interchangeable items. The substance of the charge is that the merits of the dispute get lost in arguments over arbitrability, the form of the grievance, technical rules as to the admissibility of evidence, the application of precedent, reliance upon transcripts, briefs, etc.

These charges need not, of course, be taken entirely uncritically. Arbitrators are inclined to agree, for instance, that the weakest link in the arbitration process is often the woefully inadequate state of preparation in which the parties approach the hearing. Some of this could be remedied by a little more attention to what might be classified as "formalities." More will be said about this later. There are also experienced and respected lawyers representing both sides who feel strongly that loose practices on the part of arbitrators in admitting irrelevant evidence unduly prolong and complicate cases. Some of this showed up in a 1963 survey which the American Bar Association's Committee on Arbitration conducted. A few of the comments bear repeating:

. . . in my experience arbitrators do not limit purposeless and irrelevant evidence, and thereby do unnecessarily increase the cost of the hearings. I have a favorite expression, that if someone would offer a telephone directory it would be received as evidence whether it had any bearing on the case or not. An arbitrator tends to allow all evidence, whether by document or testimony to be placed in the record, and later decide whether the evidence is relevant. This does unnecessarily extend the hearing and increases the cost.

. . . . .

While it is true that the normal rules of evidence may be relaxed during an arbitral proceeding, it is my experience that arbitrators, instead of relaxing the rules, often disregard them and permit endless testimony which is both repetitive and in some instances completely irrelevant. This of course tends to increase the cost of the hearings. In addition there is the "wear and tear" on opposing counsel who have to sit through long examinations which will in no way affect the arbitrator's award since the testimony is repetitious, not in substantiation of the issues and in some cases merely for the purpose of satisfying a client that he has done his duty by testifying.

I might add, parenthetically, that not only do arbitrators permit purpose-less and irrelevant evidence during the hearing but they compound the felony by reciting this needless part of the record in their opinions. This frequently is confusing to the parties and completely wasteful.[1]

The fact that some of the criticisms are contradictory must not be allowed to hide the fact that there are problems which deserve serious consideration. On the question of time-lag there is documentation, though unfortunately the existing surveys are not entirely additive. In 1957 the American Arbitration Association published an analysis of 1,183 cases drawn from its 1954 file of cases.[2] In 1958 Arthur Ross related the results of his examination of approximately 75 to 150 cases drawn from decisions published in the *Labor Arbitration Reports*.[3] And in the spring of 1964 the General Counsel of the Federal Mediation and Conciliation Service, Mr. H. T. Herrick, gave some preliminary figures derived from approximately 250 cases drawn at random from the 1963 Service files.[4] Some of the figures can be matched up, and when this is done the result is as follows:

CHART 1

Date	Survey Auspices	Average Lapse of Time from Demand to Decision
1954	AAA	97.5 days
1963	FMCS	154 days

CHART 2

Date of Cases	Survey Auspices	Average Lapse of Time from Grievance to Hearing	Average Lapse of Time from Hearing to Decision
1945–46	Ross	99.9 days	27.8 days
1955–56	Ross	111.7 days	45.9 days
1963	FMCS	167 days	73 days

[1] ABA Comm. on Labor Arbitration Report No. 10 (1963).
[2] American Arbitration Ass'n, *Procedural and Substantive Aspects of Labor-Management Arbitration*, 12 Arb. J. (n.s.) 67 (1957).
[3] Ross, *The Well-Aged Arbitration Case*, 11 Ind. & Lab. Rel. Rev. 262 (1958).
[4] Address by H. T. Herrick, General Counsel, Federal Mediation and Conciliation Service, to Cleveland arbitrators, Spring, 1964.

CHART 3

Date of Survey	Auspices	Grievance to Demand	Demand to Appointment	Appointment to Hearing	Hearing to Decision
1963	FMCS	86 days	30 days[a]	51 days	73 days

[a] Three days for the FMCS to make the appointment and 27 days for the parties to reply.

Methodological differences in the surveys preclude placing too heavy reliance on comparative results. We do not know in the Ross and FMCS samples, for instance, how many cases involved transcripts and briefs, but we are told that in the AAA survey there were transcripts in about one-quarter of the cases. Nevertheless, a clear trend in the direction of more time is evident. This trend is confirmed by at least one other measure. We used as evidence the discharge cases from the files of the Federal Mediation and Conciliation Service already mentioned (100 decided in 1951-52, 100 in 1956-57, and 100 in 1962-63). Again, discharge cases were taken in order to make the three samples as nearly comparable as possible. From the files we then constructed a graph which shows the lapse of time from the date of the arbitrator's appointment until the date of the award in each of the three periods. It shows that even in discharge cases it took about two weeks longer in 1962-63 to get a case decided than in 1951-52. Since discharge cases are usually decided more expeditiously than others, it is the trend in these cases rather than the total elapsed time which is significant.

The rapid growth in grievance arbitration, which is documented in chapter 1, is partly responsible for the fact that it now takes much longer to process cases. Numerical reduction in union membership has sometimes caused a cut-back on staff services just when demand for arbitration is increasing. Multiplant companies often utilize a traveling central staff to try cases and this factor must be fitted into the equation. Experienced arbitrators are more in demand than ever and therefore less readily available. And insofar as the parties tend to rely on already busy lawyers to represent them, a further delay is experienced as schedules are accommodated.

Some of the increase in formalities is doubtless traceable to the fact that since the Supreme Court's decision in the *Lincoln Mills* case in 1957 the law has played a much more important part in the arbitration process than it did previously.[5] The new General Electric-IUE contract, for instance, deliberately reduces the power which the Supreme Court found to reside in the arbitrator in the *Steelworker Trilogy*.[6] In the GE contract, grievances are carefully defined so that some go to arbitration by right while others can go only by common consent. Arbitrability may be questioned and, if it is, arbitration can only proceed after a court order. Then, the court order must specify the issues to be arbitrated, and the arbitrator has no authority to consider issues other than those which are specified. To cap it all off the contract includes the following clause: "No matter will be considered arbitrable unless it is found that the parties clearly agreed that the subject involved would be arbitrable in light of the principles of arbitrability set forth in this Article and no court or arbitrator shall or may proceed under any presumption that a request to arbitrate is arbitrable." [7]

One wonders also whether there isn't a certain inevitability about the life cycle of administrative processes which tends to move them inexorably from the simple toward the complex. A clear illustration of this is found in the field of workmen's compensation. In the early years of the century proponents of workmen's compensation laws were sure that such statutes would, by withdrawing work injury cases from the courts, thereafter insure an inexpensive, expeditious, and informal procedure. But by 1953 two of the foremost students of that subject would write: "The evidence is clear that workmen's compensation has left unfulfilled most of its major original objectives."[8] ". . . advances have been made at the expense of increasing complexity, ambiguity, litigiousness, and costliness in the whole process. . . ."[9]

Since the arbitration process is not cast from a common mold, it is hard to analyze problems of time-lag and excessive formalities in a general context. On the other hand, the variety is so extensive that there is no choice but to attempt generalizations, while admitting at the outset that they may not apply to any given situation. For convenience of analysis it is easiest to divide the problem into

---

[5] Textile Workers Union v. Lincoln Mills, 353 U.S. 448 (1957); see ch. 1, pp. 21–29.

[6] COLLECTIVE BARGAINING NEGOTIATIONS & CONTRACTS 20:801, 817ff. (1963).

[7] *Id.* at 819.

[8] H. A. & Anne Somers, *Workmen's Compensation: Unfulfilled Promise,* 7 IND. & LAB. REL. REV. 32, 33 (1953).

[9] *Ibid.*

three stages: pre-hearing problems, hearing problems, and post-hearing problems.

PRE-HEARING PROBLEMS

There is little that outsiders can do to help the parties speed up the time which it now takes from the demand for arbitration to the date of the hearing. Chart 3 shows, for instance, that it takes almost a month for the parties to agree upon and get an arbitrator appointed from the time the Federal Mediation and Conciliation Service gives them a panel. These same figures show that it is fifty-one days from the time an arbitrator is appointed until the date of the hearing. It is impossible to know how much of this time is attributable to the parties and how much is due to the difficulty in finding an open date on the arbitrator's calendar. Insofar as it is caused by the unavailability of the arbitrator the only answer appears to be an increased willingness on the part of companies and unions to experiment with new arbitrators. That subject is discussed elsewhere in this volume, and the argument is advanced that there is less risk than the parties seem to think on this score.[10]

More constructive criticism can be directed at the pre-hearing formalities. Most arbitrators can agree that in the typical *ad hoc* case, and even in some umpire situations, the pre-hearing preparation is not what it should be. In the usual case the arbitrator knows nothing at all about the case until he arrives at the hearing. The actual grievance may state a complaint without alleging a specific contract violation, and the company's answer may simply say, "Grievance denied." At the hearing a good deal of time may be wasted in reaching agreement on what it is that the arbitrator is to decide. When the issue is finally framed it may be one to which the parties are not prepared to speak. The hearing is likely to go on, even so, because there will be a reluctance to incur the additional expense of a reconvened meeting, and the out-of-town company and union representatives who are present may be busy later. Because of his lack of knowledge about the case, the arbitrator will be unprepared to ask meaningful questions, and it may be decision time before he realizes what he should have asked and didn't. At that point his choice is to reconvene the hearing and ask for the information, which may turn out to be inconsequential, or go

---

[10] See ch. 4.

ahead and make a decision without it. The arbitrator is likely to go ahead with his decision since another day of hearing will probably be resisted by the parties. A heavy premium is thus placed on the arbitrator's general experience and on his sensitivity to factors which have not been adequately presented.

In the phraseology of the courts, it is the "pleadings" which are weak in arbitration. Despite the fact that the parties are critical of formalities in arbitration, perhaps the situation could be improved by looking at the court experience with similar problems.

One of the most dismal pages in legal history relates to the injustices which arose out of tricky and highly technical rules with respect to pleading. More recently the rules have been completely revised, but there is now a frank recognition that pleadings alone will seldom be adequate to inform the parties properly of the nature of the lawsuit.[11] Therefore the rules now provide for discovery and pre-trial conference. Let us look at these techniques to see if they would have any value in arbitration.

Under the Federal Rules of Civil Procedure the principal devices for discovery are set forth in Rules 26 through 37.[12] Included are provisions for depositions, interrogatories, and requests for the production of documents. Additionally, there are provisions for obtaining the physical and mental examinations of parties and for requests for admission of facts and genuineness of documents.

Properly used, discovery might be useful in arbitration, but on balance the disadvantages seem to outweigh the advantages. The mechanics of the device almost inevitably create an adversary atmosphere, and there would be an almost irresistible impulse to "go fishing." More important, discovery does not go to the heart of the problem. Companies and unions are usually willing to give each other information bearing on a grievance. The difficulty is that they are often not equipped to know what they need or how to go ahead and get it. Thus if X alleges that he was entitled to a promotion which went to Y, it may turn out that the core of his complaint is that in the past the company has always promoted the senior man without inquiry into his qualifications. Too often the case ar-

---

[11] Chandler, *Discovery and Pre-Trial Procedure in Federal Courts*, 21 Okla. L. Rev. 321 (1959); Clark, *Simplified Pleading*, 2 F.R.D. 456 (1948); Pike, *Some Current Trends in the Construction of the Federal Rules*, 9 Geo. Wash. L. Rev. 26 (1940); Shields, *Advantages to a Trial Lawyer of a Pre-Trial Conference*, 23 F.R.D. 342 (1959).

[12] Fed. R. Civ. P. 26–37.

rives at arbitration without any satisfactory evidence as to what the company has done in the past.

There is another reason why discovery is unlikely to contribute much to the arbitration process. The heart of the successful discovery process is the interrogatory, and the drafting of interrogatories is a job for a skilled practitioner. Further expense would be incurred in hiring such assistance, and this the parties would prefer to avoid.

If discovery procedures seem to offer little promise, how about the pre-trial conference? Under pre-trial rules, before the case is brought to trial the parties meet with the judge (or with another judge who will not hear the case, or perhaps with some other designated officer of the court) for the purpose of stipulating facts, clarifying the theory of the case, and exploring the possibilities for settlement without going to trial.[13]

An effective grievance procedure is, by definition, a sort of pre-trial conference. In its steps the parties normally have at least three chances, short of arbitration, to examine and settle the case. Unfortunately, they often fail to explore thoroughly the chances of settlement. Some examples will serve to illustrate the point.

X was discharged for causing a "quickie" strike by driving his automobile across the driveway to the plant and blocking traffic during the hour when employees were reporting to work. He insisted that he had not come to work that day, but he was unable to prove his whereabouts or to account for the undeniable fact that his car was blocking the driveway. At the hearing the company guard, who had seen the car drive across the road and had seen the occupant get out, testified. On seeing the grievant for the first time he stated that this was not the man who got out of the car. Other testimony developed the fact that a member of the grievant's car pool had borrowed his car and committed the rule infraction. Clearly the company had fired the wrong man.

In another case, the company did what parties to an arbitration seldom do: it deliberately withheld from the union knowledge of the fact that it had a second witness in a case which would otherwise put the word of a foreman against the word of a production worker. When the second witness appeared at the hearing the union was

---

[13] Holtzoff, *Federal Pre-Trial Procedure*, 11 Am. U. Intra. L. Rev. 21 (1962); see, generally, Nims, Pre-Trial (1950); Murrah, *Pre-Trial Procedure*, 14 F.R.D. 417 (1953) (good bibliography).

naturally irked. In an umpire context he might not have been allowed to testify, but in an *ad hoc* proceeding it would normally
be allowed. The testimony of the second witness might very well
be the deciding element in such a case.

In a third case the company attorney and the union's international
representative came into the case, as they so often do, only the night
before the hearing. They had time for only brief conversations with
their constituents. In one of the issues the company was defending
a rate on a new job against a claim by the grievant that it was
more like Job A, which was higher-rated, than like Job B, which
paid less. To the attorney's utter astonishment, the company's industrial engineer, when asked how he thought the two jobs compared,
responded that he too thought the job in question was a little
more like A than B!

Many cases go to arbitration which should be settled in the
course of an efficient grievance procedure. The fact remains that
not all grievance procedures are efficient and that the parties will
not always take the proper steps to improve them.

Might a pre-arbitration conference procedure, patterned after the
pre-trial conference, serve a useful purpose in some cases? The success of the pre-trial conference is heavily dependent on the judge,
or other court officer, and there is no readily available counterpart
on the arbitration side. The arbitrator might be utilized, but there
are at least two disadvantages to this. One is that some parties
vigorously oppose the idea of having the same man who will ultimately judge the case attempt to mediate it. (The same criticism
applies in the courts, of course.) The other is that the arbitrator
will have to be paid for his time, and since most grievances can be
heard on the merits in a day the parties feel that they would be
unnecessarily wasting money. This attitude is unlikely to change
although it may be penny-wise and pound-foolish since many
cases would be settled without the additional expense of study-
time and the preparation of an opinion.

A possible solution to this problem is the establishment of a formal apprenticeship system, a device which ought to be given
serious consideration because it has a good many advantages. This
system would require the cooperation of professional arbitrators,
the appointing services, and the parties. Let us look at it in a little
more detail.

No one doubts that the arbitration load is increasing all the time, and that the experienced arbitrators do not have time to handle all the cases which arise. At the same time, the parties are reluctant to experiment with new arbitrators. It is a historical fact that many of the present arbitrators got their experience with the War Labor Board, often while serving in junior positions under the guidance of more senior executives. By and large these young men did well and learned quickly. There is now an opportunity in the arbitration field to duplicate some of that experience. A great many cases come to arbitration without being properly prepared and without the opportunities for settlement being fully explored. A pre-arbitration conference would settle some of these cases and greatly improve the presentation of others by sharpening the questions and encouraging the parties to prepare better. Apprentice arbitrators could serve as neutral chairmen in pre-arbitration conferences in much the same way that the young assistants of the War Labor Board era served as assistants on cases which were scheduled for possible hearing before the Board. At a modest per diem rate they could meet with the parties and discuss the case. Several advantages would flow from such an experience. The parties would benefit by eliminating some cases and better preparing others which did go to arbitration. Apprentice arbitrators would be given the experience which parties want them to have before they become journeymen arbitrators. The load on experienced arbitrators would be relieved, and a continuing source of supply for new arbitrators would be established. Finally, the whole effort would have a sound foundation in experience in that all experiments to date seem to show that the best way to train acceptable new arbitrators is to have them work with older and already accepted arbitrators.[14]

One possibility, then, for improving pre-hearing aspects of the arbitration process is to work out an apprentice system for conducting pre-arbitration conferences. The same general system could be used in connection with the hearing and post-hearing stages, but comment on that will be reserved for the moment.

There is another pre-hearing device which, if widely adopted, would immensely improve present procedures. In the better-run umpire systems, e.g., General Motors and U.S. Steel, each side prepares a *pre-hearing* statement and largely dispenses with a *post-*

---

[14] D. Jones & R. Smith, *Management and Labor Appraisals and Criticisms of the Arbitration Process: A Report with Comments*, 62 MICH. L. REV. 1115, 1137 (1964).

hearing statement. A pre-hearing statement has several advantages. In the first place, it forces the parties to explore the case so that they are able to write about it. Second, reducing matters to writing often exposes weaknesses in the case which are somehow glossed over in oral preparation. Third, the arbitrator knows in advance of the case what he is to hear and he is therefore better qualified to ask intelligent questions about the case. Such a procedure is not novel. A recent example to which public attention has been directed involves the Ingersoll-Rand Company and the Steelworkers Union. In that system, with Israel Ben Scheiber serving as umpire, the parties exchange brief written statements of the grievances and facts, and of their views on contract interpretation, application, and their mutual obligations. A joint statement of facts is submitted if the parties can agree on one; otherwise two are tendered. After reviewing the advance information, the umpire holds hearings and asks questions. The parties may make statements on their positions, limited to points covered in the advance materials. Thereafter, decisions are rendered, not all of which are accompanied by opinions.

Pre-hearing statements are not much used in *ad hoc* cases at the present time. If the parties could be persuaded of their value perhaps they would be. There would be the problem of training local people to prepare statements (lawyers are still used in a minority of the cases), or in providing central services from union or company headquarters. This problem could be met, just as companies and unions meet other training problems, if they considered it of sufficient importance.

In short, the pre-hearing aspects of arbitration can be improved if the parties want them to be and if arbitrators and the appointing services are willing to provide some imaginative leadership. More will be said on that score in the concluding chapter.

THE HEARING STAGE

If the suggestions which have already been made for the pre-hearing stage were widely adopted the hearing would automatically improve. No time would be wasted in defining the issue, facts which were not in dispute would be stipulated in advance, there would be less need for a transcript, the arbitrator would know enough about the case to ask the questions which he deemed wise, and the hearing would be much more expeditious.

Insofar as there is no delay in establishing hearing dates because the arbitrator is unavailable earlier, the apprentice system would help resolve the difficulty. The steel companies have experimented satisfactorily with the use of hearing officers whose draft decisions are subject to the approval of the permanent umpire. A number of the junior associates who got started under that system are now established arbitrators in their own right.

It is easier to operate an apprentice system within the framework of a permanent umpire system, but it is not impossible even in the *ad hoc* situation. With the cooperation of the appointing agencies, established arbitrators could affiliate with junior associates. Such associates could conduct hearings and prepare draft opinions which would be discussed with and approved by the senior man. The parties would understand the nature of the junior-senior relationship and a single fee would be charged, with the financial relationship between junior and senior left to them.

Even if time-lag problems could be worked out through some of the devices suggested above, there would remain complaints about the "technicalities" of the hearing. Many of these have to do with the handling of evidence. There are those who complain that rules of evidence introduce an unneeded note of formality into the arbitration proceeding, and others who complain because arbitrators don't exclude many things that they deem irrelevant. This is not really a dispute about the rules of evidence at all, though most of the critics phrase it in those terms. Fundamentally, it is a question of policy on which there are different viewpoints. On the one hand, there are those who say that the arbitration hearing's prime function is to let people say what they want to say since it is a part of the therapeutic process known as the grievance procedure. Thus, it is more important to "waste" time hearing irrelevancies than to conduct a more expeditious but less satisfying hearing for those who think they have a grievance. On the other hand, there are those who believe that the therapy ought to be taken care of short of arbitration and that by the time the dispute reaches the arbitration level every effort should be made to make the proceeding as efficient as possible. These differences in view, which are not likely to be reconciled, arguably shouldn't be because the parties are permitted a greater flexibility in deciding what kind of arbitration they want.

Another evidentiary problem which is a frequent subject of controversy in arbitration has to do with the burden of proof. Mere mention of the subject causes some people to engage in a heated discourse about the introduction into arbitration of useless and misleading technicalities borrowed from the courts. Others see in the concept only a device for promoting fair and orderly proceedings.

Part of the difficulty in talking about burden of proof is that the term means several different things and is often used without careful definition. It can mean the burden of pleading, the burden of producing evidence, and the burden of persuasion. When used in the sense of burden of persuasion, it involves further questions as to the quantum of evidence, or standard of proof, which will be required to prevail in the particular case.

Insofar as the term "burden of proof" is used to mean the burden of pleading, it clearly has no meaning in the arbitration field because there are no comparable technical rules with respect to stating a cause of action or a defense. There is, on the other hand, a good deal of quibbling about who has the burden of producing evidence. This is an unrewarding argument over a problem which is made difficult only if one confuses the question of going forward with the evidence with the separable question of who has the burden of persuasion. Logic, good sense, and the expeditious conduct of the hearing dictate that the company go forward with the evidence in many situations simply because there is no other way to get the facts in the record. In discipline and discharge cases this is now largely accepted, but it applies equally to other kinds of cases. Thus, seniority is often alleged to have been violated on layoff or promotion on the grounds that the senior man was entitled to the job and didn't get it. Suppose the contract contains a clause requiring that the senior man must be qualified in order to take the job and the company takes the position that he is not qualified in the particular case. Since the company made the decision that the senior man was not qualified the logical way to proceed is to have the company offer its evidence first. Presumably it knows why it disqualified the man, while the union may or may not know. For the union to go forward necessitates the introduction of evidence which may prove to be both unnecessary and irrelevant. This is so apparent that one can explain the company's reluctance to proceed in such cases only on the ground that it fears it is being asked to accept the burden of persuasion, as distinguished from the burden of producing evidence.

Because controversies over the burden of proof question so often fail to specify that it is only the burden of persuasion which is in dispute, great impatience is expressed with the whole subject and it frequently becomes an annoying "technicality." Arbitrators largely avoid addressing themselves to the question, and in a great many cases there is no necessity for doing so. The fact remains that many cases cannot be resolved without making a decision both as to who has the burden of persuasion and as to what quantum of evidence is required. Let us look at some specific examples.

X was discharged by his employer for stealing. He was also arrested, on complaint of the company, and was, at the time of the arbitration hearing, suing the company for false arrest. The evidence which was adduced at the arbitration hearing, in which X was contending that he had not been fired for just cause, showed the following: X worked on the third shift as a fork lift operator. Part of his job was to transport pigs of lead from one part of the plant to another. The plant yard was lighted, and during the night a plant guard, who was stationed on a rooftop, saw X make repeated trips, carrying pigs of lead, from one of the buildings to a spot alongside the fence which bounded the company's property. Unfortunately, the guard could not see X unload the pigs since this was done behind a small shed where there was a narrow passageway between the shed and the fence. The guard did observe that X returned from each trip with an empty fork lift.

When the guard became convinced that X was preparing to take the pigs, he reported the matter to his supervisor and was instructed to keep watch on X for the balance of the night. During the evening lunch break, X was observed moving his quarter-ton truck to a parking place exactly opposite the spot in the fence where he had deposited the pigs. All this the guard once more reported. Suspecting that X could be caught red-handed, two or three guards followed him as he left the plant and approached his truck. For unaccountable reasons the guards then "goofed." Without waiting for X to lift the fence (which was newly cut next to the pigs) they apprehended him, called the police, and charged him with stealing.

At the hearing X denied that he had transported the pigs to the fence, denied that he had cut the fence, and denied that he had any intention of stealing. He explained that he moved his truck during the lunch hour to have it more conveniently located when work was over. Had the guards waited a moment longer before they seized

X the case would have been open and shut. By pouncing on him prematurely they left the company with a case strongly supported by circumstantial evidence, but perhaps without proof beyond all reasonable doubt. As a matter of fact, the company subsequently dropped criminal charges against X and settled his suit for false arrest. In a sense this constituted an admission on the company's part that it could not, in a criminal proceeding, prove its case beyond all reasonable doubt.

In the arbitration proceeding the company readily accepted the burden of going forward with the evidence because it had all the facts which were necessary to the presentation. Because in discharge cases it is now well understood that the burden of persuasion is on the company, there was no dispute about this. A real question re-mained, however, of what quantum of evidence the company must produce. In the criminal case, then pending before the courts, the standard would be proof beyond all reasonable doubt. Should it be the same in arbitration? One could argue that it should, on the ground that a discharge for stealing would "permanently brand an employee just as surely as a criminal conviction would."[15] On the other hand, there are innumerable civil suits based upon alleged criminal acts in which the courts do not impose a standard of beyond all reason-able doubt as they would in criminal cases. Some such cases clearly involve social stigma, such as legitimacy proceedings. A mere pre-ponderance of evidence is usually sufficient in such cases, though sometimes the proof must be clear and convincing.

The significant point is that a decision cannot be made without first deciding not only who has the burden of persuasion, but what quantum of evidence is required. To evade the latter problem is to leave the parties without guidance for the future. If the company must indeed prove its case beyond all reasonable doubt it will have to decide whether the police methods which this may require are worth the cost in terms of plant relations. The arbitrator who makes the decision must likewise face the policy implications of what he is doing. Finally, the individual and the union are entitled to know in deciding whether to bring the case to arbitration what quantum of evidence the company must produce.

It is not important for present purposes to arrive at a "correct"

---

[15] Aaron, *Some Procedural Problems in Arbitration*, 1 VAND. L. REV. 733, 742 (1957).

rule in such a case. The important thing is to recognize that the burden of persuasion aspect of the burden of proof problem does have meaning in the arbitral context. The above case suggests that the quantum of evidence which is required may be different in arbitral and court proceedings. This distinction is carried further by another example.

Y was discharged for manhandling a foreman. He was also guilty of some other less serious associated offense which he admitted. Y complained that he was not discharged for just cause, and in the arbitration proceeding the parties stipulated that he should not be discharged unless it was found that he had used physical force on the foreman. As it turned out there was only the word of one man against another. The foreman insisted that Y had grabbed him, picked him up, and thrown him several feet. Admittedly no physical damage was done to the foreman. Y maintained that he had not touched his supervisor. Several witnesses testified for the company that following the incident the foreman had reported the offense to them, and that he had appeared agitated. Several witnesses testified for the union that they had had repeated difficulty with this particular foreman and that he was a known liar. Neither the foreman nor Y made a particularly impressive witness.

Because the case involved a discharge the company was prepared to accept both the burden of going forward with the evidence and the burden of persuasion. But what was the proper quantum of evidence to satisfy the burden of persuasion? In a civil court case the test would presumably be simply the preponderance of evidence. An arbitrator might think that a more appropriate standard would be clear and convincing proof because of other factors which he may wish to consider. On the facts of the case, Y had twelve years of good service with the company. His job rights were substantial and his fringe benefits important. Unemployment was high. Discharge under such circumstances would make it difficult to find a new job. Should the discharge be sustained because it seemed somewhat more likely that the foreman was telling the truth than that Y was, in which case the preponderance test would be met, or should the quantum of evidence be more exacting?

Both of the above cases suggest that there is a burden of persuasion problem in arbitration, just as there is in the courts, but that the proper quantum of evidence may appropriately differ in the two tribunals. The court experience is relevant, but it must be adapted to the industrial scene. A clear illustration of this is seen in a seniority case when a promotion is involved.

Many collective bargaining contracts provide that job vacancies shall be filled by the senior man provided he is qualified. In the arbitration proceeding which results from a claim that this clause has been violated an early question will arise as to whether the company or the union has the burden of going forward with the evidence, and more particularly who has the burden of persuasion with its accompanying quantum of evidence problem. The arbitrator will doubtless urge the company to go ahead with its evidence since this will expedite the hearing. The company will probably do so without much resistance, but will disclaim any intimation that it has the burden of persuasion. At the mention of this problem the arbitrator is likely to make soothing sounds about the "burden of proof" not being very important anyway and the hearing may end without anything further being said on the subject. In nine cases out of ten it may make little difference whether anything further is said about the burden of persuasion. But in the tenth case the arbitrator will find that it is a toss-up in his mind as to whether the man is qualified for the job or not. One function of the burden of proof concept is to assign the burden of persuasion to one side or the other. If it is six of one and a half-dozen of the other whether the man is qualified, who gets the decision? If the burden is on the union to show that the man is qualified, it has failed to prove its case regardless of the standard of proof. If the burden is on the company to show that the man is unqualified it has suffered a similar failure. Thus, much as arbitrators would like to say that there is no problem associated with burden of proof, and much as they avoid this question in their opinions, it is hard to see how a decision can be reached without making some judgment as to who must persuade the arbitrator of the validity of his position.

There is a somewhat analogous situation in the courts which illustrates both the fact that the courts do assign the burden of persuasion in such cases, and that it would be difficult to adopt the court rule in arbitration tribunals. In the law of contract there are "satisfaction" cases, in which one party agrees to perform to the satisfaction of another. Often personal services are involved. Sometimes after the services are performed the second party refuses to fulfill his part of the contract on the ground that he is not "satisfied" with the performance of the first party. The party of the first part, now known as the plaintiff, may sue for breach of contract, alleging that he has complied with all conditions precedent and that the defendant second party now refuses to perform. In the civil courts it would fall to the plaintiff to show that the defendant was, in fact, not "satisfied." How could he do this? In matters of taste, opinion, or judgment the defendant need only have a good faith dissatisfaction, however unreasonable it may be, in order to avoid a breach of the contract by his own refusal to perform. Evidence tending to show that he ought to have been satisfied, or evidence of faithful or reasonable performance, is usually excluded. Evidence that some reason other than "satisfaction" was really behind the defendant's refusal to perform would be appropriate. And in cases where satisfaction on the part of the defendant involved commercial values, mechanical fitness, or utility a "reasonable man" standard might be used. In any event, the burden of persuasion is clearly on the plaintiff.

If the rule in the contract satisfaction cases were carried over into arbitration, it would mean that the union would have the burden of persuading the arbitrator that the senior man was qualified. Perhaps this should be the case, but no arbitrator could carry the analogy further and say that if the company in good faith thought the man was unqualified, however unreasonable this view might be, it had not breached the contract. To so rule would be to destroy the whole concept of seniority. Thus the arbitrator is helped by the court analogy only insofar as it says to him that the burden of persuasion should be on the union. Even that suggestion will have to be weighed in the light of the difference between a labor-management contract and a personal service contract at law. Management flexibility and efficiency may be maximized by a rule which requires the union to show that a senior man is qualified when he bids for the job. Seniority considerations will be furthered by a rule which places the burden on the company of showing that the man is unqualified.

In the final analysis, burden of proof discussions are not irrelevant in the arbitration context, provided one realizes that he is talking principally about the burden of persuasion. Any adjudicative process requires some rule as to who must persuade the tribunal of the justness of his cause. In this light, complaints about the "technicalities" of the subject are unjustified. It is equally clear, however, that arbitrators will have to work out appropriate rules not only as to who has the burden of persuasion, but what quantum of evidence is required, and that they will have to do so with little regard for what may seem to be analogous court situations.

POST-HEARING PROBLEMS

If the figures which were included at the outset of this chapter are correct, and admittedly they are incomplete, the time lapse between the hearing and a decision has increased from just under thirty days in 1945 to just over seventy days in 1963. In the intervening year of 1955 the figure was forty-five days, which suggests that the time is increasing with the years.

It should not be difficult to agree that one of the virtues of grievance arbitration is that it is supposed to provide expeditious answers to questions which are in dispute. One can hardly say that a process is expeditious which requires seventy days from the date of hearing to the date of decision.

It is possible to identify several obvious reasons for the delay which follows the hearing. A verbatim transcript of the hearing will seldom be provided in less than two weeks after the hearing, and it may take as long as six weeks. Briefs are normally written only after the transcript is available, and busy lawyers may need as much as a month, and rarely less than two weeks, to prepare their comments. Finally, the arbitrator is normally given at least thirty days within which to prepare his decision. It is time to take a serious look at the necessity for any of this delay.

The argument has already been made that the arbitration process would be improved by a shift from post- to pre-hearing briefs. The parties would better organize their cases, the arbitrator would be better informed and could ask better questions at the hearing, transcripts would be rendered largely unnecessary, and oral arguments could conclude the hearing. Such a procedure would be resisted by many of the lawyers who practice in the field, but this would be largely because they are accustomed to a different procedure. More pre-hearing time might be required on their part, but less post-hearing time would be necessary. In any event, since lawyers are not present in all cases, their wishes should not be controlling.

If a shift could be made from post- to pre-hearing briefs the principal time-lag would then be in getting the arbitrator's decision. Here too the parties ought to try a radical departure from present methods. There is no reason why immediate decisions could not be made in most cases. From personal experience, and from talking with other arbitrators, I conclude that in a large percentage of the cases the arbitrator has a clear feeling at the end of the hearing as to how he is going to decide the case. He would often be quite willing to render a judgment immediately. He tends to be reluctant to do this only because our tradition is to the contrary and he is apt to be accused of giving a decision without thinking about it.

That it is possible to function efficiently, with fairness and equity for all, in an adjudicatory system which produces decisions at the conclusion of the hearing, is evidenced by the system in Great Britain. The English trial court judge will almost always, at the conclusion of the case, give an oral opinion, stating the reasons for his conclusion. On appeal the court has the trial court record, consisting of a notice of appeal, pleadings, relevant documents, and the judgment below, along with any relevant evidence. The appellate hearing is then largely devoted to oral argument. Lawyers do not file written briefs, and decisions are usually given orally immediately on conclusion of the arguments. Few cases are published and precedent is accordingly less relied upon.

Oral decisions by appellate judges in England are delivered extemporaneously and recorded in shorthand. One copy of an appellate decision will be available to barristers and judges in a library in London, but in practice the decisions are rarely dug out for future use. Some decisions are published, but whether this will happen rests in the hands of a group of barristers employed by the publishers of the officially sanctioned, but not officially operated, *Law Reports*.

There is a greater degree of specialization among both judges and lawyers in England, but this is no different than the American arbitration tribunal where both the arbitrator and the parties tend to be specialized.

Sometimes British judges reserve judgment, but even in those instances the winning side will be designated, although the reasons will be supplied later. This technique appears to be used at all levels of the British system except in the House of Lords, where decisions are usually reserved.[16]

It can hardly be argued that labor arbitration cases are so complex as to make a system of decisions at the end of the hearing impossible. There are, it is true, some extraordinarily complicated cases on which

---

[16] See KIRALFY, THE ENGLISH LEGAL SYSTEM 286–97, 333–34 (2d ed. 1956); Karlen, *Appeals in England and the United States*, 78 L.Q. REV. 371 (1962); Karlen, *The Court of Appeal in England*, 72 YALE L.J. 226 (1962).

no arbitrator would care to render a decision without a good deal of thought and consultation. But there are a vast number of cases, particularly among the *ad hoc* group, in which there would be no difficulty at all in giving immediate decisions. The question is not whether such a system would work, but whether the parties are sufficiently interested in problems of time-lag and formality to try new methods. When the American Arbitration Association announced that its panel members were willing to render decisions of this kind there were no takers during the ensuing months. Surely this is more because the parties do not fully appreciate the possibilities in this kind of decision-making than because they have thoughtfully rejected it. The fact that immediate decisions were forthcoming would not need to eliminate written opinions. The latter do have value in developing an industrial jurisprudence which is useful to the parties. But the opinions could follow at a later date, thus greatly speeding up the actual administration of the grievance procedure.

SUMMARY AND CONCLUSIONS

There is a serious problem of time-lag which is developing in the labor arbitration field. There is also a less well understood and less well articulated feeling that unnecessary "formalities" are taking over. It is difficult to talk about such problems in a general way, because the practice is so diversified. Much of what can be said therefore tends to apply to *ad hoc* rather than umpire cases, though this is not entirely true.

Despite complaints about undue "formalities," arbitration practice would be greatly improved if the parties would better prepare in advance of the hearing. One way to do this, and a way which is already utilized by some of the better umpire systems, would involve the preparation of advance briefs setting forth the facts and arguments on which each side would rely. When the courts ran into similar difficulties in the state of preparedness of cases, discovery and pre-trial conference procedures were developed to improve the administration of justice. Discovery procedures have been discussed in the arbitration context, but seem to offer little affirmative aid. A pre-arbitration hearing procedure might, however, be a highly constructive development. To provide the personnel for such a system the arbitrators and the appointing agencies would have to develop an apprentice system. This would have several advantages, including the settlement of many cases which would never reach the arbitration stage, and the training of new arbitrators to relieve the burden on those who are now too busy.

In the actual hearing stage, the procedure would be simplified and expedited if the parties prepared pre-hearing briefs. On the other hand, troublesome problems of evidence which now annoy the parties will remain because they arise in part out of a difference in philosophy about arbitration itself. Those who believe that some of the value of the arbitration hearing is therapeutic will prefer to see evidence handled on a wide-open basis, while those who see this as a waste of time will continue to argue that arbitrators should better control the hearing.

One "technicality" that creates frequent arguments relates to the burden of proof concept. These arguments flow more from imprecise analysis than anything else. Insofar as burden of proof thinking includes the problem of the burden of persuasion, it is highly relevant to arbitration proceedings simply because every decision-making process requires some rules for the resolution of cases which hang in the balance. Arbitrators will necessarily evolve burden of persuasion concepts, but in doing so they will not be greatly helped by court analogies because the different environments in which court and arbitration cases take place will require differences in treatment.

Once the hearing is over, more and more delay in getting a decision is occurring. If the parties are serious about improving this situation they can take two steps, neither of which is untried, which will make an immediate improvement. They can, on the one hand, provide pre-hearing statements rather than post-hearing briefs and simply conclude the case with oral arguments. Next, they can dispense with their insistence on a waiting period, followed by written opinions, in favor of immediate oral opinions from the arbitrator. Reliance on oral opinions at the end of cases would not preclude subsequent written opinions, which may have real value to the parties in developing a system of industrial jurisprudence.

In short, there are problems of time-lag and formalities. They are not insoluble, but they do require the parties to experiment. This they have not shown great willingness to do. The question is one of desire. Do the parties really want a change from the present methods?

Chapter 4

PREDICTABILITY IN ARBITRATION

In 1960 the late Karl N. Llewellyn, then a Professor of Law at the University of Chicago, published a book entitled *The Common Law Tradition—Deciding Appeals*. Starting with the assumption that the bar had lost confidence in the reckonability of results before appellate courts, Professor Llewellyn sought to show that by employing guidelines which he set forth in his book lawyers could predict the likely outcome of particular cases in particular courts. He was careful, of course, not to equate predictability with absolute certainty. On that score he said: "I reject as useless and misleading the dichotomy which infected so much writing of the '20's and '30's: absolute or 100 per cent certainty versus anything else at all as being '*un-certainty*.' I see no absolute certainty of outcome in any aspect of legal life, and think that no man should ever have imagined that any such things could be, or could be worth serious consideration." [1]

To one interested in the field of labor arbitration the Llewellyn book opened up a fascinating area of speculation. To what extent, and under what circumstances, were grievance decisions predictable? The mere question evoked memories of scattered conversations over the years: of the permanent umpire in a large industry who once said that the parties told him they could almost always predict what he would do with a given case; of the management counsel who told me that they would never take X as an arbitrator in a discharge case because he is a fine man but constitutionally unable to discharge anyone; of the government conciliator who said that management often likes Jesuit priests in discipline or discharge cases because the Jesuits have a strong sense of discipline; of the local union leader who said that he could accurately predict the outcome of 75 per cent of his cases no matter who heard them; of the great reluctance expressed by labor and management representatives to experiment with inexperienced arbitrators because decisions might be "unpredictable."

One could see immediately, of course, that an analysis of predict-

---

[1] LLEWELLYN, THE COMMON LAW TRADITION—DECIDING APPEALS 17 (1960).

ability in labor arbitration would be quite unlike the problem with the appellate courts. In the first place, the arbitration tribunal is a curious combination of trial and appellate court. It is the last step in the grievance procedure, and in that sense appellate, but it is also often the first full-scale exploration of the facts and therefore more akin to a trial court.[2] Arbitrators, unlike judges, do not have a common professional background, nor are they all trained in the same system of thinking. (It should be mentioned, however, that the core of the arbitration fraternity has been composed of alumni of the War Labor Board and that these men have shared a common philosophy.) Most arbitration opinions are not published so that, unlike the case of the courts, it is impossible to read the entire product of a given arbitrator's work except in the permanent umpire systems, where the parties keep a complete file of all past opinions. Much is made in arbitration of the fact that there is no such thing as binding precedent derived from similar cases decided between other companies and unions. The fact that the company and the union must continue to work together puts the whole decision-making process in a somewhat different context than in the courts. The range of cases in arbitration is more limited than in the courts, though it is easy to draw the erroneous conclusion that all arbitration questions are analogous to suits for breach of contract in the courts. The labor contract is more than just a contract; it is also a charter, a treaty, and a code of conduct.[3]

There are doubtless many other differences in the problem of predictability in appellate courts and among arbitrators, but enough has been said to make the point. One thing, however, requires emphasis. Llewellyn was concerned because he sensed a prevailing attitude throughout the bar that appellate decisions were unpredictable. In the labor-management field this does not appear to be so. On the contrary, if labor and management people's conversations are to be relied upon, they think decisions are predictable *provided they know who the arbitrator will be,* or, perhaps even more broadly, *provided the arbitrator is an experienced professional* as indicated, let us say, by membership in the National Academy of Arbitrators. For those unfamiliar with the field, so broad an endorsement of professional

---

[2] For a further development of this subject see Fleming, *Reflections on the Nature of Labor Arbitration,* 61 MICH. L. REV. 1245 (1963).

[3] J. I. Case Co. v. NLRB, 321 U.S. 332 (1944); Cox, *Reflections upon Labor Arbitration,* 72 HARV. L. REV. 1482 (1959).

arbitrators might seem to eliminate the need for pursuing further the question of predictability in arbitration. One of the many reasons that this is not so is that, as the arbitration case load continues to grow, experienced arbitrators are unable to keep up with it, and the best laid plans for bringing new arbitrators into the field have not so far been very successful.[4]

As I thought about the problem of predictability in arbitration, three lines of experimentation gradually opened up. Each would test some facet of the problem, though none would be all-inclusive. The experiments speak for themselves.

EXPERIMENT NO. 1

In my office were a number of complete arbitration cases — transcripts, exhibits, briefs, and my decisions. In my class were a number of third-year law students, only one semester away from being members of the bar. What would happen if the two were put together and the students were told, in the absence of my decisions, to study the cases and write appropriate decisions? Some immediate reservations were apparent. The students were without experience in the industrial relations field, and they would have to deal with dead records which might not accurately reflect the nuances of the hearing. On the other hand, their very lack of experience would place a premium on resort to the literature in the field, and if they were told that their awards had to reflect citations to appropriate authorities it would be a good test of the extent to which a uniform industrial jurisprudence could be said to be emerging.

The students liked the idea — by that time they like any idea that seems to move them closer to life! I deliberately chose cases which are the grist of the arbitration mill, i.e., discipline and discharge, and straight contract interpretations. There were no cases which would raise novel points. I then divided the students into teams of two, not so that they could work together in writing a decision (each was, in fact, required to write his own decision), but so that each would have another student to talk to about the problems in this rather unfamiliar field. It happened that the class included three graduate students who were already members of the bar. Each of

---

[4] D. Jones & R. Smith, *Management and Labor Appraisals and Criticisms of the Arbitration Process: A Report with Comments*, 62 MICH. L. REV. 1115, 1132 (1964).

them was assigned a case alone, and the cases they got were more difficult.

Practically all of the students had taken a basic course in labor law, and we were, at the time of the experiment, engaged in a four-week discussion of labor arbitration in class. They knew of the basic texts in the field, and they had available complete sets of published arbitration decisions. They were told that their decisions would be graded, but that the grade would have nothing to do with the way the decision went. The grade would, as in the case of examinations with which they were long familiar, depend on the way in which the argument was developed and the issues analyzed. They had no hint of how I had decided the case, and the opinions were not available in print.

A total of twenty-one cases was distributed to the students. Of these, three involved the imposition of discipline, ten were discharge cases, seven were straight contract interpretations of various kinds, and one was a combination of contract interpretation and bargaining history.

Since most students were assigned in teams, there were more decisions than cases. In most instances though not all, the team members agreed upon a result though their opinions were different. The purpose in examining their results alongside mine was to compare decisions by novices with those of an experienced arbitrator; whether my decisions were "right" was irrelevant in this context.

The results, when all the decisions were in, were as follows:

There were 3 discipline cases, and a total of 5 opinions. Of the 5, 4 agreed with my decision on the basic question of whether the discipline could be sustained or had to be reversed. There were minor variations in assigning some lesser penalty.

There were 10 discharge cases, and a total of 18 opinions. Of the 18, 11 were in agreement with my decision as to whether the discharge should be sustained or the man reinstated. Again, there were variations on the imposition of lesser penalties.

There were 7 contract interpretation cases, and a total of 13 opinions. Of the 13, 12 were in agreement with my interpretation of the contract.

There was one case which involved a contract interpretation which was complicated by some bargaining history. In that case there were 2 opinions, neither of which agreed with mine.

Something more than the bare statistics can be given with respect to the results. The biggest discrepancy was in the discharge cases, and the least in the contract interpretation cases. On the face of it that made some sense, because the contract interpretation cases were unencumbered by important equities and both the students and I came to the problem out of a law background. On the other hand, the discharge cases often involved questions of crediblity in which the students had been denied the opportunity of viewing the witnesses.

A little more probing into the discharge cases revealed even more. Six of the seven opinions which differed from my own in end result were in connection with three cases. As I looked back on those three cases I found that in one of them I was probably wrong, and in the other two it was clear that my decision was against the weight of the authority. In the latter two cases, I had been impressed with the equities and it is possible that had the students actually heard the cases, as distinguished from working with the records, they too might have reached a different result.

The most difficult and controversial of all the discharge cases had been assigned to one of the graduate students. It was one of those nasty cases in which the atmosphere of the hearing is charged and the lawyers outdo themselves in puffing their respective claims in their briefs. Any decision would be ill-received, particularly one which involved reinstatement. I had nevertheless decided in favor of reinstatement because I thought a clear principle was involved. The company had changed its rules on an important point and had not publicized this fact to its employees. True, one could find the change in a lengthy rule book, but the record was clear that it had not been called to the attention of the employees. My decision was met by bitter criticism from the company and was only enforced in the face of a strike threat. The student, removed from some of the heat of the immediate hearing, came up with the same decision heavily documented by similar opinions in reported cases. He did not, however, have to bear the heat which the hearing had generated. Would that have made a difference in his decision?

The one contract interpretation-bargaining history case, in which both opinions differed from mine, deserves special comment. It involved past pension credits and there were great equities on the side of the employees. I thought, and still think, that the bargaining history made quite clear the fact that the employees did not have the pension credits which they sought. Neither of the students agreed, though one of them tried to straddle the issue in such a way that his award was probably unenforceable. Of all the cases, this one perhaps placed more emphasis upon experience in the industrial relations world than did any of the others.

The experiment, limited though it was, seems to me to suggest two general conclusions:

1. In straight contract interpretation cases which are uncomplicated by subtle industrial relations considerations, law-trained decision-makers are likely to come up with the same result. How important it is that they be law-trained is hard to judge, but it is probably important since it provides a common discipline.

2. In the discipline and discharge areas there is now a sufficient body of experience in the published cases and texts to guide an inexperienced decision-maker to the "general rule." This assumes, of course, that the arbitrator is aware of and has available to him the existing literature, and that there are not unusual equities involved in the case.

If these conclusions are valid, they are of some importance. Discipline and discharge cases annually constitute at least a quarter of the total of all cases. (In 1962 an analysis of the American Arbitration Association total case load showed that just over 27 per cent of the cases involved discipline and discharge.) This being so, if there is in such cases a "general rule" which can be derived from the reported decisions and the texts, the outcome of such cases seemingly will not be much different whether they are decided by experienced or relatively inexperienced men.

The next biggest category of arbitration decisions involves seniority; again the figure is around 25 per cent. (Similar American Arbitration Association figures for 1962 showed over 26 per cent of the total to be seniority cases.) These cases are often straight contract interpretation cases, though certainly not without subtlety or industrial relations nuance. Many of them are not too complicated, and could be referred to law-trained arbitrators with fairly uniform results if the student experiment is any test.

These conclusions may be controversial, but let us leave them for the moment and turn to the second experiment.

EXPERIMENT NO. 2

While the first experiment was under way it happened that I was asked to decide a case on briefs without a hearing. This procedure, though not common, is used occasionally. There was one unique aspect of this case. It had in fact been heard and there was a transcript. There were also exhibits and briefs. While the decision was pending, the arbitrator had suddenly died. The parties did not wish to go through the hearing again and they therefore agreed that the case should be decided by another arbitrator.

After I had studied the case and rendered a decision it occurred to me that opinions in this case from inexperienced decision-makers would supplement the first experiment in at least one important respect. This time none of us would have been exposed to any of the witnesses and all of our knowledge would be drawn from the paper materials which were before us.

A brief statement of facts will make the case more understandable. X Company installed some new machinery on a packaging line. The union was notified, the line was put in operation, and some jobs were eliminated. There was in the plant the usual rule against supervisors working. While the new machinery was being installed one of the supervisors was working with it and this, aggravated by general tension arising out of the job dislocation, caused complaints to reach the steward. It happened that the steward was newly elected and not experienced. He therefore called for assistance from a former steward who was a relief man and who legitimately worked in various parts of the plant. The two of them visited the site of the new machinery, asked some questions, got little information, and left. There were several other visits to the machinery on the part of the stewards, all with unsatisfactory results. Late in the afternoon, not long before quitting time, a walkout suddenly occurred. The company promptly telephoned the business agent to order the men back to work. He did so and the walkout was over. Thereupon the company gave Y, the former steward, a two-week disciplinary layoff for leading an unauthorized work stoppage.

The union denied that Y had led the walkout, and therefore denied that any disciplinary penalty was properly imposed. But it also argued that because of the language of a particular clause in the contract *no* penalty *could be imposed* so long as the men promptly returned to work when ordered by the union.

The company argued that the penalty was justified because Y could be sufficiently identified as the ringleader of the walkout. It insisted with great vigor that the clause in controversy certainly did not warrant the interpretation that the company *could not* impose discipline in such a situation.

The contractual clause, about which the parties were arguing, read as follows:

In the event any employee or group of employees covered by this agreement shall, during the term of this Agreement, engage in any strike, slowdown, walkout or other concerted stoppage of work, the Union agrees, as soon as practicable after being notified by the Company, to direct such employee or group of employees to resume work. Should such employee or group of employees fail to resume work upon being so directed or should the Union fail to give such directions as soon as practicable, such failure shall be cause for discharge or such disciplinary action as the Company may care to take with regard to the employees concerned.

There was no dispute on the record that there had been a walkout, that the union did, on being notified, order the men back to work, or that they did go back to work. Thus the contractual question, arising out of the above language, was whether discipline could be imposed on individual employees even if they did walk out so long as they promptly returned when requested by a union official. There was some evidence of previous walkouts in which no discipline had been imposed, but the evidence was unclear as to whether on those occasions the company had been able to identify any leader.

As I reviewed the case, I thought that two things were clear: (1) the company's evidence against Y as a ringleader in the walkout was very skimpy, there being at least as good and perhaps stronger evidence against one or two others (both stewards) who had not been disciplined, and (2) the union's insistence that the company could not impose discipline in a walkout so long as the men returned to work was clearly inconsistent with normal procedures in such a case. Since the parties agreed in the course of the hearing that the disputed clause had been put in the contract to relieve the union of liability for damages for illegal walkouts, there was no reason to believe (though its wording might be subject to such an interpretation) that the clause was designed to prevent the company from imposing discipline.

I ruled that the discipline was wrongfully imposed since it could not be supported by evidence that Y was the ringleader and was in any event discriminatory. I also said in the course of the opinion that the clause in question could not be interpreted as the union suggested and that in a case in which the company properly exercised discipline it would be justified.

Whether my decision was right or wrong in any of these cases is not, of course, the point. Right or wrong, it represented the judgment of an experienced arbitrator, and the experiment was designed to see whether inexperienced decision-makers would reach the same result. I thought they might not because I sensed in the case one subtlety which inexperience might gloss over. The arbitration case law is so clear that a company may not impose discriminatory discipline, and the evidence for disciplining Y was so skimpy, that I could not believe this was the main point in the case. On the contrary, I thought it was a test case to see what the contractual clause meant. If my interpretation was right, a decision which glossed over that point and spoke only to the question of whether Y was properly disciplined would not be responsive to the main reason for bringing the case in the first place. The question was whether inexperienced decision-makers would sense this.

For this experiment I chose two top-notch individuals, both of whom had graduated from law school and had been admitted to the bar. One was currently a teaching assistant while doing graduate work. The other was my research assistant. Neither had any experience in the labor-management field, but both had superior academic records. Both were given exactly the same materials I had had at the time I had worked on the case. This time they worked separately, and their instructions were the same: take the case and write a decision which can be supported by the textbook and case authorities; decide it any way you want to, but be sure you can document your decision. Neither knew how I had decided the case, nor was there any discussion of it which would give them any hints.

In due course their decisions came in. Both said that the discipline could not be justified since the evidence was skimpy and the penalty was discriminatory. The conclusion was in each case loaded with documentation. So far there was no surprise, for the case rule in arbitration is so clear on this point that they could hardly have missed it. The more important question was what they would do with the question of the company's right to impose discipline under the controversial clause. Having found that the evidence would not support discipline in any event, they could, in good lawyer fashion, have said that they were not required to answer that question since it would not affect the result. Neither did this. Both talked about the clause, both analyzed it with some care, both cited authorities to the effect that the clause could not mean what the union said it did.

In short, both of these inexperienced decision-makers reached exactly the same decision that I had. Their opinions were heavily loaded with documentation, whereas mine was not, but this was because they were instructed to do it this way. They saw the need for resolving the question of the company's right to impose discipline in future cases. There was no loose or dangerous language in their opinions.

I see this experiment as further documentation for the results of the first experiment, though admittedly the two inexperienced individuals who worked on the second case both had superior records. It was a discipline case in which the "general rule" was easily obtainable from the published decisions and the textbooks. Those who were making the decisions had access to the books and they knew how to use them. As to the contract interpretation point, three law-trained individuals made the same interpretation of the contract, though only one (myself) had any experience in the industrial relations field.

The stage is now set for Experiment No. 3, which was by far the most complicated of the three.

EXPERIMENT NO. 3

To what extent would a group of professional arbitrators and a group of experienced practitioners who normally represented labor or management clients be able to agree in advance upon the outcome of an arbitration case? The question was intriguing, but the difficulties of constructing an adequate test would be enormous. What kind of a case would one use in such an experiment? If routine, would this not automatically load the answer in favor of agreement? If difficult, would this not have just the opposite effect? How could one surmount the problem of working with a paper record without exposure to witnesses and counsel? Would it make any difference if a lawyer-arbitrator studied the case, or if the arbitrator was trained in another discipline? If so, would this be because of the nature of the particular case, or because lawyers think differently, or both? Are there geographical differences in the way people think about labor-management problems, so that New Yorkers might reach one conclusion and midwesterners another? These were but a few of the questions which would inevitably be asked in the wake of any experiment. Nevertheless, the idea seemed worth a serious try.

In my files was a case which involved no disagreement on the facts. It dealt with a problem that would probably be regarded as "difficult." An arbitrator who had to decide the case would not benefit much from a hearing since the facts were not in disagreement and the main lines of argument advanced by counsel could be supplied.

On the theory that there might be geographical differences in attitudes toward some questions in the labor-management field—indeed, most of us believe there are—it seemed wise to choose all of the participants from a single large midwestern city. It would not be difficult in such a city to list five well-known lawyers who represented management, and another five who represented unions. Presumably they would be typical of their colleagues.

One way to be sure that all of the arbitrators were experienced men would be to take only members of the National Academy of Arbitrators. To avoid using only lawyer-arbitrators, it would be possible in this particular city to use three economist-arbitrators and two lawyer-arbitrators.

By paying all of the participants a modest honorarium for giving the case some serious thought, it might be possible to avoid off-the-cuff judgments, provided one could get their cooperation in the first place.

A statement of the case, in substantially the form to be set forth shortly, was prepared. Attached was a copy of the contract in almost complete form so that those who studied the case would not be restricted only to those clauses which counsel had argued were relevant. Before the case was sent out the proposed participants were asked whether they would cooperate in the study. Their response was gratifying.

Each of the arbitrators was asked to prepare a memorandum decision indicating the nature of his award and the reasons for it. The lawyers were asked the following six questions:

1. Assuming that the alternatives for your client were: (1) to accept the other party's view, (2) to try to devise a compromise solution, or (3) to go to arbitration, which alternative would you advise your client to take?

2. If the only alternatives were: (1) to accept the other party's view, or (2) to go to arbitration, which alternative would you advise your client to take?

3. If the case went to arbitration, how confident would you feel that you would get a ruling in favor of your client? Very confident? Confident? Doubtful?

4. Assuming the case was heard by one of the experienced arbitrators, would the result be likely to vary with the arbitrator? Would it, for instance, make any difference whether he was a lawyer-arbitrator or an economist-arbitrator? Please explain.

5. If the case went to arbitration, how do you believe it would be de-

cided, and what reasoning would the arbitrator use to justify his award? Please develop this answer fully.

6. Do you have any other observations which you believe to be relevant and which are not included in the above?

Since it is difficult to evaluate the answers without knowing about the case which was under review, the case is stated below except that, for the sake of brevity, only the contract clauses which were deemed relevant are included.

The Case of Company X

X is engaged in the manufacture and sale of food products. It maintains a plant for the production of yeast, vinegar, and other allied products in the Middle West, and it also operates eight other plants in various parts of the country.

In the midwestern plant the company regularly employs three production workers in the preparation and treatment of molasses for fermentation purposes. Each of the three employees works on a different but consecutive shift on each day of the scheduled work week, and he is responsible for the processing of molasses during his shift. In order to equalize working conditions (including shift differentials), the three employees rotate shifts every two weeks. Thus in any given six-week period each employee will have worked a two-week stint on each of the three shifts. The fermentation process is such that one of the three men must always come to work on Sunday for the other production work to get under way properly on Monday morning.

Prior to the negotiation of the present contract, the three molasses department employees worked under the six-week cycle which is shown on Schedule A below. It will be seen that this schedule calls for five days and forty hours of work each week from each individual. However, in two of the six weeks, one of the five working days will be on Sunday, for which the contract provides double-time pay. Thus the net result is that each man works forty hours during the week, but in two of these weeks he receives forty-eight hours pay. Schedule A also shows that each of the three men works six consecutive days once during the six-week cycle.

During the course of bargaining for the present contract, the union insisted that the new contract contain a clause under which time-and-one-half would be paid for work on a sixth consecutive day. This demand was bitterly resisted by the company, but in the face of a strike threat a last-minute concession was made, and section

7(g) was incorporated in the new contract. It read: "For work performed on a seventh consecutive day, employees shall be paid at double time. For work performed on a sixth consecutive day, other than a Sunday or holiday, employees shall be paid at the rate of time-and-one-half."

The new contract was signed on April 3. On April 20 the company announced a new work schedule (see Schedule B below) for the three molasses department employees. Schedule B calls for an identical number of hours of work and pay as Schedule A, but it is frankly designed to avoid penalty pay on a sixth consecutive day. For example, if one follows Employee No. 1 through the six-week cycle, it will be noted that in the fourth week of the cycle Employee No. 1 works Friday (which he did not under Schedule A) and that this gives him a total of six eight-hour days. With premium pay for Sunday, he receives fifty-six hours of pay for forty-eight hours of work during that week. But in the sixth week of his cycle, Employee No. 1 drops Friday from his previous schedule, thus giving him four days of work during that work week, for a total of thirty-two hours.

When the company announced the new work schedule for employees in the molasses department, the union complained that this was a violation of the contract. In support of its contention the union cited the fact that the plant had always worked a five-day, forty-hour week; that all of the plant with the exception of the molasses department was still on this basis; that various sections of the contract dealing with vacations, holidays, overtime, etc., clearly contemplated a five-day, forty-hour week; and that section 7(a) of the contract stated that the work week ran from Monday through Sunday. Finally, the union argued that when an employee was scheduled for less than forty hours of work during any one week, he was laid off. Seniority is plant-wide rather than departmental, and in case of lay offs "seniority rights in general shall govern," according to section 6(b) of the agreement. In this light the union claims that the fact that the individual will work the same number of hours and receive the same pay as he did before is immaterial.

The remedy for the alleged violation of the contract, according to the union, is that "since each of the three employees has been laid off for one day in each of the weeks in which he was scheduled for thirty-two hours of work, he should be given a full day's pay for each such day."

In support of its position, the company insisted that "there has been no cut-back in production, no reduction in work, no slackening of production requirements, no loss in pay, no reduction in the hours worked, and no loss of any kind experienced by the employees in the molasses department — no lay-off in the accepted sense of the term." Moreover, the company contended that "the essence of the grievance is a challenge of the right of the company to regulate production and schedule the work in such manner as it may determine, notwithstanding the fact that such right is unrelinquished and unrestricted in the terms and conditions of the collective bargaining agreement between the company and the union."

The grievance, filed by the three molasses department employees, was processed through the grievance procedure without being settled. In accordance with the provisions of the contract, the parties then agreed to refer the matter to arbitration. The stipulation before the Arbitration Board reads as follows: "Is the Company in violation of the Collective Bargaining Agreement when it schedules less than forty hours per week for the employees in the Molasses Department, and, if so, what is the remedy?"

"SCHEDULE A": MOLASSES PREPARATION ROTATING WORK SCHEDULE EMPLOYED *BEFORE* NEW CONTRACT 4–3–60

		M	T	W	T	F	S	S	Emp.[a] No.	Work Hours	Pay Hours
	11–7	1	1	1	1	1	.	.	1	40	40
1st wk.	7–3	2	2	2	2	2	.	.	2	40	40
	3–11	3	3	3	3	.	.	3	3	40	48
	11–7	1	1	1	1	1	.	.	1	40	40
2nd wk.	7–3	2	2	2	2	.	.	.	2	40	48
	3–11	3	3	3	3	3	.	2	3	40	40
	11–7	3	3	3	3	3	.	.	3	40	40
3rd wk.	7–3	1	1	1	1	1	.	.	1	40	40
	3–11	2	2	2	2	2	.	2	2	40	48
	11–7	3	3	3	3	3	.	.	3	40	40
4th wk.	7–3	1	1	1	1	.	.	.	1	40	48
	3–11	2	2	2	2	2	.	1	2	40	40
	11–7	2	2	2	2	2	.	.	2	40	40
5th wk.	7–3	3	3	3	3	3	.	.	3	40	40
	3–11	1	1	1	1	.	.	1	1	40	48
	11–7	2	2	2	2	2	.	.	2	40	40
6th wk.	7–3	3	3	3	3	.	.	.	3	40	48
	3–11	1	1	1	1	1	.	3	1	40	40
							Six-week total			720	768

[a]This column refers to Employee No. 1, Employee No. 2, and Employee No. 3 as individuals and does not indicate the total number of employees working on any one shift.

"SCHEDULE B": MOLASSES PREPARATION ROTATING WORK
SCHEDULE EMPLOYED *AFTER* NEW CONTRACT 4–3–60
TO PREVENT THE SIXTH CONSECUTIVE DAY

		M	T	W	T	F	S	S	Emp. No.	Work Hours	Pay Hours
	11–7	1	1	1	1	1	.	.	1	40	40
1st wk.	7–3	2	2	2	2	2	.	.	2	40	40
	3–11	3	3	3	3	.	.	3	3	40	48
	11–7	1	1	1	1	1	.	.	1	40	40
2nd wk.	7–3	2	2	2	2	2	.	.	2	48	56
	3–11	3	3	3	3	.	.	2	3	32	32
	11–7	3	3	3	3	3	.	.	3	40	40
3rd wk.	7–3	1	1	1	1	1	.	.	1	40	40
	3–11	2	2	2	2	.	.	2	2	40	48
	11–7	3	3	3	3	3	.	.	3	40	40
4th wk.	7–3	1	1	1	1	1	.	.	1	48	56
	3–11	2	2	2	2	.	.	1	2	32	32
	11–7	2	2	2	2	2	.	.	2	40	40
5th wk.	7–3	3	3	3	3	3	.	.	3	40	40
	3–11	1	1	1	1	.	.	1	1	40	48
	11–7	2	2	2	2	2	.	.	2	40	40
6th wk.	7–3	3	3	3	3	3	.	.	3	48	56
	3–11	1	1	1	1	.	.	3	1	32	32
							Six-week total			720	768

Because the collective bargaining contract is lengthy only those portions which were cited in deciding the case are reproduced herewith. (Each of the participants in the study received a copy of the complete contract.)

Section 1. (a) The Company recognizes the Union as the sole and exclusive collective bargaining agent for the Employees within the bargaining unit at its Manufacturing Division plants presently located in California, New York, Illinois, Texas, Washington, Alabama, and Ohio. The word "Employees" as used in this agreement means those employees referred to as being covered by this agreement in Section 1, of Parts II, III, IV, V, VI, VII, VIII, IX, and X hereof.

Section 6. (a) The Employee's length of service for the purpose of determining seniority rights herein will be computed from the first day of employment as a regular Employee and shall be applied to male and female Employees separately, provided however that seniority shall cease:

1. When Employee has been laid off for six (6) months or more;
2. Upon discharge for just cause;

3. Upon voluntary quitting;
4. Upon more than two (2) days' absence without notice to the employer;
5. Upon failure to return to work within seven (7) days after notice to return to work has been sent to his last known address as shown by the plant employment records.

(b) It is agreed that in all cases of promotion to job classifications covered by this Agreement, recall to or layoff in job classifications covered by this Agreement, seniority rights in general shall govern, provided, however, that any employee chosen on the basis of relative seniority has the necessary qualifications to perform the job duties.

If a man has bid for a job and has been accepted and is found to be unqualified for the new job after a fair trial he shall be returned to his previous job if it is still in operation.

If an Employee has bid for a job and has been accepted and found qualified, he cannot bid for another job in less than six (6) months after date of previous bid.

(g) The Union may bring up through the grievance and arbitration provisions the question of capability and qualification where an Employee entitled to preference by reason of seniority in filling a position covered by this Agreement has not been assigned to that position.

Section 7. (a) The work week shall run from Monday through Sunday.

(b) Work schedules shall be posted weekly and before the end of an Employee's last scheduled shift, but in all cases at least forty-eight (48) hours before they are to take effect, and shall be adhered to.

(e) All work performed over eight (8) hours in any work day or over forty (40) hours in any work week, whichever is greater, shall be paid for at the overtime rate of time and one-half.

(f) For work performed on Sunday, Employees will be paid at double time for all work performed. For work performed on a Saturday, Employees will be paid at time and one-half, except for Saturday work in weeks in which the Employee does not work on a Contract Holiday. This exception shall not apply when the Contract Holiday would have been the Employee's scheduled weekly day off even if it had not been a Holiday.

(g) For work performed on a seventh consecutive day, Employees shall be paid at double time. For work performed on a sixth consecutive day, other than a Sunday or holiday, Employees shall be paid at the rate of time and one-half.

(i) For an Employee who is eligible to receive idle holiday pay and is not scheduled to work on that day, said Employee shall be scheduled for at least five (5) days work at straight time within the work week, subject to the provisions of paragraph (f) of this Section 7.

Section 8. (b) When an Employee reports for work on a regular work day pursuant to his work schedule, the Company will guarantee him a minimum of four (4) hours pay at the rate applicable to work by him on that day if he does not work and eight (8) hours at the rate applicable to work by him on that day if he is put to work. When an Employee reports for work on a Contract Holiday or a Sunday pursuant to his work schedule, the Company will guarantee him a minimum of eight (8) hours pay, at the rate applicable to his work on that day whether or not he is put to work.

Section 10. (b) In the event that an Employee does not work on a Holiday, he shall receive a day's pay when he has worked at least thirty (30) days prior to the Holiday, performs any work in the week in which the Holiday occurs, and works on his last scheduled work day before the Holiday and his next scheduled day after the Holiday. Failure of an Employee to work in the week in which the Holiday occurs because of his layoff effective on or after the first day of the week prior to the Holiday week or because of his bona fide illness of not more than six (6) months duration shall not result in loss of Holiday pay. Failure of an Employee to work on a Holiday or on his last scheduled work day prior to the Holiday or on his next scheduled work day after the Holiday or on the fifth day of work in the week (if the Employee was not scheduled to work on the Holiday) shall result in forfeiture of Holiday pay unless such absence was caused by his bona fide illness or death in his immediate family or unless such absence is excused by the Company in its discretion for other reasons.

Section 20. (b) This Agreement, which includes any other agreements made part hereof by reference, fixes all terms and conditions of employment for the Employees whether or not specifically referred to, provided for or considered by the parties hereto and both the Company and the Union specifically waive any and all rights which each may have to compel the other to bargain collectively during the term of this Agreement to change or add to this Agreement or to reach agreement on any subject matter not covered by this Agreement, with the single exception of the subject matter of Pensions.

Predictability in the Case of Company X

The sample of opinion in the case of Company X included five professional arbitrators, five management lawyers, and five union lawyers. Answers ultimately came in from the five arbitrators and the five management lawyers, but only two of the union counsel responded. It should be said in behalf of the latter that they were not uncooperative — in one case a serious illness intervened, and two of the others became so involved in pending litigation that they were unable to produce a memorandum.

The arbitrators were asked only for a decision supported by an opinion. The lawyers were asked prior questions with respect to a possible compromise settlement, capitulation to the adversary, or advancement of the case to arbitration. Their answers are logically considered first.

The Views of the Management Lawyers

Four of the five management lawyers indicated clearly that they would seek a compromise settlement, and the fifth implied that he would do so. None of them would settle on the union's terms, and in preference to that all would proceed to arbitration. In arbitration *all* of them thought the outcome was doubtful. Four of them thought the company had probably violated the contract in at least one respect, and three thought the company would probably lose the arbitration while two thought it might win (one despite the fact that he acknowledged a contract violation).

On the question of whether the outcome of the case might vary with the individual arbitrator, all five respondents thought that it might, but not necessarily because he happened to be a lawyer rather than an economist. The flavor of the replies is best obtained from some quotations:

The result might well vary depending on whether the arbitrator was a lawyer or an economist. An economist might be more impressed with the company's argument, particularly that there is no loss of pay. A lawyer would be more likely to follow the language of the contract and to rule this is a reduction or layoff.

Assuming the case was heard by an experienced arbitrator the result probably would not vary, i.e., it would make little difference whether the arbitrator was a lawyer or an economist. . . . If the neutral was inexperienced, then probably the decision would vary depending upon whether his background was in law or economics. One legally trained would be likely to give greater emphasis to the absence of a provision in the contract prohibiting the company from changing work schedules and to the inference that under Section 7(a) the company has the power to schedule work. In addition, he might find the answer to the claim that the parties intended to provide a "forty hour week" by the doctrine of substantial performance, i.e., each employee does receive an average of forty hours pay a week over a short given period of time. He is likely to stress that the agreement contains no guaranteed work week.

I feel that the result would vary from arbitrator to arbitrator, depending primarily upon the particular arbitrator's personal feeling regarding the scope of the management prerogative. . . . The decision may also vary depending upon whether the arbitrator is a lawyer or an economist. If the arbitrator were a lawyer, the contractual clauses which the union claims were violated, would probably undergo close scrutiny in an effort to determine whether the clauses are material to the issues and if so were they actually violated. . . . The economist, minus the technical legal background, may tend to slide over these issues. The economist, on the other hand, will probably tend to view the case as a whole, rather than the piecing together of facts and legal conclusions which make up the whole.

I believe that the results of the arbitration would be likely to vary with the arbitrator . . . but I do not believe that the mere fact that an arbitrator is a lawyer or is an economist would necessarily explain the difference in results. I believe the differences are more individually oriented. It may be that lawyers who are not too experienced in arbitration would be inclined to use traditional rules of construction and to use precedents more than the non-lawyer arbitrators, but among the more experienced arbitrators, I do not believe any such difference is too significant.

If the case were heard by one of the experienced arbitrators, I think the result would be likely to vary with the arbitrator. I don't think it would make much difference whether the arbitrator was a lawyer or an economist. . . . Much more depends on the background and experience of the particular arbitrator to whom the case is submitted, and whether his decisions show a tendency to give companies a relatively free hand in running the plant, or a tendency to restrict companies to past practice where changes are not specifically authorized by the union contract.

At first blush there is some inconsistency between the fact that three of the five management lawyers say that the company will *probably* lose the case in arbitration, and their statements that the result will vary with the arbitrator. This inconsistency is reconciled if one remembers that in all cases counsel said the outcome of the case was *doubtful*.

The contractual provisions which management counsel thought controlled the case were substantially the same in all cases, though the interpretations differed. All acknowledged that the contract did not contain a management clause, but two of them thought that the provisions of section 7 indicated an intention by the parties to give management the power to schedule. Three of the five counsel thought that the seniority clause of the contract had probably been violated in that there was a layoff on the occasion of the four-day week, but one of the three thought that an arbitrator might be persuaded that it was not a layoff. One of the five thought it was clear that there was a layoff because management could no more balance hours over a six-week cycle than over a six-month cycle, and to permit it to do the latter would be to destroy completely the seniority clause. Another, who felt that the union would win the case, was convinced that the seniority clause had not been violated, but that the company had unilaterally changed a working condition without bargaining with the union about it. The lone lawyer who found no violation of the contract reasoned that section 7 gave management the right to schedule, the contract contained no guarantee of a five-day, forty-hour week, there was no layoff, and there was no evidence that the parties agreed when 7(g) was added to the contract that the company would not change the schedule to avoid the payment of premium pay.

Since two of the respondents thought that the company might prevail, they did not need to provide for an arbitral remedy. Two would apparently order the company to restore the old schedule. One of the two reasoned that this would call for payment for hours missed during the short weeks, but the other did not mention the subject. Finally, one lawyer thought that the only necessary remedy was to give bumping rights to senior employees during the short work weeks, provided that they had the necessary qualifications.

It would be fair to say that the layoff problem was the one which most bothered management lawyers. Three of them thought there was a layoff, though one hoped an arbitrator would not think so.

The Views of the Union Lawyers

There were only two answers from union lawyers, but both were given in some detail and they formed a very interesting contrast. Both thought the contract had been violated, though for quite different reasons, and both thought that the union could not accept management's view of the case. They agreed that in arbitration the union would win. As to the possibilities of compromise, they were at far poles, but this was because they viewed the contract violation differently. One said that while there was no guaranteed five-day work week under section 7, it was clear that this was what the parties had in mind and that the company could not change the work week simply to avoid the payment of premium pay. Stated another way, "the Company would immediately reject any contention that the employees are not bound to report for a five-day forty-hour week. There must be some *quid pro quo* in this language. This *quid pro quo* would appear to be the right to an expectation of a normal five-day forty-hour week." He also thought there was a layoff under the seniority clause. Given these clear contractual violations, this lawyer thought that the possibilities for compromise were slim. In his language: "I am hard put to imagine how a suitable compromise could be managed in this instance which would encompass the objectives of both the employer and the union. The two positions seem to be mutually exclusive. In view of this and the unacceptability of the first alternative, the only thing left to do would be to proceed with arbitration, and I would so advise my client."

The other union lawyer thought that most of the contractual arguments were "unimpressive and unimportant smoke screens" for the real issue, which was whether it was a breach of contract for the company to make unilateral changes in the previously existing work schedules. He had no doubt that the answer to this question was in the affirmative, but he traced the contractual breach largely to section 1(a) of the contract. For this reason he said of the possibilities of compromise:

Standing alone, an attempted compromise is a better undertaking than an uncertain arbitration case. But there are even more persuasive reasons why a compromise should be sought. Here we have no loss of jobs, no loss of employee earnings, no loss of union membership, and no attempt to disestablish the union itself. Thus, if the Union would exchange its forgiveness for what has already taken place for the Company's promise to hereafter avoid unilateral action and recognize a duty to bargain, a most important principle would be firmly established under circumstances causing no real harm to the Union or its members.

In addition, such a compromise seems advisable under the doctrine of casting bread upon the waters. Nothing adds more to the success of future negotiations than a history of giving in when it was not necessary to give in.

One of the union lawyers thought that it wouldn't make any difference in the outcome of the case whether it was heard by an arbitrator trained as an economist or a lawyer, provided the arbitrator followed the mandate of the law with respect to bargaining. The other lawyer would prefer that a lawyer hear the case. He reasoned as follows:

A lawyer arbitrator would be my preference since this is a legal question which would demand knowledge of contract law. The question for decision is whether the employer is in compliance with his legal obligations, regardless of supposed moral or economic justification for "stretching" the interpretation of this contract. Most non-lawyer arbitrators with whom I have had contact either do not recognize contract interpretations or are swayed by considerations other than legal. There is a real possibility that an economist arbitrator might be more disposed to accept the employer's view that the overall *annual* income of the employees remains the same and that the change was made for economic reasons. This overlooks two factors; first, that the employer by contract is on a week-to-week work and pay schedule, and secondly, that while the annual income may be the same as it would have been under the previous contract, it is not the same as it would have been under the newly negotiated contract had it not been for the employer's deviation therefrom.

On the question of the proper remedy both lawyers would presumably require the company to reinstate the Schedule A work week. One would provide back pay for losses sustained, while the other says that employees are not entitled to any pay because they have not suffered any loss. The latter would go further and order the company to bargain with the union about any change (after re-establishing the old work week), but he believes the arbitrator should make no provision for what happens if the parties are unable to agree in bargaining.

Though the two union lawyers phrase their estimates of the contractual problem in the X Company case somewhat differently, their theories tend to converge. Both believe that the company committed itself to a five-day, forty-hour week. Both believe that the contract was violated when the company made a unilateral change. One thinks that the contract was violated because specific provisions of the contract, such as those dealing with layoff, were violated, while the other disagrees but thinks the company violated its duty to bargain which is implied from the fact that it recognizes the union as the proper agent for bargaining over wages, hours, and working conditions.

The Views of the Arbitrators

The views of the arbitrators in this case are particularly interesting because we know, as we come to them, that five of the seven adversary lawyers who looked at the case said that the union would probably win, and a sixth thought that the contract had been violated by the company though he hoped to persuade the arbitrator to the contrary.

The five arbitrators consisted of two lawyers and three economists. All were experienced, all were members of the National Academy of Arbitrators. Two, one lawyer and one economist, said that the union would win the case. Three, one lawyer and two economists, said that the company would win the case! The lawyer who thought that the company would prevail was "very clear" about this. The lawyer who believed that the union would win thought the case was difficult, but was "confident" that he was right in deciding for the union. The three economists all thought the case was difficult. One said that once he had made up his mind in favor of the union he had "little doubt" about the correctness of the decision. One said that he was "moderately clear to clear" that he was right in holding for the company, and the third simply said that it was a novel case in his experience and that he missed the benefit of a hearing.

None of the arbitrators thought there had been a layoff under the terms of the contract, and only one (the lawyer who decided for the company) thought this was a serious question. (His view was that even if there had been a layoff, which he doubted, the union had shown no desire on the part of the three employees to bump into other jobs.) The one economist who held for the union did so by reasoning that while there was no guarantee of a five-day, forty-hour week, this was the underlying assumption of the parties and a usage to that effect had been established. He then made this usage a part of the contract. The lawyer who held for the union relied on section 7(a), which established a work week running from Monday through Sunday. While admitting that such a clause had other purposes, he concluded that the basic unit of work was the week, that the week was Monday through Sunday, and that by having four days in one week and six in another the company changed the work week. If the company could do this over a six-week cycle, he reasoned, it could do it over a longer cycle and in either event it would be a violation of the contract.

One of the economists who held for the company said that section 7(a) was in the contract only to satisfy the Fair Labor Standards Act, that there was nothing else in the contract which limited the company to a five-day, forty-hour week, that no one had been hurt by the substitution of Schedule B for Schedule A, and that section 20(b) of the contract indicated that there were no restrictions on management other than those imposed by the written language of the contract. The other economist found nothing in the contract which limited the company's right to change the schedule. Moreover, since no harm was done anyone by the change, which was not capricious, since there was no "past practice" clause, he would rule for the company.

The lawyer who ruled for the company pointed out the lack of a "past practice" clause and the necessity for sticking to the written language of the contract. He thought the company might have been guilty of an unfair labor practice for making a unilateral change without bargaining, but this was none of the arbitrator's business. Seeing nothing in section 7 which limited the company's right to change the schedule, he believed that section 7(a) dealing with the Monday through Sunday work week was in the contract for other reasons, took a strong management rights position even in the absence of a specific clause in the contract, and finally thought that whether or not there had been a layoff was the principal question.

An incidental but interesting sidelight of the opinions related to the question of why section 7(a) — the penalty clause for the sixth consecutive day of work — was put in the contract. The economist who ruled in favor of the union said of this clause: "A reasonable conclusion is that the union was not seeking to change the company's manufacturing technique or the pattern of its operations in such circumstances; it was seeking rather to enhance earnings." One of the economists who ruled in favor of the company said of this same clause: "In most instances 'penalty' clauses, such as those requiring premium pay for a sixth or seventh consecutive work day or for work performed on a Saturday or Sunday, are more designed to discourage such employment than to increase the incomes of employees. Insofar as this is true it would be reasonable to conclude that an employer retains freedom to develop schedules to avoid penalty work days so long as he does not in the process violate other provisions of the Agreement under which he operates." One of the union lawyers, who said that the union would win the case in arbitration, nevertheless said this about section 7(a): "Students of industrial relations well know that premium pay provisions of this nature are designed to discourage, not encourage, work on designated premium pay days and it is fanciful to read into them an obligation to freeze pre-existing work schedules so that employees will be guaranteed an increase in earnings."

Since only two of the five arbitrators ruled in favor of the union they were the only ones who had to devise a remedy and their solution was exactly the same. Schedule B was in violation of the contract; therefore the company would either have to revert to Schedule A or devise a new schedule that conformed to the five-day pattern. For the period in which Schedule B had been in effect the grievants were entitled to the pay which they would have received had the old schedule been continued.

Reflections on Predictability in the Case of Company X

If four out of five of the arbitrators had decided the X Company case in favor of the union the experiment would have been mechanically perfect. This was the result which five out of seven of the adversary lawyers predicted, and even the two who thought the company might win would not have been surprised had the union won. But the results did not turn out this way and we must now reflect on what this means in terms of predictability. Several things immediately come to mind.

In the first place, the Company X case was, by practically universal admission, "difficult." Despite the fact that five of the seven lawyers who looked at it said they thought the union would prevail, none of them felt very confident of this, and all of them thought that the result might differ with the arbitrator.

Second, the lawyers were asked to speculate about the outcome generally, not the outcome before a particular arbitrator. Had the lawyers been given the names of the five arbitrators, all of whom were from the same city and would have been known to the practitioners, they might very well have predicted differently. One of the arbitrators commented, for instance, that his result (which favored the company) ought to have been predictable to any lawyer who had prior acquaintance with his work. (The difficulty of being familiar with a particular arbitrator's views is compounded, however, by the fact that few opinions are published, and some of the best known arbitrators rarely publish any of their opinions.)

Third, the case involved the management prerogative question and this is a question on which arbitrators often hold known, but quite different, views. Three of the management lawyers mentioned this in responding to the question of whether the outcome would vary with the arbitrator. They recognized that an arbitrator who believed in a strong management rights theory would be more likely to award in favor of the company, while one who held contrary views would be less likely to.

In the fourth place, there was an undertone of possible bad faith involved in the case and that always tends to make predictability more difficult. The company had accepted the penalty pay for a sixth consecutive day clause only in the face of a strike threat. Immediately after signing the contract, it sought to avoid the effect of the clause. To some this would appear to be bad faith, though to others it would appear to be only legitimate concern with costs. A hint of the importance which this factor might have played in the case is seen in the comments of several of the lawyers, and in the opinions of the two lawyer-arbitrators. The lawyer-arbitrator who decided for the company said that he thought there was a possible unfair labor practice involved in the unilateral schedule change, but that this was a matter for the NLRB. The lawyer-arbitrator who ruled for the union pitched his decision to section 7(a) of the contract (the Monday through Sunday work-week clause), but between the lines one suspected he thought the company was guilty of bad faith in bargaining and that he used section 7(a) to tie the result more closely to the contractual language.

Fifth, there was a noticeable miscalculation among the lawyers as to the theory on which the arbitrators would decide the case. Four of the seven lawyers thought that there was a layoff as the result of Schedule B, but none of the arbitrators thought this was so, and only one of the arbitrators even gave it very serious attention. Since the lawyers unquestionably gave this hypothetical case less time than they would have a real case, and since they had no clients to talk to, it is quite possible that in a real case they would not have given so much credence to the layoff theory.

Finally, both the predictions of the lawyers and the opinions of the arbitrators were based upon a paper record. They were not exposed to a hearing, and though the facts were not in dispute a hearing would have supplied some "feel" for the case which could not be obtained in a brief recapitulation of it. Several of the respondents suggested a need for more information. (But high on the list of "famous last words" of arbitrators is the phrase, "I need more information!")

SOME GENERAL CONCLUSIONS

In the early part of this chapter it was suggested that the results of Experiment No. 1 (and even Experiment No. 2) would support two tentative conclusions, which were:

1. In straight contract interpretation cases which are uncompli-

cated by subtle industrial relations considerations, law-trained decision-makers are likely to come up with the same results.

2. In the discipline and discharge areas there is now a sufficient
body of experience in the published cases and texts to guide an
inexperienced decision-maker to the "general rule."

Experiment No. 3 suggests that in difficult cases predictability can
not be put on any such broad basis, but that it might be related to
individual arbitrators. Thus if the management prerogative question
is involved, it is possible to ascertain an individual arbitrator's views
on that subject from published decisions.

If these over-all conclusions are accurate, and those who believe
they are not will find substantial grounds for disagreement, they
support the proposition that labor and management can make an
educated guess as to the outcome of even difficult cases by studying
the views of experienced arbitrators, and that in the routine cases
(which constitute a large percentage of the total) they ought not
to be so concerned about trying new arbitrators. The latter conclusion is particularly important at a time when there is a need for
new faces in the arbitration fraternity. The cooperative program
being carried on by the National Academy of Arbitrators, the Federal
Mediation and Conciliation Service, and the American Arbitration
Association is intended to introduce new arbitrators who, in the
judgment of all three sponsoring agencies, will prove to be competent. It is very arguable that the decisions of these men, in routine
cases at least, will not vary from decisions rendered by experienced
arbitrators.

Out of these modest experiments have come at least two other
questions which offer interesting possibilities for research.

It was noticeable in the decisions of the arbitrators that even the
same results were often justified on different grounds. To what
extent would this be true if one could test it on a large sample?
(Llewellyn reported that in his study of the appellate courts one
of the judges who sat on a court whose opinions were studied said
that "the outcome was pretty certain about 8 times out of 10, as
soon as the court got their minds around the case, but that there
was no such certainty about the ground of the decision." [5] If it is
true that arbitrators will come out with the same result but for different reasons, why is this so? Is it because experienced professional

_____

[5] *Supra* note 1, at 25 n. 16.

arbitrators get a "feel" for the case which leads them to the same result though they may rationalize it differently? Are the successful arbitrators the ones who have the sense of "feel," and if so, where do they get it? Are they unusually sensitive people who learn at least as much about a case from what they feel as what they hear?

A closely related question is to what extent the success or failure of an arbitrator depends not on his decisions, but on what labor and management representatives think of him. Stated another way, is what labor and management people think about an arbitrator determined by his decisions? To some that will seem like a foolish question, but there is evidence that it is not. Observation alone documents the conclusion that it is not always the most knowledgeable arbitrator who is the most successful. In addition there is a recent survey, conducted by the Missouri Bar Association and Prentice-Hall, Inc., which indicates that clients do not consider results the most important factor in forming an opinion about the attorneys who serve them. By analogy, results may be less important than other factors in determining what labor and management representatives think of their arbitrators.

The Missouri survey asked laymen and lawyers the factors which each thought contributed the most and the least to their relationship. The following charts summarize the results:[6]

CHART 1. POSITIVE FACTORS

Laymen	Lawyers
1. Friendliness	1. Results
2. Promptness	2. Honesty
3. Courtesy	3. Efficiency
4. Not condescending	4. Personality
5. Keeping client informed	5. Education

CHART 2. NEGATIVE FACTORS

Laymen	Lawyers
1. Superior attitude	1. Procrastination
2. Bored; indifferent	2. Failure to inform
3. Impatient; impersonal; failure to inform	3. Lack of frankness
4. Rude; brusque	4. Lack of courtesy

[6] Richter, *What the Layman Thinks of Lawyers: A Survey Report*, 9 STUDENT LAW. J. 8 (1964).

In commenting on the charts, the Director of Information for the Missouri Bar said:

On Chart 1, we have the factors which each considers to be most helpful to the relationship. Note the importance placed by the client on the human aspects. More than 50 per cent of the users said that their lawyer's friendliness was the thing about the relationship which impressed them most. Next in importance to the client was the lawyer's promptness, his courtesy and the fact that he was not condescending and that he kept the client informed.

The lawyers, however, considered other factors more important. They listed as number one, results! And yet only 2 per cent of the clients mentioned results as the cause of any dissatisfaction! This seems to refute the generally held assumption that winning is all-important to client satisfaction. According to the findings of the Survey, losing does not necessarily cause the client to be dissatisfied with the service of his lawyer.

. . . .

The variance in views between the client and attorney regarding factors helpful or harmful to the relationship is emphasized even more strongly when we consider them from the negative side. In Chart 2 we see again that the human elements seem to be causing the most friction in the relationship between the attorney and the client.

No knowledgeable student of arbitration would argue that an arbitrator's decisions are irrelevant to his success. On the other hand, it is an observed phenomenon that men of equal knowledge and equally sound judgment are not equally sought after as arbitrators. What would one find out if he conducted a survey among labor and management representatives and arbitrators about the factors which each thinks to be most important to a rewarding relationship? Perhaps the answer to this question would be helpful in keeping new arbitrators going once they got started.

Chapter 5

INDIVIDUAL RIGHTS IN ARBITRATION

Collective bargaining, to which we are committed as a way of life in the world of labor-management affairs, necessarily involves agreements between companies and unions. An integral part of the agreements is the grievance procedure culminating in final and binding arbitration. Since the contract is between the company and the union, the grievance machinery is usually in their control. Occasionally this leads to unsatisfactory results from the standpoint of the individual employee, and a good deal of attention has been devoted to the question of the respective roles of the individual employee and the union in processing the grievance.[1] At the arbitration level the question is particularly troublesome because the individual may wish to take advantage of the final step in the grievance procedure though this meets with the approval of neither the company nor the union.

Vast though the literature on this subject is, changes within the past year suggest that we are on the threshold of new developments. For this reason a review of the situation is warranted.

A brief word of background is necessary before the current materials are examined. Individual complaints about the grievance procedure tend to fall into two broad categories. The first encompasses those cases in which the union refuses to process the individual's grievance at all, and the second relates to situations in which a settlement is reached which is not satisfactory to the individual.

---

[1] Aaron, *Some Aspects of the Union's Duty of Fair Representation*, 22 Ohio St. L.J. 39 (1961); Blumrosen, *Legal Protection for Critical Job Interests: Union-Management Autonomy Versus Employee Autonomy*, 13 Rutgers L. Rev. 631 (1959); Blumrosen, *The Worker and Three Phases of Unionism: Administrative and Judicial Control of the Worker-Union Relationship*, 61 Mich. L. Rev. 1435 (1963); Cox, *The Duty of Fair Representation*, 2 Vill. L. Rev. 151 (1957); Cox, *Rights Under a Labor Agreement*, 69 Harv. L. Rev. 601 (1956); Hanslowe, *The Collective Agreement and the Duty of Fair Representation*, 14 Lab. L.J. 1052 (1963); Hanslowe, *Individual Rights in Collective Labor Relations*, 45 Cornell L.Q. 25 (1959); Summers, *Collective Power and Individual Rights in the Collective Agreement — A Comparison of Swedish and American Law*, 72 Yale L.J. 421 (1963); Summers, *Individual Rights in Collective Agreements in Arbitration*, 37 N.Y.U.L. Rev. 362 (1962); Summers, *Individual Rights in Collective Agreements: A Preliminary Analysis*, 9 Buffalo L. Rev. 239 (1960).

Within these broad categories there are many variations. The union may refuse to process the grievance because the individual is not a member, because he has engaged in hostile activity on behalf of another union, because he is a member of the political opposition, or because it is an obviously spurious claim. By the same token, a settlement which is unsatisfactory to the individual may be the result of a "trade" for a more meritorious grievance, a judgment that the claim of the individual is inferior to that of another employee who has a conflicting interest, a reprisal for past behavior which has been obnoxious to the union leadership, or a good faith conclusion that the grievance is without merit. No one doubts that in the overwhelming number of cases in either of the two broad categories a fair solution is reached and no problem is raised. But because the potential for invidious treatment exists in all human organizations one must face the question of what remedies, if any, are to be provided in that situation.

As to those cases in which the union refuses to process the grievance, Professor Aaron has pointed out that there are at least three identifiable points of view as to what should be done about it.

Some argue that inasmuch as the union's principal reason for being is to improve the economic and social position of its members, the individual member should have a vested right to use the grievance and arbitration provisions of the applicable collective agreement.[2] Others believe that the union must be given a free hand to evaluate the individual's claim in terms of the collective interest and therefore must be allowed to refuse to process the grievance, so long as it acts in good faith.[3] A third position is that the individual employee should be permitted to compel the union to process meritorious grievances involving only the "critical job interests" of discharge, compensation, and seniority.[4]

Insofar as the union has been willing to handle grievances, the courts have been reluctant to interfere with settlements, on the ground that the law does not guarantee employees more than the right to participate in and reject settlements made without their consent.[5] The famous 1945 case of *Elgin, Joliet & Eastern Ry. Co. v.*

---

[2] E.g., *Report of the Comm. on Improvement of Administration of Union-Management Agreements*, 50 Nw. U.L. Rev. 143, 156 (1955).

[3] E.g., Cox, *Rights Under a Labor Agreement*, 69 HARV. L. REV. 601 (1956).

[4] Aaron, *The Individual's Legal Rights as an Employee*, 86 Mo. LABOR REV. 666, 671–72 (1963) (footnotes renumbered). The "critical job interests" theory is from Blumrosen, *Legal Protection for Critical Job Interests: Union-Management Activity Versus Employee Autonomy*, 13 RUTGERS L. REV. 631 (1959).

[5] Aaron, *supra* note 4.

Burley brought a warning from the Supreme Court that unions could not bind individuals to a financial settlement which they did not approve,[6] but on rehearing the court considerably softened its view so that the employee could not stand idly by while the union settled and then claim that he did not approve.[7]

There have been other cases, almost always involving the race issue, in which employees have alleged that they were being discriminated against for reasons irrelevant to the contract. These cases have resulted in a series of decisions in which the courts have read into the National Labor Relations Act an implied obligation on the part of the union to represent its members fairly and without discrimination for irrelevant and invidious reasons.[8]

Along with these cases there has been a steady stream of other situations, most often involving conflicting seniority claims, in which one group of employees has asked the court to intervene because another group of employees was being preferred by agreement between the company and the union. The best known of these cases is *Ford Motor Co. v. Huffman,* in which the aid of the court was invoked on the ground that the company and the union had, in reaching an agreement upon seniority, violated the Selective Service Act by allowing seniority credit for time spent in the service *prior to employment,* and also violated the union's statutory duty toward the employees under the National Labor Relations Act.[9] With respect to the latter point the court said: "Inevitably differences arise in the manner and degree to which the terms of any negotiated agreement affect individual employees and classes of employees. The mere existence of such differences does not make them invalid. The complete satisfaction of all who are represented is hardly to be expected. A wide range of reasonableness must be allowed a statutory bargaining representative in serving the unit it represents, subject always to complete good faith and honesty of purpose in the exercise of its discretion."[10]

State courts, in which similar actions were brought, did not always share the Supreme Court's view of the flexibility which the union

---

[6] Elgin, Joliet & Eastern Ry. Co. v. Burley, 325 U.S. 711, 16 L.R.R.M. 749 (1945).

[7] *Id., aff'd on rehearing,* 326 U.S. 801, 17 L.R.R.M. 899 (1946).

[8] Syres v. Oil Workers, 350 U.S. 892, 37 L.R.R.M. 2068 (1955); NLRB v. Wallace, 323 U.S. 248, 15 L.R.R.M. 697 (1944). Cf. Steele v. Louisville & N.R.R., 323 U.S. 192, 15 L.R.R.M. 708 (1944).

[9] 345 U.S. 330, 31 L.R.R.M. 2548 (1953).

[10] *Id.* at 338, 31 L.R.R.M. 2551.

might exercise in such situations. In *Clark v. Hein-Werner Corp.*, the Wisconsin Supreme Court said: "Where the interests of two groups of employees are diametrically opposed to each other and the union espouses the cause of one in the arbitration, it follows as a matter of law that there has been no fair representation of the other group. This is true even though, in choosing the cause . . . to espouse, the union acts completely objectively and with the best of motives."[11]

A final preliminary comment remains. At the grass-roots level one hears much about the necessity felt within unions for allowing spurious grievances to go to arbitration lest the union be charged by an irate member with violation of the Landrum-Griffin Act. In any analysis of the current state of the law that problem deserves some consideration.

THE CURRENT SITUATION

Developments during the last year suggest that one who would be abreast of the law with respect to individual rights in grievances which may culminate in arbitration must pay heed to what is happening in three separate areas. One relates to litigation under the Landrum-Griffin Act, and can be dealt with briefly. Another pertains to new theories of unfair labor practices under the Taft-Hartley Act. The third relates to some recent court decisions.

The Landrum-Griffin Act

Two sections of the Labor-Management Reporting and Disclosure Act of 1959 have been suggested as having a bearing on the freedom of a union in disposing of grievances which might go to arbitration. The first, section 101(a)(4), provides that the union may not limit the right of a member to institute an action although it may require him to exhaust reasonable internal remedies before instituting legal or administrative procedures against the union or its officers, provided such internal procedures do not take more than four months. This section was originally believed by some to emasculate union grievance screening.[12] Continued concern seems unwarranted, however, since no recent litigation has refuted the early decisions stating that 101(a)(4) gives the right to sue only to protect rights

---

[11] 8 Wis. 2d 264, 272, 99 N.W.2d 132, 137, 45 L.R.R.M. 2137, 2140–41 (1959).

[12] E.g., Meany, *Get Crooks, Not Unions*, 66 AMERICAN FEDERATIONIST 2 (July 1959).

given in Title I of the Act, that is, freedom of speech and assembly, nomination of candidates in union elections, etc.[13]

The other section of Landrum-Griffin which may be relevant to the processing of grievances is section 501(a) and (b). That section imposes upon union officers a fiduciary responsibility and allows a suit in the nature of a derivative stockholder's suit, in which the individual can sue the officers "to recover damages or secure an accounting or other appropriate relief for the benefit of the labor organization." Fiduciaries are usually concerned with the purse; however, section 501 may encompass a broader meaning of the fiduciary obligation. Some support for this view is found in the supplementary views of five members of the House Education and Labor Committee who said of provisions identical to those finally enacted:

We affirm that the Committee bill is broader and stronger than the provisions of s. 1555 which relate to fiduciary responsibilities. S. 1555 applied the fiduciary principle to union officials only in the handling of "money or other property" . . . apparently leaving other questions to the common law of the several states. Although the common law covers the matter, we considered it important to write the fiduciary principle explicitly into Federal labor legislation. Accordingly, the Committee bill extends the fiduciary principle to all the activities of union officials and other union agents and principals.

The general principles stated in the bill are familiar to the courts, both State and Federal, and therefore incorporate a large body of existing law applicable to trustees, and a wide variety of agents. The detailed application of these fiduciary principles to a particular trustee, officer, or agent has always depended upon the character in which he was engaged.[14]

This view was recently adopted in *Johnson v. Nelson* in which union members sued two local officers who allegedly violated their fiduciary obligation in refusing to sign checks for expenses approved by the union majority.[15] In rejecting the defendants' narrow pecuniary interpretation of the Act, the Court said: "Careful analysis of Title V refutes the notion that that statute is narrow in its terms and scope and that it is limited solely to pecuniary responsibilities or the proper or improper use of funds."[16]

Just how far beyond pecuniary responsibility section 501 may go

---

[13] E.g., Allen v. Local 820, Teamsters Union, 185 F. Supp. 492, 45 L.R.R.M. 3067 (D.N.J. 1960).

[14] H.R. Rep. No. 741, 86th Cong., 1st Sess. 77 (1959) (supplementary views of Representatives Elliott, Green, Thompson, Udall, and O'Hara).

[15] 325 F.2d 646, 55 L.R.R.M. 2060 (8th Cir. 1963).

[16] *Id.* at 649, 55 L.R.R.M. 2062.

is uncertain. There is support for the view that section 501 may call forth a new body of federal law in the same way that section 301 does.[17] It is also true that state fiduciary principles appear to be sparse and somewhat confused in this area. It is therefore possible but unlikely that section 501 will add to relief currently available.

The Taft-Hartley Act

For twenty years or more the courts have held that both the National Labor Relations Act and the Railway Labor Act impose on unions the duty of fair representation. In the words of *Steele*, the union must "represent non-union or minority union members . . . without hostile discrimination fairly, impartially, and in good faith."[18] Most of the court cases have dealt with racial discrimination but there have been very few cases taken to court. Probably this means that the cost is too high. It is therefore of interest to know in what areas, if any, the NLRB will bear the burden of the litigation.

Until this past year the National Labor Relations Board had confined itself to threatening to rescind the certification of a union which failed in its duty to represent all members of the bargaining unit fairly,[19] and to holding that a discriminatory agreement represented no bar to an election proceeding.[20] Neither remedy was very useful. With the *Miranda* case, however, the Board embarked on a new route.[21] The theory of the Board in that case deserves careful examination because refusal of the Second Circuit to enforce the Board's order has not deterred the Board from continuing to apply its theory of the case.[22] A strong dissent in the

---

[17] Ratner, *Some Contemporary Observations on Section 301*, 52 GEO. L.J. 260 (1964).

[18] Steele v. Louisville & N.R.R., *supra* note 8, at 204, 15 L.R.R.M. at 713.

[19] E.g., Pittsburgh Plate Glass Co., 111 N.L.R.B. 1210, 35 L.R.R.M. 1658 (1955).

[20] Pioneer Bus Co., 140 N.L.R.B. 54, 51 L.R.R.M. 1546 (1962).

[21] Miranda Fuel Co., 140 N.L.R.B. 181, 51 L.R.R.M. 1584 (1962), *enforcement denied*, 326 F.2d 172, 54 L.R.R.M. 2715 (2d Cir. 1963).

[22] Local 1367, Int'l Longshoremen's Ass'n, Case No. 23-CB-476, 55 L.R.R.M. 138 (Trial Examiner 1964) (racial discrimination in job allocation violates 8(b)(1)(A) and 8(b)(2)); Local 453, UAW, Case Nos. 13-CB-1372, 13-CA-5409 (Trial Examiner 1964) (racial discrimination in seniority reduction violates 8(b)(1)(A) and 8(b)(2); Hughes Tool Co., Case No. 23-CB-429, 23-RC-1758, IR-93-63 (Trial Examiner 1963) (refusal to process grievance because of race violates 8(b)(1)(A), 8(b)(2), and 8(b)(3)). Cf. Houston Typographical Union, 145 N.L.R.B. No. 153, 1964 CCH N.L.R.B. P 12, 908 (1964) (no violation under *Miranda* rule since work rule agreed on was not arbitrary);

Second Circuit, plus some support from the critics, has encouraged the Board to feel that it may have more success in the future.[23]

Miranda was not a race case. On the contrary, it involved a white truck driver by the name of Lopuch who worked for the Miranda Fuel Co. in the state of Ohio. Lopuch was a member of the union and had worked for the company for some eight or nine years. The business was seasonal and the contract between the company and the union contained a clause which permitted drivers to ask for a leave of absence from April 15 to October 15 without losing their places on the seniority roster. Lopuch took such a leave, departing on Friday, April 12, rather than waiting for Monday, April 15. His employer saw no reason to believe that the early departure would prejudice his seniority rights in view of the fact that it was the end of the week anyway. Lopuch failed to report back on October 15 because of illness. When he finally did report, about the end of October, the union took the position that he had lost his seniority because of failure to comply with the October 15 return date. When it was explained that Lopuch was ill, and his later return was therefore excusable, the union took the position that he should lose his seniority because he left work before April 15. With considerable reluctance Miranda bowed to the wishes of the union and put Lopuch at the bottom of the seniority list.

Miranda first went to the Supreme Court on another question. On remand the company was charged with a violation of section 8(a)(1) and (3), and the union with a violation of section 8(b)(1)(A), and (2). By a vote of three to two the Board concluded that the union owed a duty under the terms of section 9(a) to represent the individual fairly, that when it failed to do so this resulted in a violation of section 7, and that when section 7 was violated this in turn involved unfair labor practices under the subsections of

Teamsters Union, 145 N.L.R.B. No. 25, 54 L.R.R.M. 1356 (1963) (discrimination against part-time employees not shown to be arbitrary); Typographical Union, 144 N.L.R.B. No. 146, 54 L.R.R.M. 1281 (1963) (no violation because action not arbitrary); Operating Engineers Union, 144 N.L.R.B. No. 127, 54 L.R.R.M. 1235 (1963) (negligent failure to refer does not violate 8(b)(1)(A) and 8(b)(2)); Local 12, Rubber Workers, Case No. 10-CB-1362 (Trial Examiner 1964) (*Miranda* interpreted not to require union to take action against company's racially discriminatory conditions).

[23] NLRB v. Miranda Fuel Co., 362 F.2d 172, 180, 54 L.R.R.M. 2715, 2722 (2d Cir. 1963) (dissenting opinion); Sovern, *Race Discrimination and the National Labor Relations Act: The Brave New World of Miranda*, 16th ANN. N.Y. CONF. ON LABOR 3 (1963).

section 8 which are cited above. The Board found that section 7 "gives employees the right to be free from unfair or irrelevant or invidious treatment by their exclusive bargaining agent in matters affecting their employment." [24] If the employer accedes to a union request to violate the section 7 rights of the individual, it too becomes guilty of a section 7 violation, and thereby is involved with section 8(a)(1). In addition, the Board said that "a statutory bargaining representative and an employer also respectively violate section 8(a)(3) when, for arbitrary, or irrelevant reasons or upon the basis of an unfair classification, the union attempts to cause or does cause an employer to derogate the employment status of an employee." [25]

The Second Circuit refused to enforce the Board's order on the ground that discrimination against an employee affecting the terms and conditions of his employment could not constitute an unfair labor practice under section 8 so long as it was wholly unrelated to any union consideration. [26] However, in three opinions by as many judges, only Judge Medina, writing the principal opinion, rejected the section 7-8(b)(1)(A) theory. Judge Lumbard, in a concurring opinion, expressly refused to discuss 8(b)(1)(A) because of the weak factual situation in the case. [27] Judge Friendly examined only the 8(b)(2)-8(a)(3) theory in his dissenting opinion. [28] In subsequent cases the Board has continued to apply both theories, and it is evident that there will be other court tests.

In *Metal Workers Union*, the Board majority found violations of 8(b)(1)(A), 8(b)(2), and 8(b)(3) in a race case involving the failure of an all-white local to process the grievance of a Negro who belonged to a jointly certified Negro local. [29] Agreeing with the majority that the joint certification ought to be revoked, two members of the Board also found an 8(b)(1)(A) violation, based, however, not on the breach of duty of fair representation found by the trial examiner and the majority, but apparently resulting from the Negro's non-membership in the white local.

If the Board is ultimately sustained in its view that breach of the

---

[24] Miranda Fuel Co., 140 N.L.R.B. 181, 185, 51 L.R.R.M. 1584, 1587 (1962).
[25] *Id.* at 186, 51 L.R.R.M. at 1587.
[26] NLRB v. Miranda Fuel Co., 362 F.2d 172, 54 L.R.R.M. 2715 (2d Cir. 1963).
[27] *Id.* at 180, 54 L.R.R.M. at 2721.
[28] *Id.* at 180, 54 L.R.R.M. at 2722.
[29] 147 N.L.R.B. No. 166, 56 L.R.R.M. 1289 (1964).

union's duty to represent an individual fairly within the bargaining unit constitutes an unfair labor practice, the union must obviously reflect on the significance of this development as it relates to the handling of grievances. In that connection it is worth noting as well that in a 1963 administrative decision the Board's General Counsel refused to process a charge that the settling of an individual grievance in the employee's absence constituted an unfair labor practice. The contract did not call for the individual's presence after a certain step in the grievance procedure, and the General Counsel said: "even assuming the applicability of the Section 9(a) proviso to this situation, the individual had been permitted to initially present his own grievance. Moreover, the legislative history of the proviso substantiated the view that it was intended to be permissive in nature insofar as employers were concerned in that it enabled them to deal with individual employees in the adjustment of grievances without violating Section 8(a)(5) but imposed no obligation upon them to do so." [30]

More will be said later about the possible effect of *Miranda* on grievance handling.

The Court Decisions

During any given year there are, of course, innumerable court decisions related to the question of grievance handling. Most of the decisions follow along fairly predictable paths, though the outcome is not always certain. Two decisions during the past year warrant particular consideration because they do seem to add to the present state of the law. Both apply federal law though one comes from the Supreme Court of the State of New Jersey.

The first of the cases is *Donnelly v. United Fruit Co.*[31] In that case the plaintiff, Donnelly, had been employed by the United Fruit Company as an assistant purser. He was a member of the union, there was a collective bargaining contract, and the contract contained a clause which permitted the company to fire for cause. Grievances could be processed through arbitration if the union so desired.

Donnelly was fired for inefficiency. He then asked his union representative to investigate the case and the latter did so. At that point the union declined to take the case any further, advising Donnelly

---

[30] Administrative Decision, General Counsel, No. SR-2721, 63-2 CCH N.L.R.B. P 12, 745 (1963).

[31] 40 N.J. 61, 190 A.2d 825, 53 L.R.R.M. 2271 (1963).

that he had no case. There were some subsequent meetings but ultimately the union representative advised Donnelly that neither the company nor the union was willing to go to arbitration. Subsequently, before the New York Supreme Court Donnelly sought a declaratory judgment against the company alone that the discharge was improper. The company obtained a summary judgment in its favor without prejudice. The present action was then brought in the Superior Court of New Jersey against both the company and the union. Damages were sought. The claim against the company was for wrongful discharge and refusal to arbitrate, while the claim against the union was simply that it wrongfully refused to arbitrate. The trial court granted summary judgments for both defendants, relying on previous New Jersey cases and the fact that the collective bargaining agreement conferred no individual right on the plaintiff to insist that the union process his grievance. On review, the Supreme Court of New Jersey treated the action as one for breach of contract under section 301 of the Taft-Hartley Act, and therefore governed by federal law. After an extensive review of the problem it then held that as to "grievances" relating to individual rights (such as discharge) the plaintiff (Donnelly) had an absolute right under section 9(a) to process and have adjusted his grievance. Since the union refused to take the case to arbitration, the court held that Donnelly should have asked the company to arbitrate, this being the preferred method of handling such cases. In the arbitration, said the court, the union would have a right to be present and to argue contractual implications of the case, but Donnelly had the right to control the proceeding, including the choice of arbitrators. On the ticklish question of costs, the court left the decision to the arbitrator, suggesting that if he found that Donnelly had a valid claim which the union should have processed, or if he found that the union had failed to accord Donnelly fair treatment in refusing to process the case, he might require the union to pay half of the expenses of arbitration. In the absence of such a finding the individual would have to bear his share of the cost of arbitration.

Having established a procedure by which an individual could utilize the arbitration machinery, the Supreme Court nevertheless ended up denying Donnelly any relief. The reason was that "if the employee's individual right under section 9(a) is to be regarded as integrated with the collective bargaining agreement, then consistency requires the same limitation of the employee's right to institute a damage suit against the union until such a demand by the employee and refusal by the employer have occurred. Concededly, Donnelly took no such step in this case." [32]

Without pausing for further comment at this time, it is interesting to note that following the *Donnelly* decision the American Bar Association's Labor Law Section took a quick tally of New Jersey labor lawyers in an effort to find out how they interpreted the effect of *Donnelly*. Some thought that to avoid litigation by individuals the union would now have to take every discharge case, meritorious or not, to arbitration. Others felt that the union's obligation had decreased because doubtful cases could now be discarded on the theory that the individual could pursue his own remedy.[33]

The second court case, and in many ways the most interesting, is *Humphrey v. Moore*, which was decided by the United States Supreme Court on January 6, 1964.[34] That case involved the Teamsters Union and two auto transport companies. Both companies transported Ford cars and Ford ultimately had need for only one of them. The two companies then worked out a new territorial arrangement under which X took the area in question. The employees of both companies were represented by the same union. Since X did not need all of the employees of both companies a question arose as to the proper allocation of jobs among present employees. Ultimately it was agreed that the seniority of the two sets of employees would be integrated. It turned out that Y was the older company so that X ended up with a work force constituted largely of Y's men. The individuals who had formerly been employed by X then protested that the union and the company had exceeded their contractual powers in making such an agreement, and that in any event the union had unfairly discriminated against some of its members. The Kentucky state court which heard the case was asked to enjoin the company and the union from carrying out the agreement or to give damages in the alternative. The trial court dismissed the claim, but the Court of Appeals reversed and granted a permanent injunction. Among other things the Court of Appeals said that the decision could not stand since the situation involved

---

[32] *Id.* at 96, 19 A.2d at 843, 53 L.R.R.M. at 2285.

[33] *Report of the Comm. on State Labor Legislation*, ABA Sect. of Lab. Rel. Law 158 (1964).

[34] 375 U.S. 335, 55 L.R.R.M. 2031 (1964).

antagonistic interests of two sets of employees represented by the same union advocate.[35]

The United States Supreme Court granted certiorari. In its subsequent decision the court agreed that a claim that the company and the union had exceeded their authority under the contract stated a cause of action under section 301 which required the application of federal law to the case. For reasons which are much less clear the court also agreed that the claim that the union violated its duty of fair representation to the employees of X also stated a cause of action under section 301 because it too alleged a breach of contract. Since the contract did not contain a specific clause which required the union to represent its members fairly, the court had to find that it was a part of the contract by implication. This was, of course, exactly what the court had done before when it implied such a duty under section 9 of the Taft-Hartley Act, but no such *contractual* duty had previously been articulated.

Having found that a proper cause of action was stated, the court then proceeded to deny recovery on both counts because the contract did authorize the action which the parties had taken, and because there was no showing that the union had been guilty of a lack of "good faith and honesty of purpose in the exercise of its discretion" within the rule of the *Huffman* case.[36]

While Justice Goldberg agreed with the end result, he dissented vigorously from the reasoning by which the court reached its result. As to the allegation that the company and the union had exceeded their powers under the contract he said:

A mutually acceptable grievance settlement between an employer and a union . . . cannot be challenged by an individual dissenting employee under § 301(a) on the ground that the parties exceeded their contractual powers in making the settlement. It is true that this Court, in a series of decisions dealing with labor arbitration, has recognized that the powers of an arbitrator arise from and are defined by the collective bargaining agreement. . . . But the power of the union and the employer jointly to settle a grievance dispute is not so limited. The parties are free by joint action to modify, amend, and supplement their original collective bargaining agreement.[37]

---

[35] Moore v. Local 89, Teamsters Union, 356 S.W.2d 241, 49 L.R.R.M. 2677 (Ky. 1962).

[36] Ford Motor Co. v. Huffman, *supra* note 9, at 338, 31 L.R.R.M. at 2551.

[37] Humphrey v. Moore, *supra* note 34, at 352-53, 55 L.R.R.M. at 2039.

On the matter of an implied contractual duty of fair representation, Justice Goldberg said:

I read the decisions of this Court to hold that an individual employee has a right to a remedy against a union breaching its duty of fair representation — a duty derived not from the collective bargaining contract but implied from the union's rights and responsibility conferred by federal labor statutes.[38]

We should not and, indeed, we need not strain, therefore, as the Court does, to convert a breach of the union's duty to individual employees into a breach of the collective bargaining agreement between the employer and the union.[39]

Mr. Justice Douglas agreed with Justice Goldberg that the action was not properly brought as a 301 action and should, therefore, have been resolved in the state courts. On the merits, however, he thought the majority of the court was right.[40]

Mr. Justice Harlan agreed with the majority on the propriety of a 301 action on the allegation that the parties had exceeded their power under the contract, but with Justice Goldberg on the impropriety of a 301 action which alleged breach of an implied contractual duty of fair representation.[41] As to the latter he raised a preemption question which will have to be faced in the future. If the allegation of unfair union representation gives rise only to a cause of action for violation of a duty implicit in the National Labor Relations Act, would not such a cause be preempted under the rule of the second *Garmon* case? [42]

Humphrey v. Moore is significant for at least one other reason. It appears to lay to rest the rule of the Kentucky Court of Appeals that there is a per se inadequacy of representation any time a union represents employees having antagonistic interests. This, of course, was the rule of *Clark v. Hein-Werner*, referred to earlier.[43] In reversing the Kentucky court the Supreme Court once more reaffirmed *Ford Motor Co. v. Huffman*.[44] The language is so unmistakably clear that there can hardly be doubt in the future. Said the court:

---

[38] *Id.* at 355–56, 55 L.R.R.M. at 2040.
[39] *Id.* at 357, 55 L.R.R.M. at 2041.
[40] *Id.* at 351, 55 L.R.R.M. at 2042.
[41] *Id.* at 359, 55 L.R.R.M. at 2041.
[42] San Diego Bldg. Trades Council v. Garmon, 359 U.S. 236, 43 L.R.R.M. 2838 (1959).
[43] Clark v. Hein-Werner Corp., *supra* note 11.
[44] Ford Motor Co. v. Huffman, *supra* note 9.

But we are not ready to find a breach of the collective bargaining agent's duty of fair representation in taking a good faith position contrary to that of some individuals whom it represents nor in supporting the position of one group of employees against that of another. . . . Just as a union must be free to sift out wholly frivolous grievances which would only clog the grievance process, so it must be free to take a position on the not so frivolous disputes. Nor should it be neutralized when the issue is chiefly between two sets of employees. Conflict between employees represented by the same union is a recurrent fact. To remove or gag the union in these cases would surely weaken the collective bargaining and grievance processes.[45]

After disposing of the question of antagonistic interests within the union, the court did say that there was a remaining question of whether the employees of X, if they were going to be opposed by the union, were "deprived of a fair hearing by having inadequate representation at the hearing." [46] On investigating this question, the court found that the employees had notice of the hearing, that three stewards representing them went to the hearing at union expense, and that they were given every opportunity to state their case. At an earlier stage in the grievance procedure when the company and the union representatives were meeting to decide what to do about merging the seniority lists, the employees of X had not requested that the hearing be continued until they could secure further representation, and they never suggested what "they could have added to the hearing by way of facts or theory if they had been differently represented." [47] Under the circumstances the court thought it would be mere idle speculation to say that the result would have been different had the matter been differently presented.

Thus, certain points peripheral to the central problem of individual rights, though still important, may be noted in summation. First, despite persistent suggestions to the contrary, there is little evidence that Landrum-Griffin provisions are having any appreciable legal effect upon grievance handling and arbitration. Second, *Humphrey v. Moore* has laid to rest doubts about the union's capacity to represent antagonistic interests but has emphasized the due process requirements of notice and hearing.

---

[45] Humphrey v. Moore, *supra* note 34, at 349-50, 55 L.R.R.M. at 2037-38.
[46] *Id.* at 350, 55 L.R.R.M. at 2038.
[47] *Ibid.*

THE CURRENT ALTERNATIVES

The current choices for protection of individual rights in arbitration seem clearly to include the approaches of *Miranda, Donnelly,* and *Humphrey.* In evaluating each, it is helpful to go beyond the reasoning of the opinions and analyze the problems which are involved.

In *Miranda* the Board finds that failure on the part of a union to represent a member fairly constitutes an unfair labor practice. Acquiescence by the employer in a union request from which such a charge arises will involve the employer in the unfair labor practice. This interpretation of the Act has been rejected by the Second Circuit, but the Board continues to assert its view and it is likely that another circuit will eventually agree. If and when it does so the stage will be set for certiorari and a ruling from the Supreme Court. A ruling favorable to the Board's position will not necessarily mean that an unfair refusal to carry a grievance to arbitration will constitute an unfair labor practice, but it will be hard to distinguish the two situations.

If the National Labor Relations Board is ultimately successful in persuading the courts to accept the *Miranda* doctrine, the effect will be to expand the Board's role in supervising collective bargaining. Judge Medina saw this clearly in the Second Circuit's review of the *Miranda* ruling. He said, "Were we to support the doctrine thus propounded the power and jurisdiction of the Board would be vastly extended and increased. . . ."[48] He also thought that "the machinery of the Board and the remedies applied in the enforcement of findings of unfair labor practices, as defined in the Act, are not suited to the task of deciding general questions of private wrongs unrelated to union activities, suffered by employees as a result of tortious conduct by either employers or labor unions."[49]

An important policy question is thus posed. If one feels strongly that there ought to be an inexpensive remedy available to the employee who can prove that the union has been unfair in refusing to take his grievance to arbitration, there is logic in having the Board take jurisdiction of such cases. The employee will then run no risk that the cost of litigation will be prohibitive. On the other hand, the net result will be to subject one more area of collective bar-

---

[48] NLRB v. Miranda Fuel Co., *supra* note 26, at 177, 54 L.R.R.M. at 2719.
[49] *Id.* at 180, 54 L.R.R.M. at 2721.

gaining to supervision at the hands of the government. This gives rise to a certain uneasiness. Moreover, there is the question of whether the Board can devise a suitable remedy, though that problem may be put aside for the moment.

On the policy question, it is reasonable to inquire into the proportions of the problem before trying to make any decision as to the role which the NLRB should play in cases of this kind. In this connection Professor Summers, who has perhaps given this whole problem more careful study than anyone else, reports two items of special interest. The first is that "more than three-fourths of the reported cases in which individuals have sought legal protection of their rights under a collective agreement have arisen out of disciplinary discharges." [50] This is a strong argument in favor of a remedy at the hands of the NLRB since discharge, particularly if unjust, is especially unfair when one considers the difficulty of finding new jobs because of high unemployment. Certainly, too, one of the prime objectives in today's bargaining is job security for the individual.

Summers' second item is that in Sweden, where the individual is permitted to bring suit in the Labor Court to protect his rights, "the Labor Court has not been flooded with individual suits; such suits have constituted less than two per cent of all cases coming before the court." [51] The Swedish experience thus suggests that the NLRB will not be deluged with cases. This point may be confirmed by yet another bit of evidence. For some time critics of the Board have expressed concern about certain of its decisions in that they seemed to inject the Board into collective bargaining to an unwarranted degree. Perhaps the best example was the *Borg-Warner* case, in which the Board upset a contract between the Borg-Warner Company and the UAW on the ground that the company had committed an unfair labor practice by making bargaining contingent on a clause which involved all employees, whether members of the union or not, in a strike vote. [52] Since there was no doubt about the legality of the clause for which the company contended, and

---

[50] Summers, *Individual Rights in Collective Agreements: A Preliminary Analysis*, 9 BUFFALO L. REV. 239, 252 (1960).

[51] Summers, *Collective Power and Individual Rights in the Collective Agreement — A Comparison of Swedish and American Law*, 72 YALE L.J. 421, 453 (1963).

[52] Wooster Div. of Borg-Warner Corp., 113 N.L.R.B. 1288 (1955), *enforced*, 236 F.2d 898 (6th Cir. 1956), *rev'd in part*, 356 U.S. 342 (1958).

there was no finding that it had not bargained in good faith, the Board was vigorously criticized for finding the company guilty of an unfair labor practice. The gist of the criticism was that the Board was unduly injecting itself into the bargaining process. In a recent study the Board has tried to evaluate this criticism. With specific reference to *Borg-Warner*, the Chairman of the Board reported:

The Borg-Warner decision has been almost universally condemned by all legal and academic commentators as imposing a strait-jacket upon collective bargaining. Indeed, the literature is rife with hostile speculations about the dangerous consequences of this decision.

It may be that our critics are right, and it would be helpful to have the evidence for their views. We do have [a] report of what the Board has done in the five years after Borg-Warner. In this period of time, there were only 35 out of the 1008 closed cases in which the Agency either formally or informally found a violation involving a mandatory subject matter of bargaining. In *none* of these cases did a Borg-Warner type of situation occur.[53]

In 1955 the American Bar Association's Committee on Improvement of Union-Management Agreements reported that over two-thirds of the lawyers who replied to its questionnaire "stated that in their experience they found that meritorious grievances were at times ignored or surrendered because of political pressures within the union." [54] At the same time, the Committee reported that "the number of instances in which unfairness occurs is relatively small." [55] This fact, coupled with the post–*Borg-Warner* history outlined above, suggests that enunciation of a Board doctrine of an unfair labor practice based upon failure to represent the employee fairly in the grievance procedure would not constitute an undue interference with bargaining nor impose a significant burden on the Board.

The new law of *Humphrey v. Moore* is the holding that there is an implied contractual obligation, arising out of the collective bargaining agreement, that the union will fairly represent its members. Such a ruling is significant for several reasons. In the first place, it creates a wholly new cause of action. Second, it federalizes the law which will be applied in such cases since a 301 action,

---

[53] McCulloch, *Effects of NLRB Rules on Good-Faith Bargaining*, 56 L.R.R.M. 120, 124-25 (1964).

[54] *Report of the Committee on Improvement of Administration of Union-Management Agreements*, 50 Nw. U.L. Rev. 143, 156 (1955).

[55] *Id.* at 155.

though properly brought in either a state or federal court,[56] is to be decided by the application of federal law.[57] Finally, it seems to avoid the preemption problem because a breach of contract claim, even by an individual, properly qualifies as a section 301 action,[58] and 301 actions are not preempted by the *Garmon* rule.[59]

A contractual cause of action for unfair representation would expand the role which the courts now play in overseeing collective bargaining. Justice Goldberg was as concerned about this as was Judge Medina in the *Miranda* case.

In a long concluding paragraph Justice Goldberg said:

. . . in this Court's fashioning of a federal law of collective bargaining, it is of the utmost importance that the law reflect the realities of industrial life and the nature of the collective bargaining process. We should not assume that doctrines evolved in other contexts will be equally well adapted to the collective bargaining process. Of course, we must protect the rights of the individual. It must not be forgotten, however, that many individual rights, such as the seniority rights involved in this case, in fact arise from the concerted exercise of the right to bargain collectively. Consequently, the understandable desire to protect the individual should not emasculate the right to bargain by placing undue restraints upon the contracting parties. Similarly in safeguarding the individual against the misconduct of the bargaining agent we must recognize that the employer's interests are inevitably involved whenever the labor contract is set aside in order to vindicate the individual's right against the union. The employer's interest should not be lightly denied where there are other remedies available to insure that a union will respect the rights of its constituents. Nor should trial-type hearing standards or conceptions of vested contractual rights be applied so as to hinder the employer and the union in their joint endeavor to adapt the collective bargaining relationship to the exigencies of economic life. I have deemed it necessary to state my views separately because I believe that the Court's analysis in part runs contrary to these principles.[60]

Even if we assume that there is now an action under section 301 for breach of an implied obligation to represent the individual employee fairly, many questions remain. What kind of conduct on the part of the union will constitute a failure to represent fairly?

---

[56] Charles Dowd Box Co. v. Courtney, 368 U.S. 502, 49 L.R.R.M. 2619 (1962).

[57] Local 174, Teamsters Union v. Lucas Flour Co., 369 U.S. 95, 49 L.R.R.M. 2717 (1962) (state court must apply federal law); Textile Workers Union v. Lincoln Mills, 353 U.S. 448, 40 L.R.R.M. 2113 (1957) (federal court is to devise federal law of labor contracts).

[58] Smith v. Evening News Ass'n, 371 U.S. 195, 51 L.R.R.M. 2646 (1962).

[59] *Ibid.*

[60] Humphrey v. Moore, *supra* note 34, at 358–59, 55 L.R.R.M. at 2041.

Are there some kinds of grievances which the individual has an absolute right to take to arbitration? If so, what are they? If the court orders arbitration, will it be bilateral, involving the company and the individual, or trilateral, involving the company, the individual, and the union? Who will pay for the arbitration? On the question of who pays, should it make any difference whether or not the grievance is meritorious?

As to conduct which might constitute a failure to represent fairly, about all we know from the *Humphrey* decision itself is that antagonistic interests within the union will not alone be ground for claiming any dereliction on the union's part. A much more difficult test for the court would be stated in a factual situation patterned after *Union News Co. v. Hildreth.*[61] In that case the company operated a lunch counter in a railway station. Food costs were so far out of line that the company became convinced that either food or money was being stolen. Guilt could not be pinned on any individual (out of a group of about twelve) and the company wanted to discharge all of them. Ultimately a compromise was reached with the union under which half of the employees would be laid off and replaced with another group. It was further agreed that if costs came down it would indicate that the guilty employees were among those on layoff and the layoff would then be converted to discharge. As it turned out, the layoffs were completely effective in restoring the normal cost ratio and the union then acceded to the discharges. Hildreth, a waitress with ten years of experience, was among those discharged. There was no proof of her personal guilt, and the collective bargaining contract protected employees against discharge except for just cause. Hildreth sought the aid of the union in contesting her discharge, but it refused because of its earlier agreement with the company. She then sued without success, the court holding that the agreement between the company and the union was entered into in good faith, and that such an agreement was permitted under the terms of the contract.

In making its decision in the *Union News* case the Sixth Circuit was without benefit of the Supreme Court's subsequent ruling in *Humphrey* that there was an implied contractual obligation of good faith representation. Would this have made any difference in the out-

---

[61] 295 F.2d 658 (6th Cir. 1961), *adhered to when reviewed in light of Smith v. Evening News Ass'n*, 315 F.2d 548 (6th Cir. 1963).

come? It is not clear that it would, though the case gives rise to some real doubts, as Professor Blumrosen has pointed out in the following comment:

The court recognized that there was no basis for inferring that any of the laid-off employees were more guilty of theft than those who remained at work. There was simply no proof of individual guilt. The contract prohibited discharge without just cause and provided for arbitration. In labor arbitration the burden of proof of just cause is normally on the employer. When a criminal act is alleged, this burden is substantial. In all probability, an arbitrator would not have sustained the discharge of these employees. But union and company had agreed to dispense with proof of the guilt of the laid-off employees. Thus, the union deprived the employees of a hearing before an arbitrator in which, on the evidence adduced, they would probably have prevailed.

Gladys Hildreth could not have been deprived of any of her legal rights, no matter how insignificant, by any court on the basis of the record in this case. Yet, she was deprived of her job, despite ten years seniority, under a contract protecting her from discharge except for just cause, when her union refused to insist that her case be reviewed on its merits.[62]

Another approach to a decision in cases like *Union News* would be that of the New Jersey Supreme Court in the *Donnelly* case. The New Jersey Supreme Court, applying federal law in the *Donnelly* case, said that section 9(a) of the Taft-Hartley Act gives the individual employee "a statutorily-vested right to present his grievance to, and to have it determined by, his employer when the union declines to process it in his behalf." [63] This seems to be the view of the American Bar Association's Committee on Improvement of Union-Management Agreements referred to earlier, but it certainly is not the view of the Second Circuit in the recent case of *Black-Clawson Co. v. Machinists*. In that case the court said that section 9(a) did not confer "an indefeasible right upon the individual employee to compel compliance with the grievance procedure up to and including any arbitration provision. . . ." [64] To rule otherwise, said the court, would not be consonant with a sound view of labor-management relations, for "chaos would result if every disenchanted

---

[62] Blumrosen, *The Worker and Three Phases of Unionism: Administrative and Judicial Control of the Worker-Union Relationship*, 61 MICH. L. REV. 1435, 1492 (1963).

[63] Donnelly v. United Fruit Co., 40 N.J. 61, 87, 190 A. 2d 825, 839, 53 L.R.R.M. 2271, 2281 (1963).

[64] Black-Clawson Co. v. Int'l Ass'n of Machinists, 313 F.2d 179, 185, 52 L.R.R.M. 2038, 2042 (2d Cir. 1962).

employee, every disturbed employee, and every employee who harbored dislike for his employer, could harass both the union and the employer by processing grievances through the various steps of the grievance procedure and ultimately by bringing an action to compel arbitration in the face of clear contractual provisions intended to channel the enforcement remedy through the union." [65]

In view of the evidence cited earlier, it is doubtful that the consequences of holding that section 9(a) gives employees a vested right to process grievances, even through arbitration, would be as doleful as the Second Circuit suggests, but there is strong support for the view of section 9(a) which that court adopts. In this situation it would be possible for the court to adopt the compromise position advocated by Blumrosen. [66]

Ultimately both the NLRB, if it follows the suggested *Miranda* route, and the courts, if they apply either the contractual theory of the *Humphrey* case or the vested rights theory of the *Donnelly* case, will have to face the question of a proper remedy. If the collective bargaining contract contains an agreement to arbitrate, as it does in the overwhelming majority of the contracts, the logical remedial order is to direct the parties to proceed to arbitration. This will effectuate the contract, take advantage of the public policy which favors arbitration, and insure that the dispute will come before the kind of tribunal best equipped to deal with it. The individual grievant must obviously be allowed to participate in the choice of an arbitration; otherwise suspicions of hostility to his interests will only be renewed. But it is equally apparent that the union must also participate in the choice of an arbitrator and in the ensuing hearing. The reasons for this conclusion have been apparent ever since the Supreme Court decided the *J. I. Case* matter in 1944. [67] There is a certain tension between individual and group interests and if both are to be protected both must be represented.

THE COST PROBLEM

The cost problem seems to have most plagued those who believe that trilateral arbitrations must be permitted. The problem *is* a very complicated one in which, for instance, the equities may change

---

[65] *Id.* at 186, 52 L.R.R.M. at 2043.

[66] Blumrosen, *Legal Protection for Critical Job Interests: Union-Management Autonomy Versus Employee Autonomy*, 13 RUTGERS L. REV. 631 (1959).

[67] J. I. Case Co. v. NLRB, 321 U.S. 332, 14 L.R.R.M. 501 (1944).

depending on whether one follows the *Donnelly* theory that individuals have an absolute right to take grievances to arbitration under the proviso to section 9(a), or whether one follows a *Miranda-Humphrey* theory which would involve a preliminary finding by either the Board or a court that there had been a failure on the part of the union to represent the individual fairly. Thus, in the latter type of situation there would be less reason for excusing the union from payment of any costs than would be true in the former.

The *Donnelly* court thought that individuals had an absolute right to take unsettled grievances through all of the steps of the grievance procedure, including arbitration, and it therefore had to face the cost question on that basis. It reached the following conclusion:

If the matter is pressed to the final stage of arbitration, decision as to expenses may be left to the arbitrator. Obviously, the union should not be saddled with costs of arbitrating worthless or petty claims of disputatious employees. On the other hand, if the employee is successful and the grievance is one which in the judgment of the arbitrator should have been handled by the union, costs would follow the course fixed in the collective agreement or usually followed by custom or practice. Further, even if the employee is unsuccessful after arbitration, if his cause is colorable and presented in good faith, and in the judgment of the arbitrator refusal of the union to press it was unfair and arbitrary, he should be relieved of costs. But if he fails and has no colorable claim of a substantial nature, he must shoulder the costs. Such treatment of expenses would be consistent with the existing union-management code of the plant and would serve to integrate further the section 9(a) right of the employee with that code.[68]

Professor Summers, who also believes that the individual ought to have an absolute right under section 9(a) to carry grievances to arbitration, is a little more inclined to impose the cost in such cases on the individual. He says:

Obviously, the union cannot be saddled with the costs of presenting worthless grievances brought by mistaken or litigious employees. Therefore, if the claim is rejected the individual who insisted on an adjudication of his grievance against the wishes and judgment of the union should bear what would normally be the union's share of the cost of arbitration. Placing his financial burden on the individual will serve to discourage, in the very way on which the law normally relies, the pursuit of fanciful claims. If the individual's claim proves meritorious, the individual has performed

---

[68] Donnelly v. United Fruit Co., 40 N.J. 61, 92–93, 190 A.2d 825, 842, 53 L.R.R.M. 2271, 2283–84 (1963).

the union's function in enforcing the agreement and might logically call on the union to share the costs of arbitration. However, the union's duty to represent does not require enforcing every jot and title of the contract. If an employee is sent home for alleged loitering in the washroom, the grievance may be worth only a few dollars, establish no precedent and involve no principle. The union might reasonably refuse to spend twenty times the value of the claim to get an arbitrator's award declaring management mistaken. Or a union might decide because of limited funds not to press certain categories of grievances where the collective interest is not sufficient, and leave these grievances to individual enforcement. In such cases the individual, even though he wins, should bear the costs, for he is entitled to no more than equal protection. However, if the union refuses to prosecute only because of doubts as to the outcome in arbitration, it cannot deny responsibility for the costs after the individual, at his own risk, has dispelled those doubts by winning.

The employer continues to be responsible for his share of the arbitration costs regardless of whether the union or an individual is the prosecuting party. Though there may be fears that the employer will be harassed and burdened by litigious employees, the danger is easily exaggerated, for the financial burden on the individual in pressing the claim is relatively much greater, and there will be few who will challenge the combined forces of union and management.[69]

Professor Summers suggests no way for determining whether the union refused to proceed only because of doubts about the outcome or for calling on the union to share in the cost of arbitration. A union which declined to take the issue to arbitration in the first place is not likely to be moved by a post-hearing plea to share in the costs. The *Donnelly* court resolved this problem by saying that a decision as to the allocation of expenses should be left to the arbitrator. This is a highly unsatisfactory disposition of the matter for, as Hanslowe has pointed out, "it will take a brave arbitrator to decide that the employee ought to win the grievance which the union (and the employer) opposed, *and* that the union ought to pay the arbitrator half his fee for so deciding." [70]

If there is to be a rule that employees under a collective bargaining contract have an absolute right to take grievances through arbitration, because of the proviso to section 9(a), would it not be better to have a flat rule that in the absence of any showing of bad faith on the part of the union, the cost of the arbitration would be

---

[69] Summers, *Individual Rights in Collective Agreements and Arbitration*, 37 N.Y.U.L. Rev. 361, 403 (1962).

[70] Hanslowe, *The Collective Agreement and the Duty of Fair Representation*, 14 Lab. L.J. 1052, 1066 (1963).

shared by the company and the individual? There may be some un-fairness to the company in this, in the sense that it has bargained only to share the costs of arbitration in those cases which the union wishes to take to arbitration, but the burden is not likely to be heavy. Such a rule would dispense with any relationship between costs and success or failure in the processing of the grievance. The latter is a very dubious concept anyway, since a meritorious claim, entirely worthy of arbitration, may nevertheless be lost in a close decision, or an entirely worthy claim may be sacrificed in good faith because the cost of arbitration far outweighs the benefits to be obtained.

As to those cases in which there is a finding that the union has refused to represent the member fairly, what inequity is there in ordering the union to pay its normal share of the arbitration cost? Foreknowledge of such a rule would dispose the union against dis-crimination in the handling of grievances. If despite this knowledge the union unfairly represents the individual, there is no inequity in assessing costs against the union regardless of the merits of the case. This rule would be the same whether the proceeding contemplated an absolute right to carry grievances to arbitration (in the course of which proceeding unfair treatment on the part of the union was shown), or a *Miranda-Humphrey* type proceeding. The National Labor Relations Board, or the court, having made a finding that the union had unfairly refused to carry the issue to arbitration, would issue an order to arbitrate on a tripartite basis, with the costs al-located to the company and the union. Should the individual then wish to employ counsel of his own he would, of course, be respon-sible for that portion of the expense, and if he insisted on proce-dural arrangements (such as a transcript) which the parties did not normally employ he would likewise be responsible for that part of the expense.

SOME CONCLUSIONS ABOUT INDIVIDUAL RIGHTS IN ARBITRATION

Collective bargaining's most enduring monument may well be the rule of law which it has brought to the American industrial society. Without such a rule individuals would have infinitely less protec-tion in their working lives than they now have. Yet we remain concerned that the very collective process which offers them pro-tection may unduly subjugate individual rights. Critics have long struggled with the problem without finding a completely satisfactory solution. One aspect of the problem, and the one with which we are most immediately concerned, is the question of how accessible the arbitration machinery should be to the individual for purposes of determining his contractual rights.

We are still a long way from finally resolving the question of individual versus collective rights, but two things now seem clear. The first is that the answer, when it comes, is going to be found in the federal law. The second is that public policy now so clearly favors arbitration that such rights as the individual is found to have will include utilization of the arbitration step in the grievance machinery. The second of these conclusions follows from the whole line of Supreme Court decisions since *Lincoln Mills*,[71] and the first is a direct outgrowth of the court's decision in *Smith v. Evening News Ass'n*.[72] Once it was decided in that case that individual lawsuits asserting rights under the collective bargaining contract could be brought under section 301 of the Taft-Hartley Act, the way was open for federal protection of individual rights through one or more of the following three devices:

1. A section 301 lawsuit in which it is alleged that section 9(a) of the Taft-Hartley Act vests in the individual an absolute right to have his contractual claim determined through the grievance machinery, including arbitration.

2. A section 301 lawsuit in which it is alleged that the union is in violation of an implied condition of the collective bargaining contract in that it has failed to represent an individual fairly in his contractual claims.

3. A finding by the National Labor Relations Board that failure on the part of the union to represent an individual fairly constitutes an unfair labor practice on the part of the union, and perhaps on the part of the employer.

The first of these three possibilities, in which reliance is placed on the proviso to section 9(a), has both strong supporters and vigorous opponents. It is the position of serious students of the problem, like Summers and Dunau of the American Bar Association's Committee, and of the New Jersey court in the *Donnelly* case. It would, in many ways, be the cleanest and easiest way to handle the prob-

---

[71] Textile Workers Union v. Lincoln Mills, 353 U.S. 448, 40 L.R.R.M. 2113 (1957).

[72] Smith v. Evening News Ass'n, 371 U.S. 195, 51 L.R.R.M. 2646 (1962).

lem. It would give the individual protection (and when one re-members that many of these cases are discharges, this is important), it would not be dependent on a finding that the union had treated the individual unfairly, the expense to the individual in bringing the case would be likely to deter frivolous actions, tripartite arbitration would protect both individual and collective interests, and by application of the statute there would be less of a problem of surmounting a contractual clause which limited the use of the arbitration machinery to the company and the union. On the other hand, it is rejected by such distinguished courts as the Second Circuit, and it is admittedly based on a weak legislative history. This solution would be opposed by companies which would fear a flood of wild grievances, and by unions which would suspect that it would undermine the collective bargaining process. Given the weak legislative history on which such an interpretation of section 9(a) must rest, it seems more probable than not that the courts will ultimately reject this approach.

The second possibility rests upon an exploitation of the Supreme Court's language in *Humphrey v. Moore*. In that case the court says that there is an implied contractual obligation on the part of the union to treat individuals fairly in the course of interpreting the contract. Assuming the court meant what it said, the way is now open for an individual to bring a 301 action claiming that the union unfairly refused to process his grievance or to take it to arbitration. Under this approach the individual would not have an absolute right to utilize the arbitration machinery, but would be required to show that the union had acted unfairly. The expense of bringing the suit would still fall on the individual and his chances of success would be less. On the other hand, those who fear that the processing of individual grievances would undermine collective bargaining would have less ground for complaint because unfair treatment for the individual would engender little sympathy for the union or the company.

Finally, there is the possibility that the theory of the National Labor Relations Board in the *Miranda* case will prevail, and that it will be extended to the situation in which the union is alleged to have unfairly refused to process or take a grievance to arbitration. Despite the refusal of the Second Circuit to enforce *Miranda* there is a good chance that in a stronger case the Board will be upheld and that the Supreme Court will ultimately agree. If this comes about, the great advantage to the individual will be that he will be relieved of any of the cost of fighting the battle. Judge Medina's fears that the "machinery of the Board and the remedies applied . . . are not suited to the task of deciding general questions of private wrongs unrelated to union activities" [73] need not pose any insuperable obstacles. The Board already deals with touchy questions related to individual memberships in the union, [74] and the allegation of unfair treatment in the course of handling grievances will not be so different that the Board cannot handle it. There are, however, some tricky remedy problems if the Board acts in these cases. If the unfair labor practice charge is filed against both the union and the company, as it is likely to be under the theory of *Miranda*, a directive to both that the issue be submitted to a form of tripartite arbitration in which the individual, the union, and the company all participate in the choice of the arbitrator, and each has an opportunity to present his case, would not be out of order. But it is conceivable that the company might not be guilty of an unfair labor practice, and this could pose some problems of a remedial order running against the company as well as the union.

Is the individual any better off as the result of the developments of the last year than he was before in requiring the union to process or arbitrate his grievance? Possible forms of legal action now seem clearer than ever before, but the ultimate outcome is still wrapped in doubt. It may nevertheless be true that the greater likelihood of successful legal action against unions and/or companies for failure to accord an individual fair representation rights will itself dispose the parties to take more issues to arbitration. (In *Humphrey v. Moore*, by the time the case reached the Supreme Court, the company was no longer supporting the settlement reached in the course of the grievance procedure, but was suggesting that the issue be submitted to outside arbitration.) [75]

The old problem of how best to reconcile individual and collective interests is far from dead. It is taking some new directions, though whether a satisfactory solution will be found in any of them remains in doubt.

---

[73] *Id.* at 180, 54 L.R.R.M. at 2721.

[74] E.g., Philadelphia Sheraton Corp., 136 N.L.R.B. 888, 49 L.R.R.M. 1874 (1962).

[75] Humphrey v. Moore, *supra* note 34, at 343 n. 3, 55 L.R.R.M. at 2035 n. 3.

Chapter 6

PROBLEMS OF PROCEDURAL REGULARITY

INTRODUCTION

Procedural irregularities have troubled arbitrators, and the parties, from the inception of the industrial arbitration process. Such irregularities may take place before, during, or after the hearing. The contract may, for instance, require that before any discharge is made effective the company must notify the union representative and discuss the case with him. Suppose X is then caught drinking on the job and is fired forthwith without any discussion with the union representative. What is the significance of the contractual requirement that there be notice before discharge? Or suppose that the contract requires that job vacancies be posted and that the senior man be given the job provided he has the qualifications. The company then fills the job without considering the senior man, though on subsequent investigation it turns out that the senior man did not have the qualifications. What then? Shortly after reporting for work X is accused by his foreman of being under the influence of alcohol. Hot words are exchanged and X is sent home for the day. The grievance is processed on the question of whether X was or was not drunk. At the arbitration hearing, however, the company switches its theory to insubordination. Putting aside the question of the union's preparation to meet the charge of insubordination, is this an issue which may be injected into the hearing at the arbitration level when it has not been discussed during the course of the grievance sessions? A similar question arises when one side or the other chooses, for whatever reason, to conceal and withhold either the testimony of a key witness or the existence of a key document until the arbitration hearing. Is the question which arises then simply one of surprise, in which case it can perhaps be remedied by giving the other party adequate opportunity to investigate and answer the unanticipated evidence, or does it run deeper than that and go to the very admissibility of such evidence when it has not previously been made available?

Finally, there is the post-hearing stage at which at least two procedural problems can and often do arise. One or both of the briefs may contain a new argument which has not previously been made, though based on evidence in the record. If the argument is likely to be decisive, what opportunity, if any, should the other party be given to respond to it? In the alternative, suppose the arbitrator finds a new clause in the contract which the parties have not argued, but which he deems controlling. May the arbitrator decide the case on the basis of the clause without further reference to the parties, or must he ask their views before proceeding in this fashion? Will he be accused by the parties of arbitral feather-bedding if he prolongs the case by asking for their comments on the new clause? Will he be accused of applying a clause which neither of them thought to be applicable if he does not? If he ignores the clause and sticks strictly to the arguments which the parties have made, will he have fulfilled the proper function of an arbitrator?

These are difficult questions on which arbitrators themselves hold widely varying opinions. Moreover, such questions involve problems of fair procedure, without which industrial arbitration cannot hope to achieve stature and respect, and problems of industrial relations policy. All arbitrators are certainly concerned with fair procedure. However, the degree to which they should concern themselves with "good" industrial relations policy will be more debatable, both among arbitrators and the parties.

With this much of an introduction we may now turn to a more careful examination of the problems which arise, the ways in which arbitrators have chosen to deal with them, and some of the policy considerations which are involved.

THE PRE-HEARING STAGE

Many collective bargaining contracts contain clauses which impose upon the parties a prescribed procedure. Thus there are time limitations which apply to processing the grievance at various steps in the procedure, necessity of notice to the union with an opportunity for discussion in the event of discipline or discharge, requirements of advance notice of layoff in cases of layoff, and provisions that senior employees may be entitled to first consideration on promotion provided they have the qualifications.[1] The reason for such contractual rules and limitations is not hard to find.

---

[1] BASIC PATTERNS IN UNION CONTRACTS (5th ed. 1961).

The very purpose of the collective bargaining contract, as the late Sumner Slichter so often pointed out, is to introduce an orderly system of self-government within the plant.[2] Arbitrators have sometimes referred to such rules as rudimentary requirements of industrial due process.[3] And while it may be true that it is often the union which seeks contractual limitations on the unbridled authority of management, it is not to be supposed that there is no value to management in some of the limitations. Advance discussion of a disciplinary penalty often discloses facts which affect the propriety of the penalty and give the parties an opportunity to discuss the underlying problem, of which the rule infraction may only have been a manifestation.[4]

For our purpose it is not necessary to run the entire gamut of contractual rules in order to understand the problems which are raised for the arbitrator by procedural violations. Three areas — discipline and discharge, layoffs, and promotions — will suffice to illustrate the point.

Discipline and Discharge

Contracts frequently include a provision which requires the company, before imposing disciplinary measures or discharge, to notify the union, give the employee a written statement of the charges, and/or hold a hearing at which the employee and a union representative are present. When such procedural requirements are violated and the case ends up in arbitration, the question naturally arises as to the effect of the rule violation. A review of the reported cases indicates that the following conclusions may be drawn on this question:

1. *All* arbitrators attach importance to the contractual requirement. Some arbitrators have even held that where past practice included prior notification of discharge such practice has become a part of the contract even though no express written provision is contained therein.[5]

2. *Some* arbitrators conclude that failure to follow the contractual procedure nullifies the entire action.[6]

---

[2] Slichter, Union Policies and Industrial Management 1 (1941).

[3] Bendix-Westinghouse Corp., 33 Lab. Arb. 466 (1959).

[4] Fleming & Witte, *Grievances Under the Collective Agreement* in Unions and Union Leadership 226 (Barbash ed. 1959).

[5] Coca-Cola Bottling Co., 9 Lab. Arb. 197 (1947).

[6] Baldwin-Lima-Hamilton Corp., 19 Lab. Arb. 177 (1952).

3. *Most* arbitrators conclude that failure to comply with a contractual procedure will affect the degree of penalty which is appropriate, but not necessarily vitiate the action in its entirety.[7]

4. There are occasional cases which suggest that failure to comply with the contractual procedure will not necessarily affect the penalty at all.[8]

5. There are more reported cases of procedural defects in discipline and discharge in the early reports than in recent years. This suggests that if such clauses still exist in contracts, and it is common knowledge that they do, past arbitration decisions have caused the parties to be more careful in complying with them.

To document these conclusions satisfactorily one needs to go into a little more detail. Even when arbitrators have said that the penalty may stand despite irregularity in following the contractual procedure, they have not discounted the importance of the procedure. Thus one arbitrator thought that it was appropriate to discharge a bus driver with a bad safety record even though the employer had failed to file written charges against the driver as required by the contract. But the result was justified on the ground that the safety factor was too significant to be overlooked despite the admitted procedural defect.[9] It is, of course, noteworthy that in such a case there is a third interest involved — that of the riding public. In another case the arbitrator held that failure to issue a written reprimand, as required by the contract, did not affect the discharge because the union had acquiesced in the irregularity.[10] In another case the arbitrator held that a discharge could stand where the company had failed to give the employee his contractual right to talk to his steward before leaving company premises. However, in this case the union apparently did not argue that violation of the contractual procedure should nullify the discharge.[11] And in a case where the majority reinstated a man who had been discharged without the union having an opportunity to offer evidence in accordance with the contractual requirement that no one be discharged without an investigation, the minority dissented vigorously on the ground that previous decisions had held that procedural defects

---

[7] E.g., Kohler Bros. Sand & Gravel Co., 25 Lab. Arb. 903 (1956).

[8] E.g., Columbian Rope Co., 7 Lab. Arb. 450, 455–56 (1947).

[9] Hudson County Bus Owners Ass'n, 3 Lab. Arb. 786 (1946).

[10] Schwayder Bros., Inc., 7 Lab. Arb. 552 (1947).

[11] Douglas Aircraft Corp., 19 Lab. Arb. 716 (1952).

were harmless where the "employee voluntarily acknowledges the commission of an offense charged and is assessed a measure of discipline which is fair in relation to the offense committed. . . ."[12] Finally, in a railroad case in which the employee's contractual rights had been violated in that his chosen representative was not present at the interrogation of a certain witness, the arbitrator held that the testimony of this witness would have to be ignored, but that the employer's case could stand without it.[13]

Despite the importance which arbitrators have assigned to compliance with contractual procedures, not many of them have held that irregularities of this type will completely negate the action which has been taken. There are a few decisions of this kind,[14] but sometimes the language of the contract is very precise, as in the case in which the contract provided that no discharge should be effective prior to the ruling of the Impartial Chairman and the company then discharged the individual in advance of such a ruling.[15] In the overwhelming number of the cases arbitrators have taken the rule violation into consideration with respect to the penalty, but have not declared the entire action a nullity. Doubtless the exact nature of the award in these cases is affected by the facts of the particular case, and it is difficult to generalize. There are discharge cases in which the employer failed to consult the union in advance;[16] the employer failed to give the employee a statement of the reason for his termination;[17] the warning procedure was ignored;[18] and the employer fired a man in violation of the provision that no discharge could be effected without approval of the arbitrator except in case of theft.[19] The employee was reinstated but denied part or all of his back pay because the arbitrator concluded that the offense had, in fact, been committed, but the procedure had been violated. Conversely, there are cases in which the company failed to give the union prompt notification of the

---

[12] Railway Express Agency, Inc., 29 Lab. Arb. 409, 411 (1957).

[13] Brotherhood of R. Trainmen and N.Y. Central R.R. (Eastern Dist., Boston and Albany Div.), Special Board of Adjustment No. 289, Award No. 8, Claim No. 2 (1959).

[14] See e.g., Baldwin-Lima-Hamilton Corp., 19 Lab. Arb. 177 (1952).

[15] Modernage Furniture Corp., 4 Lab. Arb. 220 (1946).

[16] Hayes Mfg. Corp., 17 Lab. Arb. 412 (1951).

[17] Die Tool & Eng'r Co., 3 Lab. Arb. 156 (1946).

[18] Cedartown Textiles, Inc., 8 Lab. Arb. 360 (1947).

[19] Lou Seidman & Co., 9 Lab. Arb. 653 (1948).

dismissal; [20] the discharged employee was refused permission to call a foreman to the grievance hearing despite the contractual guarantee that the employee could call anyone who could shed light on the grievance; [21] the employer failed to file the required written complaint;[22] employees were summarily discharged without the requisite hearing in the presence of union representatives; [23] and the discharge was sustained but the employees given back pay from the date of the discharge to the date of the award or some other appropriate date. In other cases the discharge of an employee for insubordination was commuted to a five-day layoff because, among other reasons, the employer had failed to follow the contractual requirement that he notify the union of the discharge; [24] and discharged employees were given an additional two weeks' pay because the employer violated the contractual requirement that two weeks' prior notice be given of a contemplated discharge even though the employees were given two weeks' pay at the time of discharge.[25]

From a purely theoretical standpoint one would suppose arbitrators could take at least three positions in discipline and discharge cases in which there are procedural defects: (1) that unless there is strict compliance with the procedural requirements the whole action will be nullified; (2) that the requirements are of significance only where the employee can show that he has been prejudiced by failure to comply therewith; or (3) that the requirements are important, and that any failure to comply will be penalized, but that the action taken is not thereby rendered null and void. The first of these positions would seem to be generally undesirable for a number of reasons. The procedural irregularity may not have been prejudicial in any sense of the word, the emphasis upon technicalities would be inconsistent with the informal atmosphere of the arbitration process, and the end result could on many occasions be quite ludicrous. If, for instance, an employee gets drunk on the job and starts smashing valuable machinery with a sledge hammer, it would hardly seem appropriate to nullify his discharge on the sole ground that it was in violation of a contractual requirement

[20] National Lead Co., 13 Lab. Arb. 28 (1949).
[21] Pittsburgh Plate Glass Co., 8 Lab. Arb. 317 (1947).
[22] Schreider Trucking Co., 5 Lab. Arb. 430 (1946).
[23] Torrington Co., 1 Lab. Arb. 35 (1945).
[24] Ranney Refrigerator Co., 5 Lab. Arb. 621 (1946).
[25] New York Tribune, Inc., 8 Lab. Arb. 410 (1947).

that the union be given advance notice. The second position has considerable merit in that it focuses on what is, after all, the significant point. Granted there has been a failure to comply with the procedure required by the contract, has this dereliction in any way prejudiced the employee? If he can show that it has, he has then obviously been deprived of a fair opportunity to present his side of the grievance and the past action should be set aside. There is, nevertheless, a defect in this approach. It tends to minimize the importance of a regularized procedure in a matter of considerable importance to both the company and the union, and to place a premium on value judgments as to when action will result in prejudice to the individual and when it will not. In the clear case this may make no difference, but in the marginal situation it may change the whole result. It is a recognized fact in all human negotiations that it is easier to modify a proposed action before it is taken than afterwards. Thus, in requiring by contract that the company discuss a discharge with the union before effectuating it, the union is given an opportunity to forestall the action and persuade the company that some lesser penalty might better serve the purpose. In such a case it may be hard to prove that the employee has been prejudiced by failure to comply with the procedure, but certainly his situation is psychologically quite different. The third approach, which is the one most arbitrators have taken, has the virtue of penalizing failure to comply with the contractual procedure, thereby encouraging compliance with it, but not necessarily obviating all that has been done. The decision may, on occasion, quite outrage one of the parties. When a company has discharged an employee for an offense which everyone can concede is worthy of discharge, it may be shocked to be told that it must nevertheless pay the culprit his wages between the time of the discharge and the date of the arbitration award because it failed to follow the procedural requirements of the contract. This sense of outrage will most likely assure the company's making sure the contract is followed the next time. Is this, then, a bad result? The steady decline in reported cases involving procedural defects suggests that such arbitration decisions may have been influential in persuading the parties that rules, once made, are to be complied with.

Layoff Problems

The provision found in so many collective bargaining contracts requiring advance notice of a layoff serves a somewhat different purpose than the similar provision related to disciplinary action. The employee who is about to be laid off wants to know about it not so much in order to talk the company out of it, for so long as his seniority is respected he has little possibility of this. Rather, he wants to know as much in advance as possible so that he may adjust his private plans to his change in status. Thus the notice of layoff becomes a part of the substance of the transaction. Moreover, in the normal layoff the company is able to plan ahead and it does not resist the idea of advance notice. The tensions which are invoked in disciplinary and discharge cases are not involved. The exception to this, of course, is the layoff which is occasioned by an emergency beyond the control of the company.

In light of the above, it is not surprising that the cases almost universally hold that where the company has violated the notice provisions of the layoff procedure liability is incurred. The difficult cases have been those in which the sudden layoff is beyond the control of the company and it seeks relief from the notice provisions of the contract. Even in such situations if the notice provision of the contract is unqualified, arbitrators have usually held that is binding despite the company's inability to do anything about the cause of the shutdown.[26] Sometimes a modified result is attained by applying principles of contract law under the doctrine of impossibility.[27] Thus the company is excused from performance to the extent to which performance is genuinely impossible, but not thereafter. Part of the period of notice may then be excused without waiving the entire requirement. Some contracts recognize the problem and take care of it in that fashion.

Promotions

Promotion cases often involve a different kind of problem in procedural regularity. The discipline and layoff cases tend to involve specific contractual requirements which have, for one reason or another, not been met. Promotion cases, on the other hand, often involve only a general standard with the question then being one of whether the procedure which the company utilized in complying with that standard was "fair." Obviously this gives the arbitrator much greater latitude for the application of his own views, for he is then faced not only with assessing the importance of compliance with a given standard, but deciding what the standard is in the first place.

---

[26] E.g., Greer Hydraulics, Inc., 29 Lab. Arb. 706 (1957).
[27] 6 WILLISTON, CONTRACTS, § 1956 (rev. ed. 1938).

Illustrative cases in this area are frequently found in the telephone industry. A typical contract clause will provide that in selecting employees for promotion the company "shall adhere to the principle that seniority shall govern if all other qualifications of the individuals being considered are determined by the company to be substantially equal." The decision of the company is then final unless it is shown to have acted "arbitrarily or in bad faith."

Under one such clause an arbitrator held, in 1951, that the clause had been violated because company supervisors, in evaluating applicants, read "substantially equal" to mean "exactly equal."[28] Following this decision the company installed an elaborate system for evaluating applicants so that the same error could not happen again. But in a subsequent case an arbitrator held that the company had not followed its own system with the end result that its action had been "arbitrary."[29] In another telephone company case almost exactly the same sequence of events took place.[30] A similar situation, outside the telephone industry, involved a contract which provided that in cases of transfers, promotions, and increases or decreases of the working force, length of service, ability, skill, efficiency, and physical fitness should be considered. Seniority would then govern if employees had the "necessary" ability, skill, efficiency, and physical fitness. In choosing employees for certain vacancies the company utilized a battery of tests developed at its request by a university research agency. The arbitrator thought it was improper for the company to rely on these tests to the exclusion of all other factors because "those attributes are in point only to the extent of establishing a standard of satisfactory capacity for such employees as can achieve it, and from there seniority prevails."[31] Thus any attempt to follow the test to the exclusion of seniority was improper. And in a situation in which the company agreed to promote men in accordance with their seniority, provided the employee had the aptitude, ability, and efficiency to handle the job, the arbitrator held that it could not automatically eliminate from consideration an applicant who did not have a high school education, though it could consider this insofar as such a factor could be shown to be relevant.[32]

---

[28] Southern Bell Tel. & Tel. Co., 16 Lab. Arb. 1 (1951).
[29] Southern Bell Tel. & Tel. Co., 8 Am. Lab. Arb. Awards # 70,335 (1957).
[30] American Tel. & Tel. Co., 25 Lab. Arb. 256 (1955).
[31] Ball Brothers Co., 27 Lab. Arb. 353, 356 (1956).
[32] Union Oil Co., 17 Lab. Arb. 62 (1951).

In short, where the parties have agreed to a general standard, arbitrators have not been reluctant to inquire into the procedures by which such general standards are effectuated. And insofar as such procedures are capricious, or may lead to unfair results, they have been rejected. Such a conclusion, incidentally, often leads the arbitrator into an even more difficult question — that of the proper remedy — which is beyond the scope of the present inquiry. The arbitrator may get into the case in the first place because a rejected applicant, usually having greater seniority than the successful bidder, grieves. At the hearing the evidence may show that the procedure used in choosing the employee for the vacancy was defective, but it may furnish no basis whatsoever for deciding whether the grievant would be qualified if a proper procedure had been utilized. The hearing may, on the other hand, disclose that the grievant is not qualified. Simply to declare the job open, as is sometimes done,[33] may be less than satisfactory because commitments have been made which will lead to the suspicion that the same result will ultimately be reached after a new and ostensibly fair proceeding. To promote an unqualified man will be to ignore the contract, and also to expose to possible discharge a man who is not competent to do the work. In situations of this kind arbitrators have sometimes sought a compromise under which the party which has failed to comply with the proper procedure is penalized without upsetting the substantive action which has been taken.[34]

Conclusions

If there is any basis for the claim that arbitrators have violated the fundamental rules of fairness by failing to respect procedural requirements of the contract, it is not apparent from the reported cases. As a matter of fact, quite the contrary seems to be the case. Arbitrators often go considerably beyond the requirements of fair play. Exactly why they do so is not always clear. Sometimes noncompliance may be simply a convenient peg on which to hang a decision which may otherwise appeal to the arbitrator but which he is having difficulty rationalizing. At other times the decision may represent a value judgment on the part of the arbitrator that it will be "good" for the parties to adhere strictly to their agreement. To the extent that it represents the latter the arbitrator has gone beyond his immediate function of umpiring the dispute and im-

---

[33] Sandvik Steel, Inc., 29 Lab. Arb. 747 (1957).
[34] A. O. Smith Corp., 9 Am. Lab. Arb. Awards # 70,970 (1959).

posed something of his own philosophy on the parties. In any event, there is a higher degree of uniformity in the way arbitrators treat procedural irregularities which occur before the hearing than there is those which occur either at or after the hearing, as we shall now see.

THE HEARING STAGE

Every experienced arbitrator has faced a puzzling series of questions arising out of the presentation of alleged new issues, new arguments, and new evidence at the hearing stage. These issues, arguments, and evidence are characterized as "new," of course, because they have not been presented at the previous stages in the grievance procedure. Examples of this situation are readily available. B is discharged for the violation of a safety rule, but at the hearing the company wants to show "unsatisfactory work performance," though it has not previously argued this.[35] C is discharged for excessive absenteeism and the company now wants to show, for the first time, that there are other valid grounds for the discharge.[36] D is discharged for starting a civil action against the company, but the latter now wants to show that he has committed a theft.[37] E is discharged for insubordination, but the company now wants to show that he once punched out for two other employees, contrary to company rules.[38] In a rate dispute in which the union has contended for a given classification, it now wants the arbitrator, if he finds the requested classification inappropriate, to choose a classification which has not been previously discussed.[39] In a union jurisdictional dispute one party attempts for the first time to show that the other is engaged in a boycott, though this is not a part of the charge which has brought the matter before the umpire.[40]

Whenever a situation like those cited above arises, two basic but quite separate questions arise. The first is one of procedure, the second one of policy. This difference in the nature of the two questions gives rise, in turn, to a subsidiary question, namely, should arbitrators confine themselves to procedural questions and avoid those which involve industrial relations policy? None of these ques-

---

[35] West Virginia Pulp & Paper Co., 10 Lab. Arb. 117 (1947).
[36] International Shoe Co., 7 Lab. Arb. 941 (1947).
[37] Dow Chemical Co., 32 Lab. Arb. 71 (1958).
[38] Forest Hill Foundry Co., 1 Lab. Arb. 153 (1946).
[39] Chrysler Corp. & UAW, 1 Am. Lab. Arb. Awards # 67, 258 (1944).
[40] IUE v. Sheet Metal Workers, 33 Lab. Arb. 512 (1959).

tions can be satisfactorily answered without exploring, by case example, the nature of the terms "procedure" and "policy," and then the institutional framework within which labor arbitration takes place.

When a company discharges X for violating a safety rule, and then wants to show at the hearing that he has an unsatisfactory work record, a number of procedural questions will immediately occur to the arbitrator. Is the union prepared to meet this new charge, or may it legitimately claim "surprise"? If the union is surprised should the hearing be adjourned in order that it may adequately prepare its case? Has the employee been prejudiced in any way by the company's delay in bringing forth this new charge? In view of the seriousness of the discharge penalty is there an analogy to the law of criminal pleading in which there "is a rule that on an indictment charging only a single offense the issue must be confined to that offense, and no election is allowed to lay before the jury a number of such offenses from which they are to select the one best proved"? [41]

Quite obviously the arbitrator is competent to, and indeed must, answer the above questions if the arbitration hearing is to be fair. But there are other questions which he may, or may not, answer which more nearly relate to "policy" than to "procedure." If the parties are allowed to introduce "new" material at the arbitration stage (even assuming this can be done under conditions which will fully protect the procedural rights of the other party), will this tend to undermine the whole grievance procedure of which arbitration is but the final step? And if it will tend to do this, should the arbitrator rule that no "new" material may be presented because this will be "bad" for the system of industrial jurisprudence which the parties are supposed to be developing in the plant? Or should the arbitrator take the position that the nature of the relationship between the parties is none of his business, and that the only questions which he need answer with respect to any alleged new material relate to whether either party will be prejudiced in terms of a fair hearing?

If the institution known as labor arbitration could be made to fit within a single mold, the question of the appropriate role of the arbitrator in deciding questions of "procedure" or "policy" could at least be wisely debated. But because labor arbitration does not fit

---

[41] 1 WIGMORE, EVIDENCE § 194, at 651 (3d ed. 1940).

a single model the debate is immeasurably more complicated. One can easily tick off several varieties of arbitration situations:

1. The well-established, sophisticated umpire system in which the grievance steps are well handled, and the parties firmly believe that every effort should be made to settle the matter before it is referred to arbitration.[42]

2. The well-established umpire system in which the parties nevertheless believe in giving their umpire wide latitude to proceed on his own.[43]

3. The *ad hoc* case in which the parties are sophisticated but where, for one reason or another, one party has chosen to withhold a key portion of its evidence.[44]

4. The *ad hoc* situation in which one or both parties procures counsel at the arbitration level, and where for the first time a systematic investigation and organization of the evidence is provided.

5. The *ad hoc* situation in which the parties have not procured counsel and where one or both are rank neophytes at arbitration, so that they have made little or no effort to organize the evidence prior to the hearing, and where the arbitrator must himself take over much of the examination.

6. The case in which the relationship between the parties is so bad or so suspicious that they make no real effort to resolve grievances prior to arbitration, and much of the time at the arbitration hearing may be spent in trying to ascertain the issues which are to be tried.

These are, of course, not the only situations which can arise, but they are familiar ones and they illustrate the point that there is no common denominator in the labor arbitration field. Moreover, the contract itself may control the introduction of new issues, or new evidence at the hearing stage. Thus any meaningful analysis of decisions handed down by arbitrators becomes difficult. Nevertheless an analysis may shed some further light on what arbitrators are doing in these kinds of cases and why.

Starting at the far end of the spectrum, it is common practice to deny to either party the right to present and argue an entirely new

---

[42] Alexander, *Impartial Umpireships: The General Motors-UAW Experience*, in NATIONAL ACADEMY OF ARBITRATORS, ARBITRATION AND THE LAW, PROCEEDINGS OF THE 12TH ANNUAL MEETING 108 (McKelvey ed. 1959).

[43] E.g., The agreement between the Ford Motor Co. and the UAW-AFL-CIO states in Article VII, § 13(b), that: "The Umpire may make such investigation as he may deem proper. . . ."

[44] Texas Co., 7 Lab. Arb. 735 (1947).

grievance, even though the grievance has some episodical relationship with the issue before the arbitrator. Thus where the original grievance complained about the employer's method of reducing his work force, the union was not permitted to argue claims related to recall or alleged denial of free transportation rights since no separate grievances had ever been filed on those subjects.[45] Even in this kind of situation, however, the new claim would probably be heard in the absence of any objection from the company. As was pointed out earlier, there are situations in which the parties literally make it a practice to define the issues at the arbitration hearing, and in which they then proceed upon the basis of the issues as defined. This may very well mean that such differences have never been discussed in any meaningful fashion in the grievance procedure. Under an umpire system new claims of this kind would be quite unlikely to end up before the umpire without any previous discussion between the parties. But in the *ad hoc* type of case the arbitrator has almost no opportunity to influence the development of a sound grievance procedure.

A much more frequent situation involves the kind of case in which the basic issue remains the same — "Was X discharged for just cause?" — but the rationale or the evidence changes. There are many decisions, particularly in discipline and discharge cases, in which it has been held that the company is bound by whatever reasons were given for the discharge at the time it was invoked, and may not thereafter rely upon other grounds. This is so even though the additional grounds which are now stated can be proved and if proved would probably have justified an otherwise unjustifiable action.[46] There is, however, at least one decision in which the arbitrator held that the evidence was insufficient to support a discharge on grounds of excessive absenteeism and that other reasons subsequently given could not be considered, but nevertheless denied back pay because of the additional reasons for the discharge which were advanced at the hearing.[47] Some of the cases in which the company is limited to the reasons originally given for the discharge can be traced directly to contract language. It may require that the company notify the union of *all* reasons for the discharge at the time the action is taken.[48] Or it

---

[45] American Airlines, Inc., 27 Lab. Arb. 448 (1956).
[46] Chrysler & UAW, 1 Am. Lab. Arb. Awards # 67,021 (1945).
[47] International Shoe Co., 7 Lab. Arb. 941 (1947).
[48] Forest Hill Foundry Co., 1 Lab. Arb. 153 (1946).

may simply require that before discharge an employee be given a written statement of the reasons for the discharge.[49] In either case the arbitrator need only rely upon the contract for his ruling that additional reasons for the discharge are not admissible at the arbitration hearing. There are other cases in which a similar result is reached but in which less reliance is placed upon the strict language of the contract. In such cases it is often frankly stated that to permit new grounds for past action to be stated at the arbitration hearing will undermine the grievance procedure,[50] and "void the good results which may be expected in the preliminary steps of a well functioning grievance system." [51]

It appears correct to conclude from the above cases, and others like them, that arbitrators believe it is unwise to permit new charges not previously advanced in the course of the grievance procedure to be advanced at the hearing. But one must not assume from this that any such universal rule is invoked. As has been pointed out, the official rationale for such a holding often is that the contract does not permit it. Thus the arbitrator is not imposing his views of what is "wise" upon the parties, he is simply applying a contractual agreement. Many of the cases in which the contract does not require such a restriction involve umpire situations in which the umpire, usually with the full approval of the parties, is attempting to develop a system of grievance handling which will maximize the responsibility of the parties.[52] There are, on the other hand, countless *ad hoc* situations in which the issues are never defined with any care prior to the arbitration hearing, and in which the arbitrator's sole concern is likely to be one of conducting a fair hearing in the sense that both parties are aware of the issue to be tried and have had an opportunity to prepare for it. In this kind of a proceeding there is usually little question of outlawing a given charge, but only of giving the other side adequate opportunity to prepare to meet it.

A somewhat different question is raised when the problem is not one of a new charge, but rather of new evidence relating to the same old charge. Such evidence will ordinarily fall into one of two categories: (1) newly discovered evidence or (2) deliberately withheld evidence. In either case the hybrid nature of the arbitration tribunal

---

[49] Bethlehem Steel Co., 29 Lab. Arb. 635 (1957).
[50] Dow Chemical Co., 32 Lab. Arb. 71 (1958).
[51] Chrysler Corp. & UAW, 1 Am. Lab. Arb. Awards # 67,258 (1944).
[52] Alexander, *supra* note 42, at 146.

is exposed. It is, in part, an appellate body — a court of last resort — for it ordinarily considers an issue only after the parties have tried but failed to resolve it. It is, on the other hand, akin to a trial tribunal, for seldom do the parties make an all-out effort to marshal their resources unless the case must be referred to arbitration.

Basically, new evidence (in either of the above categories) will present the arbitrator with the same questions of procedure and policy which have already been discussed. He will be concerned with whether the new evidence so surprises the other party that a fair hearing cannot be held without an adjournment with opportunity for investigation and further preparation. And in the case of deliberately withheld evidence he will have additional misgivings about the "wisdom" or the "ethics" of permitting the evidence to be introduced. These misgivings will be accompanied by doubts as to the function of the arbitrator in relation to such policy matters.

If the only problem is that in the course of preparing its case for arbitration one side or the other has developed some new arguments not previously used in the prior steps of the grievance procedure, few arbitrators are likely to find any serious question as to the receipt of the argument. As one arbitrator said:

At the hearing the Union departed somewhat from these (past) arguments and added some additional arguments. The Chairman does not believe that the new contentions raised by the Union at the hearing should be barred for the reason that they were not presented during the preliminary discussions in the grievance procedure, although the Company contends otherwise. When cases reach the last step in the grievance machinery, consisting of arbitration, it is common practice for them to be reviewed and more thoroughly prepared than they had been prior to that time. Contentions which do not change the facts or the issue, it appears to the Chairman, should always be available to the parties. A different situation is presented where important facts, as distinguished from arguments, may have been withheld during the earlier steps of the grievance machinery or where, as often occurs, an attempt is made to broaden the scope of the grievance for the first time in arbitration. Such, however, is not the case here.[53]

The fact that new evidence not previously presented in the grievance procedure is being presented does not cause its disbarment by all arbitrators. In one such case the contract provided that in discharge cases the parties should have a meeting at which "the facts concerning the case shall be made available to both parties." Sub-

---

[53] Mergenthaler Linotype Co., 15 Lab. Arb. 707, 708 (1950).

sequently, in arbitration, the union contended that the arbitration board was limited in its consideration to those items of fact presented by the company at the original meeting. The board rejected this view, saying:

The only reasonable interpretation that can be made of this sentence is that each party on the request of the other party must make available what facts it has on the case at the time. . . . There is obviously nothing in the given sentence . . . that precludes either party from introducing subsequently in the grievance steps or in the arbitration facts other than those presented in the suspension hearing. . . . Certainly the union, on behalf of a disciplined employee who believes that he has been unfairly dealt with, should not have foreclosed to it the right to present additional evidence that might be used to sustain the innocence of the employee. Similarly, the company must be recognized as not being deprived of the right to introduce additional evidence prior to final adjudication to sustain its charges against the employee. These respective rights of the parties are commonly recognized in judicial proceedings. The labor agreement of the parties does not set aside these rights.[54]

While the above decision did not limit the evidence at the arbitration hearing to that which was presented at the original grievance hearing, it did imply that the parties were under a mutual obligation to disclose to each other facts then in their possession. Another arbitrator appeared to open the door even wider for the receipt of new evidence. When the employee was discharged for incompetence, the union argued that the company did not, at the preliminary hearing between the parties, present the evidence which it later submitted to the arbitrator to prove unsatisfactory work performance, and that this evidence should therefore not be considered. The arbitrator simply replied that "the contract . . . does not restrict the Umpire to consideration of only factual evidence submitted at the first stage, or any earlier stage. . . . "[55]

Perhaps the most difficult question is whether evidence which is deliberately withheld at the earlier stages of the grievance procedure may be barred on that ground when the arbitration is held. On this arbitrators appear to hold quite different views. The case for barring such evidence is set forth in the following extract:

Arbitration is merely a method for determining a pre-existing dispute which the parties have been unable to settle in the prior steps of the grievance machinery. The arbitration hearing is not the place for presentation of new claims, although the more thorough investigation which

---

[54] American Steel & Wire Co., 5 Lab. Arb. 193, 206 (1946).
[55] Carbon Fuel Co., 1 Am. Lab. Arb. Awards # 67,327 (1946).

precedes arbitration often results in the discovery of evidence not theretofore known and of arguments not theretofore conceived. The essential facts supporting the claim of the Union should be revealed in the earlier steps of the grievance machinery if such facts are known to the Union. In the absence of such revelation, the entire purpose of the grievance machinery remains unfulfilled, and the possibilities of settlement are lost. The same, of course, is true with regard to the company's claims and existing evidence in its favor. If such evidence is not made known by one side to the other it may not be accepted for the first time in arbitration.[56]

The opposite view, namely, that the only serious question when such evidence is presented is one of "surprise," is set forth in another case:

The Union has complained that the Company did not furnish it "all information in its possession necessary to a full understanding of the subject matter of the complaint," as required by Article XIV of the contract. However, all such information was presented at the hearing, and the Union was allowed ten days, the time it asked, to consider it. That the information must be furnished at an earlier stage of grievance proceedings is not evident from the language of the contract, which only states that the Company will furnish the information "to the representative of the employee and/or Board of Review." The purpose appears to be to make sure that the representative and the Board shall have the information in time for full consideration of it; and this was so in the present instance.[57]

Something of a compromise between the above positions was struck by a third arbitrator who justified the admission of deliberately withheld evidence at the arbitration hearing on the ground that the union had contributed to the "adversary" atmosphere in which the parties conducted their affairs, and could not therefore complain about the end results.[58]

Conclusions

Both the reported cases and discussions with arbitrators indicate a wide disparity in the way they handle problems of new issues, new evidence, and new arguments presented for the first time at the arbitration hearing. However, an important caveat must be entered immediately. Differences among arbitrators on these questions may be more theoretical than real. The lack of a single model for the arbitration process confuses the question. If one prefaces his question

---

[56] Bethlehem Steel Co., 18 Lab. Arb. 366, 367 (1951).
[57] Texas Co., 7 Lab. Arb. 735, 739 (1947).
[58] Bethlehem Steel Co., 6 Lab. Arb. 617 (1947).

about the handling of new material by stating the context within which the question arises, e.g., a large corporation with a well-established umpire system, the answers are much more likely to be uniform than if the question is put in the abstract. Moreover, it is clear that in any context there is no significant difference among arbitrators as to the necessity for insisting upon procedural safeguards in the way of adjournment, further investigation, etc., which will insure the integrity and fairness of the hearing.

The one area in which there appears to be a genuine split among arbitrators relates to the matter of referring the controversy back to the parties when any new material appears upon the scene. Some arbitrators feel strongly that the arbitration process must never become in any way a substitute for the grievance machinery and collective bargaining in general. Thus in their view the proper ruling when new issues, evidence, or arguments are presented is to refer the matter back to the parties on the theory that since they have not considered the new materials, they have not exhausted the possibilities of agreement and arbitration should not proceed until they have. To do otherwise, they point out, is to undermine the collective bargaining potential between the parties and make a mockery of the grievance machinery. Other arbitrators would say that this approach is probably desirable within the context of an established umpire system, but that it is wholly unrealistic in the typical *ad hoc* situation. It is true that the two cases are not quite comparable. In the umpire situation the arbitrator has a continuing stake in the whole grievance pattern. His long-run success, as well as his tenure, may depend in large part on his success in persuading the parties to resolve most of their own difficulties. This point of view is likely to be buttressed by the more careful thought which the parties have given to their umpire system and to the ultimate objectives which they hope to achieve through it. One of those objectives will almost certainly be to resolve their own grievances insofar as this is possible. The likely result is a high degree of cooperation between the umpire and the parties toward the ultimate end of exhausting the possibilities of settlement before cases are referred to the umpire for decision. The institutional factors which are operative in the *ad hoc* case tend to exert a pressure in exactly the opposite direction. Even if he has previously arbitrated for the parties, the *ad hoc* arbitrator may know less about the relationship than does the umpire, and certainly has less control over it. He comes into the case with very little information. If material is presented at the hearing which one party contends is entirely new, the arbitrator's concern is much more likely to be with the procedural problem of giving the other side a fair opportunity to meet the new material than it is with the impact which proceeding further will have on the collective bargaining relationship between the parties. Moreover, the parties themselves are likely to resent "meddling" with their affairs in terms of any advice he may render on the development of "sound" labor relations. They may suggest that they have hired him to render a decision, not to give them gratuitous advice.

Rigid insistence upon a given pattern to be followed in the event new material is offered at the arbitration hearing would seem to be a mistake. The flexibility which has been a principal virtue of the arbitration system would be thereby diminished. Whether the issue should be referred back to the parties when something new emerges is essentially a policy question. The answer depends so much on the context within which the question arises that no uniform answer is either possible or desirable. However, if one views the question of new material solely from the vantage point of the fair process and procedure, it would seem that three questions should then be asked:

1. Is this issue, the evidence, or the argument which is now being raised genuinely new in the sense that the parties have not previously been aware of it?

2. If it is new, will its admission in any way prejudice the position of the other party, or is it purely incidental to the basic issue in the case?

3. If it is new, and if it will be prejudicial to the interest of the other party, what procedural steps should be taken to protect the interest of the surprised party?

There are some issues arising on the arbitration hearing which evoke the response of "surprise" that hardly qualify for that label. Assuming there is genuine surprise injected at the hearing, it may nevertheless not prejudice the case. New corroborative witnesses, for example, may add nothing to the principal case, and the other party may be fully protected through his right to cross-examination.

If there is real surprise, and if prejudice will result, some way must be found to give the other party an opportunity to meet the new situation. Many arbitrators apparently accept the evidence, but then give the opposing party an opportunity to investigate and request a further hearing.

There are no reported cases which have come to our attention, nor have discussions with arbitrators revealed any complaint by the parties that they have been denied a fair hearing because of surprise evidence. They may differ as to its admissibility, they may strenuously argue the effect of such a procedure on the grievance machinery, and they may deplore the ethics of the party which has deliberately withheld evidence, but there is no evidence that they feel that the procedural steps which arbitrators have taken to protect their rights to respond to surprise materials have been less than satisfactory.

THE POST-HEARING STAGE

Logically, the problem of new evidence after the record has been closed should not give rise to any particular difficulty and, in fact, it rarely does. No evidence contained in a post-hearing brief will be considered if it was not presented at the hearing. If, on the other hand, one of the parties advances a legitimate reason for reopening the hearing in order to introduce new evidence not available at the time of the hearing, the request will usually be granted. The circumstances of the individual case will control the ruling, but if one assumes that the request is in good faith and not for the purpose of unduly lengthening the hearing, most arbitrators will doubtless agree to reconvene for the purpose of receiving the evidence.[59]

The difficulty at the post-hearing stage is not with evidence but with argument. The arbitrator may sit down to consider a case only to find that one of the briefs contains an argument which was not advanced in the hearing or at any of the steps of the grievance procedure. Or, in the course of studying the record, the arbitrator may find that he is himself gradually evolving a new theory which neatly resolves the dispute but which is new to both of the parties. What then? If the arguments are based upon the evidence which is in the record is there any reason why the parties or the arbitrator should be restricted in any fashion in arguing any theory that occurs to them for purposes of reaching a decision? Perhaps this is a question which ought not to be answered without first testing it against some of the case problems which arise.

In an industrial plant making packaging products one department handled the necessary printing. Apprentices regularly worked with the journeymen so that a supply of trained men would be available if and when expanded operations became necessary. At the outset

---

[59] See Voluntary Labor Arbitration Rules, American Arbitration Ass'n, Rule 32.

of the training program the apprentices had simply worked along with the journeymen during their regular hours. Then the company decided that it would be more efficient to permit the apprentices to continue to operate the machines during the half-hour lunch periods of the regular operators, and to take their own lunch periods after the operators were back on the job. When this change was ordered the union promptly grieved, claiming in the alternative that the apprentices were either entitled to journeymen's pay for the half-hour period, or that the journeymen were entitled to an additional half-hour's pay since they "owned" the machines to which the apprentices were assigned. The dispute between the parties over this issue was referred to arbitration after they were unable to agree, and the hearing followed along the lines indicated. In its brief the union, for the first time, advanced an argument which, while related to its original contention and based upon the evidence in the record, had not previously been made. It asserted that the journeymen were entitled to this extra half-hour's pay because, though they did not work during this period, they were held responsible for the work of the apprentice, and if it was in any way defective, the blame was placed upon the journeymen. There was, indeed, evidence in the record that the journeymen were held responsible for the work of their apprentices during the lunch hour in that the mark of the journeyman appeared upon each piece of work done on his machine so that defects could be traced back to their point of origin.

What should the arbitrator do about the "new" argument in the above case? Since the brief was in the hands of the company and it had made no comment upon the union's shift in tactics, should the arbitrator be concerned? Is there any obligation on the part of the arbitrator to *ask* for comment by the company? Is there anything unfair about considering a new argument, particularly when the other party is made aware through receiving a copy of the brief that it is being advanced?

If the above case seems easy, take another one of somewhat different dimensions. The issue is a discharge, and the contract contains a clause which states, "In support of any suspension or discharge the company shall not rely on past disciplinary actions occurring prior to the preceding twelve-month period. . . . "

The issue involves the alleged insubordination of the grievant and the testimony is flatly contradictory. Barred from introducing the grievant's past disciplinary record by the clause in the contract, the company nevertheless includes in its brief a photostatic copy of his personnel record, stating that it does so not to support the discharge but only to aid the arbitrator in weighing the reliability of the various witnesses. Is it possible to conclude that the disciplinary record contained in the brief is only "argument" and not evidence? Can the union claim that the company has not only inserted evidence in its brief, but that the evidence is barred by the contract? Can the arbitrator divest himself of any prejudice he may have acquired by looking at the employee's personnel record?

Finally, can one reach any firm conclusions about how to handle a new argument advanced in the brief by one of the parties without considering the thorny problem of the case which is decided upon a theory developed by the arbitrator but unknown to the parties? Since there are not many reported cases which discuss these problems, one must rely more on discussions among arbitrators as to their views.

The safest generalization about arbitrators' views on new arguments advanced by the parties in their briefs is simply that the problem arises with sufficient frequency so that some arbitrators have developed procedures which pretty well protect them from it. Thus a leading Detroit arbitrator asks the parties at the end of the hearing to state the grounds on which they will rely in their briefs so that there can be no surprise. And one of the most experienced New York arbitrators even suggests to the parties that they indicate before the conclusion of the hearing what reported cases they will rely upon in their briefs so that the other side may respond to this in the course of its brief.

In the absence of any agreement about the use of new arguments in the brief, there is little uniformity in the views of arbitrators as to how the matter should be treated. One suspects that this diversity is more apparent than real, for when faced with a given set of facts the rulings might be quite consistent. Some arbitrators take the view that there is nothing wrong with a new argument advanced in the brief, and that as long as the other side receives a copy the arbitrator is not even under any obligation to ask the second party to comment. Other arbitrators feel that any time a substantial new argument is advanced in the brief, comment from the other party should be requested even if it has previously received a copy of the brief and made no comment. Some arbitrators qualify either view by saying that it "depends on the kind of case and the kind of argument which is made." In every discussion of the issue the point is soon raised as to whether there is any difference between a new argument raised by one of the parties, and a new argument advanced by the arbitrator in his decision. This, in turn, raises a question which needs to be explored further.

"Surprise" at the hands of the arbitrator – in the sense that his decision is based upon grounds not argued by the parties – is largely a phenomenon of the *ad hoc* cases and the increased tendency toward judicialization of the arbitration process. It could hardly have happened in the clothing industry when William Leiserson was umpiring, in the hosiery industry under George Taylor, or in the Ford Motor Co. under Harry Shulman's tenure, because none of these parties viewed the umpire as a circuit-riding judge who came into the lives of the litigants simply to hear a given dispute and then depart to render a decision. He was, on the contrary, an integral part of the company-union relationship, he was free to go anywhere and talk to anyone, and his decisions were expected to be based on much more than just the information that might be given to him in connection with the point at hand. In a substantial number of instances, the decision was, in fact, a mediated result even if it did not show this on its face. Under such a system there was little opportunity for the arbitrator to shock the parties with an unexpected analysis because his analysis had already been discussed with them. For different reasons, much the same thing is true today of the umpire system in General Motors and the United Auto Workers. There the parties carefully screen their cases, present them to the umpire stripped of a mediation context, bar new evidence or arguments not presented earlier in the grievance procedure, and expect a decision based upon their presentations. In other umpire situations, like United States Steel, there is a board on which management and labor are both represented. This insures a full discussion of the neutral chairman's line of thought with the result, once again, that there is little chance of surprising the parties.

If the umpire system offers little opportunity for surprise from the arbitrator, the exact opposite is true of the *ad hoc* system. Usually the arbitrator works alone, often finds himself confronted with a woefully inadequate presentation of the case, and even in the well-presented case he has little opportunity to think it out and ask questions which a later study of the record may convince him should have been asked. In the process of writing his decision the arbitrator faces a real dilemma. If he finds an unexpected contract clause which he deems decisive, but which the parties have not argued, what should he do? Reconvene the hearing? Ignore the clause? Write to the parties and ask them if it is relevant? Assume that it is relevant and base the decision thereon? Or suppose it isn't a new clause in the contract, it is simply a new line of argument neglected by the parties but amply justified by the evidence. Should it make any difference that one side was less well represented than the other? Is it a proper function of the arbitrator to come to the aid of one side if he believes there is a decisive argument which has not been made?

Some case illustrations will highlight the above problems even more sharply. In a steel mill a railroad dumper crew hauls raw material within the company yards. The company finds that it is necessary to weigh the cars of raw materials and installs a scale for this purpose. Arguing that the duties so involved are of a minor nature it assigns them to the conductor, and offers only to negotiate a new wage for him. The union insists that the company is without the unilateral right to assign duties, and requests that both the wage and the assignment of the duties be negotiated. Both parties come to arbitration agreeing that there is no controlling clause in the contract, and simply disputing the company's right to exercise its managerial prerogative. In deciding the case the arbitrator comes to the conclusion that the evidence supports a finding that the company knew of its manning problems during the past negotiation, but did not discuss them when the conductor's wage was being negotiated. Because of this the arbitrator concludes that the company is now bound by the previous job content unless and until the parties can agree upon a change. This is not an argument which the union made, but it is based upon evidence in the record. Is it legitimate in that kind of a case for the arbitrator to issue a decision based upon his own argument?

In a somewhat different type of case the company owned a warehouse situated a few miles from the main plant. The warehouse was leased from another owner who was responsible for its care and maintenance. When painting was required the owner hired a non-union contractor, thereby causing the painters' union to picket the warehouse. Foreseeing the dilemma which this would pose for its industrial union employees, the principal company gave part of its employees the option of coming into the main plant to work until the painters' dispute was resolved. At the same time it left a few of the industrial employees at the warehouse. When they refused to cross the picket line they were disciplined. Following their discipline the employees grieved, claiming that the record of violence in the community was such that they did not dare cross the picket line. The arbitrator held with them, but not for the reason they gave. He thought the company had violated a well-known principle of industrial jurisprudence to the effect that employees cannot be discriminatorily treated. Thus when the company chose to remove some of the employees from the scene of the picketing so that they would not be faced with the problem of crossing the picket line, it could not expose others to the same problem and then discipline them for refusing to cross. This brought the following friendly, but tart, response from the company: "We do not expect to receive an award on a position or argument we have not made; nor do we anticipate that the arbitrator will slide around the table and make the Union representatives' case for them. We do believe the case decided by the arbitrator should be the same case argued by the parties at the final local level prior to arbitration — and not a new one conceived by him." [60]

Would it have been better if the arbitrator had stuck strictly to the arguments presented by the parties in the above case? Is there any difference between applying what the arbitrator might allege to be a well-known rule against discrimination which has become a part of the common law of industrial jurisprudence, and applying a wholly new clause in the contract which the parties have not argued?

Perhaps the most troublesome case of all is the situation in which the arbitrator comes across a clause in the contract which has not been argued or even mentioned during the hearing, but which seems to be decisive. Since the contract is invariably introduced as an exhibit there will be no problem of having a basis in the record for the decision. Sometimes, of course, the problem can be avoided if the arbitrator has time to scan the contract for relevant sections about which he may then diplomatically inquire during the hearing.

An airline case, in which the company members of the board dissented, furnishes a typical example of this type of case. A group of pilots had been suspended for falsification of expense accounts, and they grieved over the penalty assessed. Though finding the pilots guilty of the offense charged, the chairman and the union board

---

[60] Letter from a company vice-president to the author, Feb. 1, 1960.

members felt that the penalty was not binding on them because the company had failed to conduct the disciplinary proceedings in accordance with the negotiated rules of the agreement. To this the company members gave the following spirited reply:

The undersigned specifically disagree with and dissent from the findings and conclusions of the neutral members of the Board with respect to the so-called faulty procedures followed by the company. The undersigned further state that by those findings the neutral member of the Board has given to portions of the collective bargaining agreement . . . a new meaning which in fact does not appear in said agreement and which was never intended. . . .

Furthermore, the undersigned also state that the matter of procedure raised by the neutral member was not an issue in this case and not subject to decision by the Board, and therefore for that reason also outside of the jurisdiction of the Board. We believe the record shows that none of the grieving pilots nor their counsel ever raised the procedural issue discussed at length by the neutral member, that this issue was only raised by the neutral member himself, and was improperly made a part of the case.[61]

Some of the sharpest criticism of arbitrators who develop their own theories or rely upon new clauses in deciding cases comes from people who advocate a much more "judicial" approach to arbitration. Unaware of the furious debate which has raged down through the years as to the proper function of a judge, they somehow assume that "judicial" means that the arbitrator will hear the arguments of the parties, retire to his quarters, strip his mind of all matters not discussed, however relevant they may appear to be, and then decide the case. Perhaps this is the way it should be — both among arbitrators and judges. In fact, courts, like arbitrators, often resort to their own theories for resolving controversies. This is illustrated by the controversial decision involving labor arbitration handed down by the Wisconsin Supreme Court in 1959. In that case a dispute arose between the company and the union as to whether certain production employees who had been promoted to supervision and then returned to the production force continued to accrue seniority.[62] An arbitrator held that they did not, in response to a grievance filed by the employees who were bumped by the action of the company in returning the supervisors to the bargaining unit.

---

[61] Unpublished award furnished the author in confidence.

[62] Clark v. Hein-Werner Corp., 8 Wis. 2d 264, 99 N.W.2d 132 (1959), *cert. denied*, 362 U.S. 962 (1960).

The supervisors, who had neither been present at the hearing nor been given any direct notice of it (except insofar as they were now once again members of the union) brought suit to enjoin enforcement of the award on the sole ground that the arbitrator had exceeded his jurisdiction. Ignoring the basis of the complaint, the trial court nevertheless granted an injunction on the ground that the complainants had been divested of property rights without due process of law. The union appealed this judgment to the Supreme Court, and the plaintiff moved for review of the action of the trial court in failing to make a finding that the arbitrator had exceeded his jurisdiction although such issue was raised by the complainant. The Supreme Court modified the trial court's opinion somewhat, but stuck to the position that the plaintiffs were not bound by the award because of not having been given proper notice of the arbitration hearing. It then brushed off the original ground of the complaint, that the arbitrator had exceeded his jurisdiction, by saying that it was unnecessary to decide in view of the earlier conclusions. The end result was that the only issue which the plaintiffs had ever themselves raised was left unanswered, though they "won" the decision.

No lawyer will suppose that the *Hein-Werner* case is in any sense atypical. Judges have from time immemorial departed from the arguments of counsel to decide cases, despite Mr. Justice Cardozo's classic admonition that the judge is not "a knight-errant, roaming at will in pursuit of his own ideal of beauty or of goodness."[63] Some judges, like Charles Wyzanski, Jr., have freely discussed the role of the trial judge in various types of cases. Speaking of antitrust cases in which the question concerned the custom of the market and what would be the consequences of a judicial decree altering those practices, he notes that the judge "is faced with the problem of determining either the appropriate standard of fair competition in trademarks or the appropriate standard for fiduciaries."[64] Counsel sometimes fail to offer relevant material and the judge then reaches his result partly on the basis of general information and partly on the basis of his own research in a library. Judge Wyzanski then goes on to observe:

This tendency of a court to inform itself has increased in recent years following the lead of the Supreme Court of the United States. Not merely in constitutional controversies and in statutory interpretation, but

---

[63] CARDOZO, THE NATURE OF THE JUDICIAL PROCESS 141 (1928).

[64] Wyzanski, *A Trial Judge's Freedom and Responsibility*, 65 HARV. L. REV. 1281, 1295 (1952).

also in formulation of judge-made rules of law, the justices have resorted, in footnotes and elsewhere, to references drawn from legislative hearings, studies by executive departments, and scholarly monographs. Such resort is sometimes defended as an extension of Mr. Brandeis' technique as counsel for the state in *Muller v. Oregon.* In Muller's case, however, Mr. Brandeis' object was to demonstrate that there was a body of informed public opinion which supported the reasonableness of the *legislative* rule of law. But in cases of which I am speaking these extra-judicial studies are drawn upon to determine what would be a reasonable *judicial* rule of law. Thus the focus of the inquiry becomes not what judgment is permissible, but what judgment is sound. And here it seems to me that the judge, before deriving any conclusions from any such extra-judicial document or information, should lay it before the parties for their criticism.

How this criticism should be offered is itself a problem not free from difficulty. In some situations, the better course may be to submit the material for examination, cross-examination and rebuttal evidence. In others, where expert criticism has primarily an argumentative character, it can be received better from the counsel table and from briefs than from the witness box. The important point is that before a judge acts upon a consideration of any kind, he ought to give the parties a chance to meet it. This opportunity is owed as a matter of fairness and also to prevent an egregious error.[65]

Insofar as one pursues the analogy between judges and arbitrators it should be noted that there are at least three important points of difference. The judge is clearly a public official, and his judicial responsibilities extend beyond the problem of the parties. The arbitrator is a private umpire whose responsibilities relate much more sharply to the parties who employ him. The judge is frankly bound by precedent, while the arbitrator says he is not. Insofar as a judge decides a case in line with a clear precedent he can hardly be said to have surprised the parties, even if they neglect to point out the precedent to him. Finally, judicial rules provide for a rehearing even before courts of last resort, while the arbitrator's decision becomes final once he signs it. Courts have been known to change their minds on rehearing but this possibility does not ordinarily even exist for the arbitrator. In this sense the arbitrator who departs on a path of his own runs the risk of doing greater damage to the parties than does that judge, for the parties can ask for an opportunity to show the judge that he was wrong. This advantage in the judicial system may be in part offset by the fact that private parties can, on receipt of a privately issued arbitration award,

---

[65] *Ibid.*

themselves agree to discard it and arrive at another solution which is more to their liking.

Conclusions

Post-hearing procedural problems are, as we have seen, largely confined to the *ad hoc* arbitration cases. And insofar as one party surprises the other — that is, catches him unprepared — the problem is invariably resolved by an appropriate procedure which gives the other party time to prepare. There are, however, two difficult and unresolved policy problems in such cases. One is the extent to which arbitrators should insist that nothing new be brought to the arbitration table that has not been presented before, on the ground that to do so undermines the collective bargaining process. The other is the attitude which arbitrators should take toward deliberately withheld evidence. The ambivalence of arbitrators about these questions is probably attributable to the lack of an agreed theory as to the role which the arbitrator is expected to play. If he is the mere agent of the parties, hired simply to give his expert judgment as to the merits of a dispute as it is presented to him, he need have no concern for the wisdom of the practices which the parties are pursuing. His sole objective will then be to see that the surprised party is given a fair opportunity to answer something which may be new to him. If, on the other hand, the arbitrator is something more than a mere agent of the parties, he may have a legitimate concern with the development of the bargaining relationship.

Some of this same ambivalence shows up when one approaches the question of the use by arbitrators of their own undiscussed theories to resolve cases before them, or the application of unargued contract clauses. Few, if any, arbitrators would probably be willing to give up the "arbitrator's prerogative" of using his best judgment as to how to resolve the case provided only that he stays within the limits of his jurisdiction. It is doubtless true that in taking this position most experienced arbitrators have been burned, and have thus grown cautious about the practice. It is reasonable to suppose that with the passage of time, and the growing sophistication of the parties in the field of arbitration, arbitrators will, and should, resort less and less to their own unargued theories or to new contract clauses for resolving cases without first discussing them with the parties. There is, at least from the point of view of the parties, a basic question of fairness involved and some of their resentment toward arbitrators on this score is no doubt justified.

Until we evolve an accepted theory as to the role of the arbitrator we will not resolve questions as to how he should deal with policy matters, or the exercise of his own unreserved judgment. In this connection we would do well to reflect on the relative recency of industrial arbitration. It is essentially a post–World War II phenomenon. A large percentage of the active arbitrators got their basic training working in the mediation context of the War Labor Board. Many of them, and other non–War Labor Board arbitrators, are college professors who teach in the field of industrial relations. Given these facts it is not surprising that few arbitrators have been willing to accept a completely passive role in which they do nothing but resolve disputes on the terms presented without ever inserting their own ideas. It should also be noted that the development of a "rule of law" within the plant is in substantial part due to the decisions of arbitrators through which the parties have come to lay down and accept regularized procedures governing their conduct. It may be seriously doubted whether such a development could have taken place had arbitrators not to a certain extent imposed their ideas of constructive labor relations on the parties.

In short, the mold within which the arbitrator is cast should not yet be confined to a single production model. The context within which cases come to arbitration is still too varied to make this a desirable development. Standards of fairness are, with rare exceptions, being met. The gray areas, which touch on the policy role of the arbitrator, are not in such urgent need of clarification that they cannot be allowed to continue to develop free of rigid rules.

Chapter 7

SOME PROBLEMS OF EVIDENCE

There are real questions with which arbitrators are struggling every day. Moreover, the way in which they are answered says a good deal about the arbitration process. And now that the Supreme Court has, through the *Steelworker Trilogy*,[1] so greatly increased the stature of labor arbitration, it behooves both arbitrators and the parties to re-examine continually the system of private jurisprudence which they are building.

Legal rules of evidence do not, of course, apply before the labor arbitrator.[2] This is not surprising since such rules were developed in connection with jury trials, and do not apply strictly in any tribunal but a jury-court.[3] The whole theory of the arbitration tribunal is that it is composed of experts who repeatedly inquire into relatively homogeneous kinds of cases. Exclusionary rules are hardly required as a precautionary measure. Indeed, as the late Harry Shulman said in his classic Oliver Wendell Holmes lecture at Harvard in 1955, "The more serious danger is not that the arbitrator will hear too much irrelevancy, but rather that he will not hear enough of the relevant."[4]

But it is not toward common-law rules of evidence, in general, that this inquiry is directed. Rather, it is toward specific rules which may apply in the sensitive area of individual rights. Broadly stated this is a due process question, not just in the legal sense of compliance with the requirements of the fifth and fourteenth amendments, but in the popular sense of action which is consistent with the fundamental principles of liberty and justice which undergird a free society. Private though an arbitration tribunal may be, the parties who appear before it have the right to expect that its procedures and

---

[1] United Steelworkers of America v. Enterprise Wheel & Car Corp., 363 U.S. 593 (1960); United Steelworkers of America v. Warrior & Gulf Nav. Co., 363 U.S. 574 (1960); United Steelworkers of America v. American Mfg. Co., 363 U.S. 564 (1960).

[2] ELKOURI & ELKOURI, HOW ARBITRATION WORKS 173 (rev. ed. 1960).

[3] 1 WIGMORE, EVIDENCE, § 4, at 27 (3d ed. 1940).

[4] Shulman, *Reason, Contract, and Law in Labor Relations*, 68 HARV. L. REV. 999, 1017 (1955).

processes will conform to fundamental standards of fairness which would be required in the case of governments. Paraphrasing a famous line from Daniel Webster, we can say, "In a tribunal like this, entirely popular, care should be taken in every part of the system, not only to do right, but to satisfy the community that right is done."[5]

THE USES OF PAST MISCONDUCT

In discipline and discharge cases, companies typically offer the record of previous derelictions on the part of the employee. In part this is because they have learned from personnel experts [6] and arbitrators [7] that progressive discipline is deemed desirable. In any event, the problem takes many forms. Does it make any difference, for instance, whether the company is using the past record to:(1) prove that the penalty which has been imposed is appropriate; (2) suggest the likelihood that the employee committed the present offense; or (3) undermine the credibility of the employee as a witness? The courts, in criminal cases, have certainly thought there was a difference. Former convictions are clearly relevant in connection with the degree of penalty.[8] But if the evidence of past misconduct is offered for the purpose of proving the likelihood that the present offense has been committed, there is what appears at first glance to be a flat rule against admission. Thus, "the doing of one act is in itself no evidence that the same or a like act was again done by the same person," and "where the doing of an act is the proposition to be proved, there can never be a direct inference from an act of former conduct to the act charged."[9] There are, however, numerous exceptions to this rule.[10] And it would be unrealistic to distinguish between "proving likelihood" and "degree of penalty" when discussing the admissibility of past misconduct in arbitration proceedings because of two fundamental differences between the arbitrator and the judge. The first is that the arbitrator sits in review of a penalty which has already been imposed by the company, while the judge has the duty of setting the penalty. Second, the judge normally

---

[5] THE WRITINGS AND SPEECHES OF DANIEL WEBSTER 163 (1903). "In a government like ours, entirely popular, care should be taken in every part of the system, not only to do right, but to satisfy the community that right is done."

[6] PIGORS & MYERS, PERSONNEL ADMINISTRATION 202 (1947).

[7] Mueller Brass Co., 3 Lab. Arb. 271 (1946).

[8] 1 WIGMORE, EVIDENCE § 81, at 511 (3d ed. 1940).

[9] *Id.* § 192, at 641–42.

[10] McCORMICK, EVIDENCE § 60, at 137 (1954).

assesses the penalty *after* the jury has decided the question of guilt or innocence, whereas the arbitrator is both judge and jury. It is impractical for the arbitrator to hear the evidence, decide whether an employee deserves to be penalized, and then return to hear evidence of past misconduct which might bear on the degree of penalty. In this connection it may be worth noting that state statutes which permit the jury to fix a criminal sentence and allow the fact of prior convictions to be considered by jurors before verdict have been severely criticized,[11] although not held unconstitutional.[12]

Past misconduct may, of course, be offered in quite different contexts. Contrast the case in which the company offers the record of the past year showing progressive steps taken to correct absenteeism with the case in which it shows an admittedly bad absenteeism record five years before followed by an intervening period of satisfactory attendance. Consider also the case in which the employer wishes to show the record of the employee with his previous employer. Except for the last case, involving the previous employer, arbitrators will almost certainly admit the evidence, although the "stale" absenteeism record may be given little weight. There is a split among arbitrators with respect to the case involving the previous employer. The company may well have known of the employee's record when it hired him, and thus condoned it; and there is more reason to believe that the evidence is being offered simply to prejudice the arbitrator against the individual. Nevertheless, some arbitrators feel that it is better to admit the evidence and weigh its credibility than to exclude it.

Instances in which the company offers an employee's past record for the purpose of suggesting the likelihood that he has committed the present offense are much more difficult to deal with. Typical examples are the following:

1. A bus driver is disciplined for negligent driving. He denies the charge, and the company offers to show that the driver has had three accidents of a similar nature during the past year and must now be considered "accident prone."

2. An employee is disciplined for drinking, gambling, or pilferage on the job. He denies the charge, and the company wishes to show

---

[11] United States v. Price, 258 F.2d 918 (3d Cir.), *cert. denied,* 358 U.S. 922 (1958).
[12] *Ibid.*

that he was given a disciplinary layoff for the same reason during the past year, and had been warned on two other occasions.

3. The same basic facts as in examples one and two, except that the previous offenses occurred while employed by a previous employer, or were offenses against the civil or criminal law (e.g., fined for being drunk and disorderly).

In all such cases there will be independent, but probably inconclusive, evidence that the employee has committed the present offense. The clear purpose of the past record is to suggest to the arbitrator the likelihood that an employee with such a past record has, in fact, committed the present offense. When questioned as to how they handle such evidence, arbitrators display a lack of uniformity. A large majority will admit the evidence and give it weight when the present offense has a functional relationship to the past offense: e.g., the "accident prone" driver. But only a minority appear to be willing to receive evidence of past offenses insofar as this bears upon a currently alleged, but functionally unrelated, offense. There is also a much greater willingness to admit evidence of past misconduct with the present employer than with either a predecessor employer or against the public order.

Finally, there is the situation in which an attempt is made to introduce the past record for the purpose of undermining the credibility of the witness. Three examples will make this type of problem clearer:

1. The contract requires that overtime be distributed equally. The company alleges that X was called at home when it was his turn, but that he did not answer. X insists that he was at home and did not receive such a call. The company then seeks to show that X has entered a similar claim in the past but that the grievance committee has never seen fit to process it beyond the first step. The implication, of course, is that not even his brethren believe X.

2. An employee is discharged for stealing, but he denies the charge. The evidence is wholly circumstantial, and the company wants to show that the employee has a record of criminal convictions for stealing despite the entry of pleas of not guilty in each case.

3. The employee is disciplined for sleeping — a charge which he denies. The contract contains a clause prohibiting introduction of an employee's past record, but the company wants to show that the employee has been disciplined in the past for this reason and has always denied the charge. The company insists that such a showing

will not be contrary to the contractual clause because it is being offered only to attack the credibility of the witness.

Most arbitrators will have little trouble with the overtime case, although they may feel that there are better ways of proving whether the telephone call was, in fact, made. Proof of prior criminal convictions will find arbitrators split, some feeling that any record outside the plant is irrelevant, but others admitting the evidence and giving it weight. The sleeping case, which comes under a contract barring evidence of past misconduct, will almost certainly find the evidence being rejected on the ground that the offer is simply being made in a way which circumvents the contract.

In discussing the law of criminal procedure, Wigmore has suggested that there are at least four reasons why information with respect to past misconduct should not be permitted to reach the judge or jury prior to a decision on the question of guilt. They are: (1) the tendency to find the defendant guilty simply because he is a likely person to do such acts; (2) the tendency to condemn for past unpunished offenses even though the defendant may not be guilty of the present charge; (3) the injustice of forcing one to defend himself against unexpected evidence or evidence which he will find it hard to combat; and (4) the possible confusion of new issues which will inevitably result.[13] Arbitrators express concern over substantially the same problems in cases which come before them. How, then, should they rule when such questions arise? If the criminal cases may be taken as a proper analogy, it would not be inconsistent with legal due process to admit the evidence. Therefore, in the last analysis, the rule which is adopted in arbitration would seem to depend on the answer to the following question: At what point does the prejudice likely to result from the receipt of evidence of past misconduct outweigh the common-sense relevance of such information? And once that question is answered, a second question arises: If the evidence of past misconduct is admitted, what weight should be given to it?

Such questions do not lend themselves to firm and unalterable answers. However, it would seem that the arbitrator would be justified in holding to the following guidelines:

1. Unless the grievant has already put in evidence of his good character, evidence of his past offenses should not be received until

---

[13] 1 WIGMORE, EVIDENCE § 194, at 650–51 (3d ed. 1940).

the record contains more than a pro forma showing with respect to the offenses charged.

2. When evidence of past misconduct is offered for the purpose of inferring that the grievant committed the present offense it should be admitted, provided it is of record and known to the grievant. Such evidence should, however, be given weight only insofar as there is a clear relationship between the kinds of offenses involved, and insofar as the events have taken place within a reasonable span of time. (Example: Repeated absenteeism proves nothing with respect to a charge of stealing, but repeated accidents may suggest that the driver is "accident prone.") [14]

3. When evidence of past misconduct is offered for the purpose of impeaching the credibility of the grievant it should be received, provided it does not appear to be offered simply to prejudice the arbitrator.

4. When evidence of past misconduct is offered in order to justify the severity of the present penalty it should normally be received. The weight to be given such evidence will then depend upon (a) the relationship between the kinds of offenses, and (b) the period of time involved. This rule should apply to past conduct both within and without the company although in general the latter evidence will carry less weight. (Example: A company hires a known alcoholic at the request of Alcoholics Anonymous. The man comes to work drunk and the company imposes discipline. Surely it is *relevant,* in terms of the leniency which can be expected from the company, that the man is a known alcoholic. To hold otherwise would be to discourage companies from the socially desirable policy of cooperating with rehabilitation agencies.)

5. A contractual limitation on the use of the past record should be broadly construed to exclude such evidence.

ACCESS TO INFORMATION IN THE FILES
OF THE OTHER PARTY

The grievance procedure gives rise to at least two types of situations in which one party desires information which is in the hands of the other. In the first case the information is sought for its own sake. Thus if A contends that he has not shared equally in the distribution of overtime, although the contract so requires, the union

---

[14] James & Dickinson, *Accident Proneness and Accident Law*, 63 HARV. L. REV. 769 (1950).

needs the records showing how the overtime has been distributed. Similarly, if B contends that his seniority is greater than that of C, the union needs to know what the company records show in this respect. In the other type of case, however, the information is expected to serve a collateral purpose. Thus if X is fired for excessive absenteeism, the union may want to see the records of a number of other employees whom it knows have been guilty of absenteeism in order to see how their lost time compares with that of X. Or if Y is the senior man and he is denied a promotion on the ground that his education is inadequate, the union may want to compare the educational qualifications of other men now on the higher job.

In the run-of-the-mill case the company and the union readily exchange information in grievance cases, both because they recognize that this will contribute to the fair and equitable settlement of the case, and because they want to avoid the cost of arbitration. The essence of the dispute may revolve around a given fact, e.g., who has the greater seniority. There would obviously be no point in hiding the seniority record in such a case. Nevertheless, there are situations in which one party declines to make available to the other information which it possesses and which is deemed by the other to be relevant to its position. The following two examples will illustrate the point:

1. A tugboat almost sinks from water which has entered the hold. The company attorney immediately interviews all crew members and obtains lengthy statements from them. Thereafter, the chief engineer is discharged for gross negligence. In trying to decide whether to take the grievance to arbitration, the union representative interviews all the crew members. In the process he becomes aware that all of them have already been interviewed by the company's attorney. Before making a decision as to whether to go to arbitration he would like to see these statements so that he will know how reliable the various witnesses are. He requests the company to let him see the transcript of such interviews, but the request is denied. What, if anything, can he do about this? If he goes to arbitration without seeing the transcripts, but asks for them after the attorney for the company has completed examining the witness, may he then have them?

2. Production and management personnel are both covered by one master insurance contract, although the benefits for management personnel are higher. Individual employees receive certificates of insurance, and a statement in the collective bargaining contract specifies

the amounts of their coverage, but neither the employee nor the union has access to the master contract. X then dies under circumstances which raise a question of whether he was entitled to the old or amended benefits, and the company insists that under the terms of the master contract he gets only the old benefits. The union then asks to see the master contract, and the company offers to have it photo-stated except for the provision showing management benefits. This the union refuses, contending that it is entitled to see the original master contract. What, if anything, can the union do about this? And if the case goes to arbitration should the arbitrator insist that the company put in evidence the complete master contract?

Faced with a similar problem in the civil courts, counsel might attempt, through use of the discovery procedure outlined in rules 26 to 37 of the Federal Rules of Civil Procedure, to obtain the information desired. But the arbitrator has no power to order discovery; and in the *ad hoc* cases there would not, in fact, even be an arbitrator at this stage. In lieu of discovery an action might be brought under the Taft-Hartley Act, contending that the reluctant party was refusing to bargain collectively by withholding the information. It is clear, of course, that good-faith bargaining requires that the company furnish the union with information which will enable it to police the collective bargaining contract.[15] But this will be a time-consuming procedure, and may be of little value to the union in deciding whether it wishes to take the grievance to arbitration. What, then, can be done? Assuming the unfair labor practice proceeding is not used, the answer seems to be that little can be done short of arbitration. If this is so, what can be expected when the question reaches the arbitration level?

If we revert to the tugboat case, an issue as to the availability of the transcript of early company interviews with the crew members is likely to be made at the time any such witnesses are examined. And if counsel is present for the union, he is almost certain to mention the *Jencks* case [16] and to contend that it is applicable. That controversial case, it will be remembered, involved a prosecution for filing a false non-Communist affidavit with the National Labor Relations Board. At the trial two important prosecution witnesses admitted making prior reports to the Federal Bureau of Investigation. The

---

[15] Cf. NLRB v. Whitin Mach. Works, 217 F.2d 593 (4th Cir. 1954), *cert. denied*, 349 U.S. 905 (1955).

[16] Jencks v. United States, 353 U.S. 657 (1957).

defense then requested the trial court to examine those reports and turn over to the defense any portions found inconsistent with the answers given by the witnesses at the trial. The denial of the request, subsequently affirmed by the Fifth Circuit,[17] was based on the theory that prior to production the defense must establish a variance between the testimony and the documents. The Supreme Court reversed on the ground that the defense could hardly know that there was an inconsistency between the testimony and the document without seeing the latter, and stated that the defendant need only show that the material sought related to the testimony. The Court also said that the defense must have access to all relevant documents irrespective of their admissibility in evidence, and disapproved any necessity for an initial testing of admissibility by the trial judge.

Jencks was, of course, a criminal trial. When counsel for a company argued before the NLRB that the *Jencks* ruling required the Board to give the company access to the Board's file data in an unfair labor practice proceeding, although the Board's rules forbade any such disclosure, the request was turned down with the statement that the *Jencks* rule applied only to criminal cases and not to proceedings before an administrative board.[18] But shortly thereafter, in *Adhesive Products Corp.*, another Board ruling to the same effect came to the Second Circuit and was reversed.[19] In that case Adhesive was being charged with failure to bargain, and in the course of the proceeding before a trial examiner a union organizer used a non-confidential written statement made to Board officials for purposes of refreshing his memory before taking the witness stand. The company asked the examiner to order the witness to turn over the statement for use in impeaching him on cross-examination and the examiner refused to so rule. On review, the court brushed off the fact that *Jencks* was a criminal trial, and expressed the view that there was no significant distinction between civil and criminal proceedings in this regard. Said the court:

Accordingly, these rules set forth in the Jencks decision provide an *a fortiori* basis for holding that the statement demanded in the case at bar should have been produced and made available for respondent's inspection if they are applicable to civil proceedings, such as administrative hear-

---

[17] Jencks v. United States, 226 F.2d 540 and 553 (5th Cir. 1955).

[18] Great Atl. & Pac. Tea Co., 118 N.L.R.B. 1280 (1957).

[19] NLRB v. Adhesive Prods. Corp., 258 F.2d 403 (2d Cir. 1958); *accord*, NLRB v. Capitol Fish Co., 294 F.2d 868 (5th Cir. 1961); Schauffler v. Local 107, Teamsters' Union, 196 F. Supp. 471 (E.D. Pa. 1960).

ings, as well as to criminal trials. In our opinion, logic compels the conclusion that these rules are applicable to an administrative hearing. . . . The production and inspection, and possible use for cross-examination purposes, of such a document could serve only to test the memory and credibility of the witness, while, in the absence of a claim of confidence or privilege, there can be no sound reason to bar such production. The request in the case at bar was not a mere fishing expedition, but rather concerned the credibility of the most important witness who testified in support of the charges.[20]

Jencks represented an exercise of the Supreme Court's power to prescribe procedures for the administration of justice in the federal courts. It was not decided on constitutional grounds, although, as Mr. Justice Brennan later said, "it would be idle to say that the commands of the Constitution were not close to the surface of the decision. . . ."[21]

If an arbitrator, in the tugboat case, denies the union access to the earlier statements of the witnesses he will probably not be guilty of denying the grievant due process of law in the legal sense — although it may not be beyond the bounds of reason to suppose that at some future date, in a proceeding to enforce an arbitration award, a grievant who had been denied access to such a statement would be held to have been deprived of due process of law. But the principle of *Jencks* is as sound for the arbitrator as for the administrative agency. The request is not a mere fishing expedition. It does concern the credibility of an important witness and should be produced.

The question of the master insurance policy raises a somewhat different issue. Here the company claims that the union is on a fishing expedition, for the question of the level of benefits for management personnel is not relevant to the issue of whether X is entitled to the new or old level of benefits. What is unsatisfactory about having the arbitrator examine the master contract to satisfy himself that the photostat is an exact copy except for the irrelevant clause showing management benefits? How can the union possibly be prejudiced by this? This is the exact procedure which Congress provided for in a statute [22] enacted to narrow the effect of the *Jencks* decision.[23]

---

[20] NLRB v. Adhesive Prods. Corp., *supra* note 19, at 408.

[21] Palermo v. United States, 360 U.S. 343, 362–63 (1959).

[22] 18 U.S.C. § 3500 (1958). That statute was upheld in *Palermo v. United States, supra* note 21.

[23] The statute applies only to criminal prosecutions and provides, *inter alia*, that no report in the possession of the United States shall be subject to subpoena or discovery until after a witness has testified, and if the United States

Since the arbitrator is usually without the power of subpoena he will not be able to force production of the documents in either the tugboat or the insurance policy cases. But this is not a serious handicap — as is evidenced by the fact that the proposed United States Arbitration Act, drafted by a committee of the National Academy of Arbitrators, does not even include such a provision. Neither side is inclined to withhold a genuinely relevant document because to do so invites an adverse ruling arising partly out of the arbitrator's inference that the document is damaging to the party withholding it.

There is doubtless a considerable temptation in arbitration proceedings to embark on "fishing" expeditions. Even so, the experienced arbitrator will have little difficulty dealing with such cases. For the rest of the cases, would not the following guidelines adequately serve the purpose?

1. In the absence of any showing of prejudice, relevant information in the hands of one party should be made available to the other party in an arbitration proceeding at the request of the arbitrator.

2. In the event the party to whom such a request is made refuses to honor it, and in the absence of a subpoena power in the hands of the arbitrator, an inference may be drawn against the party refusing to produce the evidence.

3. In a *Jencks*-type case, the principle involved in that case should be followed.

4. The arbitrator should, on request of a party, excise irrelevant portions of a document after privately inspecting it.

CONFRONTATION AND CROSS-EXAMINATION

Problems of confrontation and cross-examination are particularly troublesome in the labor arbitration field because there is likely to be a square conflict between the informality of the hearing and certain industrial relations policy considerations on the one hand, and some very sensitive personal rights and fundamental considerations of fairness on the other. Some examples will make the point clearer.

Retail stores, public utilities, and other similar businesses have a problem of customer relations. A customer in a supermarket may, for instance, complain that a certain checker is consistently overcharging him. Yet he may be unwilling to make any formal statement, and be even less willing to appear as a witness against the

---

claims that part of the material does not relate to the matter at hand, the court must inspect the statement in camera and excise irrelevant portions.

checker if disciplinary measures are taken by the company and then brought to arbitration. Or a female customer may complain that a utility service man has made improper advances to her in the course of a service call. Yet she may be unwilling to discuss the issue in more than general terms, or appear as a witness at an arbitration hearing if the company takes disciplinary action.

Another line of cases involves the peculiar problems of certain businesses in which the honesty and integrity of employees can be checked only by the use of "spotters" who, while playing the role of customers, actually watch for any irregularities. Retail stores and bus companies frequently employ such assistance. Usually it is supplied by established firms which furnish trained agents who make routine checks. To remain useful these agents must be anonymous. Their reports may identify irregularities on the part of a bus driver in dealing with fares, or on the part of a retail cashier or salesman. The employee is then confronted with the evidence, but given no opportunity to talk to the person from whom it came. And if a grievance results from disciplinary action the arbitrator finds himself presented with the question of receiving evidence from an unidentified source and without the right of confrontation or cross-examination.

There are other kinds of cases, some of them more common than either of the above examples. A substantial number of grievances involve situations in which the result hinges on the word of one management man versus one union man — but there is another employee, who is also a union member, who could testify. If, for instance, X is discharged for hitting his foreman, X may claim that he thought the foreman was about to hit him with a piece of steel. The foreman may deny that he had anything in his hand, or was in any way threatening X. Y, working at a nearby machine, may have seen the whole incident. Suppose, in fact, that after X struck the foreman Y rushed over and said to the admittedly hot-tempered X, "Are you crazy? What did you want to hit him for?" If and when the case comes to arbitration the company may not wish to call Y. Many companies simply refuse to call one production employee against another. They know that this puts him in an impossible position, for Y is then not only a "squealer," which our mores condemn, but is guilty of treason against a fellow union member as well. The latter can result in disciplinary action. The fact remains that the arbitrator's job would be much easier if he knew what Y had to say. Should he insist that Y be called? Suppose Y refuses to testify? In the absence of *Y*, suppose the foreman wants to repeat *Y*'s remark after *X* hit the foreman? Should this be permitted? Suppose the union objects?

In trying to decide how arbitrators should deal with cases of this kind, it is useful to check the court analogy. In the courts the confrontation requirement has always been considered to have two purposes, only one of which is essential. The first, and critical, purpose is to permit cross-examination. Of secondary importance is the opportunity to scrutinize the witness while testifying in order to get some feel for the truth or falsity of what he is saying. Thus, the second requirement can be dispensed with where the witness has testified at a previous hearing and been under cross-examination, and is not now available for a reason such as absence from the state, death, illness, etc.[24]

The principle of confrontation is given constitutional protection under the federal constitution, and in practically every state, in criminal cases. Wigmore has pointed out that there is a considerable carry-over into the civil law.[25]

Perhaps the most interesting analogy in the courts to the kind of cases which arise in arbitration involves the government's dismissal of employees for security reasons. Such dismissals have disturbed the courts, and indeed the nation, because of the inherent unfairness in depriving a citizen of his job and his reputation without an opportunity to know his accusers, to confront them, and to cross-examine them.[26] Counsel for government employees in such cases have long argued that the individuals were being deprived of due process. In the only case which has squarely presented the point the Supreme Court divided four to four, thereby leaving undisturbed a court of appeals case in which the court held that due process had not been denied. Said the court: "Due process of law is not applicable unless one is being deprived of something to which he has a right."[27] And since executive offices are held at the will of the appointing authority, the court thought there could be no such right.

Despite the above opinion, the Supreme Court has expressed concern about the absence of confrontation and cross-examination in two more recent cases involving security dismissals. In *Vitarelli v.*

---

[24] 5 WIGMORE, EVIDENCE § 1395 (3d ed. 1940).

[25] *Id.* § 1400, at 144.

[26] Arnold, *The American Ideal of a Fair Trial,* 9 ARK. L. REV. 311 (1955).

[27] Bailey v. Richardson, 182 F.2d 46, 58 (D.C. Cir. 1950), *aff'd per curiam,* 341 U.S. 918 (1951).

Seaton,[28] the Department of Interior had established a procedure for considering cases of dismissal for security reasons, and then failed to follow its own procedure. One of the deficiencies was that the dismissed employee was not given a chance to cross-examine one of his identified accusers. In an opinion which concurred in part and dissented in part, Mr. Justice Frankfurter made these significant comments:

An executive agency must be rigorously held to the standards by which it professes its action to be judged. . . . Accordingly, if dismissal from employment is based on a defined procedure, even though generous beyond the requirements that bind such agency, that procedure must be scrupulously observed. . . . He that takes the procedural sword shall perish with that sword.

The Secretary of the Interior concededly had untrammeled right to dismiss Vitarelli out of hand, since he had no protected employment rights. He could do so as freely as a private employer who is not bound by procedural restrictions of a collective bargaining contract.[29]

In the other case, *Green v. McElroy*,[30] the Supreme Court reversed an administrative decision which had resulted in a denial of clearance to an executive of a company doing business with the Navy, on the ground that neither Congress nor the President had authorized the procedures whereby the security clearance had been denied. The opinion contained language which caused Mr. Justice Clark to comment: "While the Court disclaims deciding this constitutional question [due process], no one reading the opinion will doubt that the explicit language of its broad sweep speaks in prophecy."[31] Particularly disturbing was the portion of the majority opinion which stated that "the right to hold specific private employment and to follow a chosen profession free from unreasonable governmental interference comes within the 'liberty' and 'property' concepts of the Fifth Amendment. . . ." [32] This proposition, thought Mr. Justice Clark, was clearly erroneous and unsupported by past cases.[33]

The thing which stands out about labor arbitration, in the kind of cases under discussion, is the amount of experimentation and horsesense procedure which are used.

---

[28] 359 U.S. 535 (1959).
[29] *Id.* at 546–47.
[30] 360 U.S. 474 (1959).
[31] *Id.* at 524.
[32] *Id.* at 492.
[33] *Id.* at 512–13.

To be specific, hearsay is almost universally accepted in preference to calling one production employee against another. The arbitrator's reasoning is fairly simple. Such a witness is, unquestionably, in an extremely difficult position — so difficult, in fact, that he may not be very reliable. Hearsay may be equally unreliable, but when it is received the party against whom it weighs, usually the union, can decide that it is better to produce the reluctant employee and encourage him to testify. To go back to the earlier example, most arbitrators will permit the foreman to say that when X hit him, Y grabbed X and said, "Are you crazy? What did you want to hit him for?" The union can always call Y to deny that he said this. If it doesn't, common sense suggests that Y probably did make the remark. And it has some weight in deciding the credibility of X in saying that he hit the foreman only when the latter came after him with a piece of steel in his hand. One arbitrator, much respected nationally, goes as far as to refuse to let one production employee testify against another. But at the same time he allows almost unlimited hearsay as to what the employee might say if called. Another distinguished arbitrator deplores the tradition of not calling bargaining unit witnesses.[34]

"Private" investigations, conducted by the arbitrator, are not infrequently authorized. Take the case of the female who complains that the utility's service man made improper advances to her. Its own investigation may convince the company that the customer is telling the truth so it fires the employee. But when the arbitration comes along she refuses to testify. The arbitrator may be, and usually is, without the power of subpoena. The union, in recognition of the problem, may be willing to authorize the arbitrator to visit the complaining customer and interview her. He may then decide the case based upon conclusions reached as a result of the interview.

In transit cases the collective bargaining contract sometimes gives formal recognition to the "private" witness. Thus article 2(g) of the 1953 agreement between the Philadelphia Transportation Company and the Transport Workers Union of America, Local 234, reads: "In case any testimony by a secret investigator of the Company is offered it shall be given only before the Chairman with no one else present

---

[34] Wirtz, *Due Process of Arbitration,* in NATIONAL ACADEMY OF ARBITRATORS, THE ARBITRATORS AND THE PARTIES, PROCEEDINGS OF THE 11TH ANNUAL MEETING 1, 18 (McKelvey ed. 1958).

and such a witness shall be referred to only by number so that his identity shall not be disclosed."

Another variation that has been worked out in at least one grocery chain calls for the acceptance, at the hearing, of customer complaints based upon company records, but then provides the union an opportunity to check privately with the customer. If discrepancies appear the arbitrator is then authorized (the subpoena power being there available) to call the customer.

Most difficult of all, perhaps, are the rare cases in which, during a recess, both counsel suggest to the arbitrator that they think a given witness was not telling the truth, counsel also suggesting that the arbitrator have a private chat with the witness afterwards to see if he can come any nearer to the truth.

Many arbitrators are unwilling, even with the consent of the parties, to talk privately with a witness if the decision is to be influenced by the results of the conference. Even when the contract authorizes the arbitrator to make such investigations as he thinks proper, the propriety of private interrogation may be challenged as it was under the General Motors agreement.[35] In some cases, as a sort of compromise, arbitrators have agreed to talk privately with witnesses provided they can then report back to both parties the substance of the information obtained. In a transit "spotter" case, one arbitrator overcame the problem of the anonymous witness by placing him behind a screen where he could be seen only by the arbitrator and counsel for both sides while he was testifying.

It is quite obvious that in this area arbitrators depart drastically from the common-law rules of evidence known to the courts. In doing so are they violating fundamental considerations of fairness which are essential to due process of law? By taking hearsay in preference to an available witness it is difficult to see that a serious due process question is involved. In practically all cases this procedure is accepted or condoned by the parties.

Private investigations offer more difficulty. Surely it can be agreed that they should never be undertaken without the consent of the parties. Even then, one may question whether the individual will be bound by the action of his union in agreeing to such a procedure.

---

[35] Alexander, *Impartial Umpireships: The General Motors — UAW Experience*, in NATIONAL ACADEMY OF ARBITRATORS, ARBITRATION AND THE LAW, PROCEEDINGS OF THE 12TH ANNUAL MEETING 108, 121 (McKelvey ed. 1959).

Communicating the results of the investigation back to the parties before decision seems preferable to no such report.

In the spotter cases it does not necessarily follow that because, as one arbitrator said, "The System may be odious, but there is no practical alternative," [36] confrontation and cross-examination cannot be provided. It may be that spotters must be utilized, but there are ways of insuring the parties an opportunity to cross-examine without revealing the identity of the witness or exposing him.

Perhaps it is possible to summarize what seem to be desirable rules as follows:

1. Depositions and former testimony of witnesses should be accepted where such witnesses are now unavailable.

2. When the alternatives are hearsay evidence versus one employee testifying against another, the choice should ordinarily lie with the parties. If the witness is available, but either is not called or declines to testify, hearsay evidence should be received in place of his testimony.

3. Private investigations by the arbitrator should be held to a minimum and conducted only with the authorization of the parties. Where possible, arrangements should be made to report back to the parties on the investigation before the arbitrator makes a final decision.

4. Where the nature of the business requires that witnesses remain anonymous, arrangements should nevertheless be made to permit counsel for the parties to confront and examine them in the presence of the arbitrator.

THE PRIVILEGE AGAINST SELF-INCRIMINATION

We know, of course, that under the federal and many state constitutions no man "shall be compelled in any criminal case to be a witness against himself." [37] And we know that despite the language which purports to limit the privilege to criminal cases, the courts have held that "the privilege of a witness not to answer incriminating questions extends to all judicial or official hearings, investigations or inquiries where persons are called upon formally to give testimony." [38] But in order to assess the role, if any, which the privilege

---

[36] Los Angeles Transit Lines, 25 Lab. Arb. 740, 741 (1955).
[37] U.S. Const. amend. V.
[38] McCORMICK, EVIDENCE § 123 (1954).

should play in arbitration proceedings, one needs to be aware of two or three other facets of the privilege as applied in the courts.

In the first place, it is only when a person has been formally accused or officially suspected of crime that he may not be questioned at all. In all other situations the witness must answer non-incriminating questions and must claim his privilege when the question is incriminating.[39] Second, many courts have held that the privilege is not breached if the accused is finger-printed, photographed, deprived of his papers and other objects in his possession, physically examined, required to submit to blood or other bodily fluid exams, required to give a specimen of his handwriting, etc.[40] Finally, the due process clause of the fourteenth amendment is not violated by a state law which permits the prosecuting attorney to comment on the failure of the defendant to take the stand.[41] Mr. Justice Cardozo once addressed himself to this point in the following language: "This too [compulsory self-incrimination] might be lost, and justice still be done. Indeed, today as in the past there are students of our penal system who look upon the immunity as a mischief rather than a benefit, and who would limit its scope, or destroy it altogether. No doubt there would remain the need to give protection against torture, physical or mental. . . . Justice, however, would not perish if the accused were subject to a duty to respond to orderly inquiry."[42]

In the purely private world of labor arbitration the constitutional protection against self-incrimination presumably has little application except insofar as it may be a desirable principle in the interest of a fair procedure. In that connection one ought to note at the outset that the proportions of the problem are almost certain to be different before the arbitrator than in the court. There are two reasons for this. The first is that the question of the privilege usually arises in a collateral, rather than direct, way in arbitration. And the second is that since the arbitrator usually has neither the power of subpoena nor the power to hold a party in contempt, the question is not really one of compelling someone to testify, but rather of whether it is permissible to draw an inference against him because he has not testified. To see the problem a little more clearly, let us examine some of the kinds of cases which arise in arbitration.

---

[39] *Id.* at 288.
[40] *Id.* at 264.
[41] Twining v. New Jersey, 211 U.S. 78 (1908).
[42] Palko v. Connecticut, 302 U.S. 319, 325–26 (1937).

Post-war ideological differences, which have given a new emphasis to security measures, account for a number of cases. Employees
have frequently been called before legislative committees and asked
about their affiliation with subversive organizations. On a number
of occasions they have refused to testify, claiming the privilege of
the fifth amendment. The employer might then discharge the individual on the ground that he is a security risk. If the employee pro-
tests he may be entitled to take the case to arbitration — thereby,
on occasion, posing a difficult internal problem for the union.[43] After
a certain amount of struggle, arbitrators now quite uniformly hold
that the employee must be reinstated where the sole cause for the
discharge is the individual's unwillingness to testify.[44] In reaching
this conclusion much emphasis has been placed upon Supreme Court
decisions, particularly *Slochower v. Board of Higher Educ.*[45] That
case involved a situation in which the New York City Charter provided that when a city employee utilized the privilege against self-
incrimination to avoid answering a question relating to his official
conduct before a legislative committee his employment would termi-
nate. Slochower was a teacher in one of the city colleges. He was
discharged without notice or a hearing when he invoked the fifth
amendment before a federal legislative committee with respect to
his membership in the Communist party. The court held that the
summary dismissal of Slochower violated the requirements of due
process of law. In his opinion Mr. Justice Clark said: "The privilege
against self-incrimination would be reduced to a hollow mockery if
its exercise could be taken as equivalent either to a confession of
guilt or a conclusive presumption of perjury." [46]

But *Slochower* was followed by *Beilan v. Board of Pub. Educ.*,[47]
in which, by a five-to-four decision, the Supreme Court held that it
did not constitute a violation of due process under the fourteenth
amendment to discharge a public school teacher for failure to cooperate by refusing to answer questions of supervisors concerning membership in subversive organizations. Although the employee had
based his position on the privilege against self-incrimination, the

---

[43] Ostrofsky v. United Steelworkers, 171 F. Supp. 782 (D. Md. 1959).

[44] R.C.A. Communications, Inc., 29 Lab. Arb. 567 (1957); Pratt & Whitney
Co., 28 Lab. Arb. 668 (1957); J. H. Day Co., 22 Lab. Arb. 751 (1954); United
Press Ass'n, 22 Lab. Arb. 679 (1954).

[45] 350 U.S. 551 (1956).

[46] *Id.* at 557.

[47] 357 U.S. 399 (1958).

Court said this was irrelevant since he was discharged not for claiming the privilege, but for refusing to cooperate.

Beilan, like *Slochower*, has found its parallel in arbitration decisions. Thus an arbitrator held that a newspaper did not have to retain editorial writers who invoked the fifth amendment.[48] And other arbitrators have held that if the plant is engaged in defense work,[49] or there is unrest in the plant,[50] the discharge of an employee who invokes the fifth amendment may be justified. There is, it should be added, another decision reinstating an individual discharged because of the alleged unrest when management made no effort to control the unrest.[51]

Aside from the security cases, arbitrators find themselves faced with occasional cases in which the plant offense gives rise both to disciplinary action and a criminal charge. When this happens the two proceedings will seldom proceed simultaneously. The result is that either the criminal trial or the arbitration may have been concluded and a decision announced before the other tribunal acts. In one such case [52] an employee was indicted for allegedly stealing tires from his employer's plant. He was suspended pending trial, in the course of which he was acquitted after claiming his privilege against self-incrimination. When the arbitration began, involving the man's discharge for the same offense, the grievant once again refused to testify. The arbitrator upheld the discharge on the ground that by refusing to explain his admitted possession of the tires, the employee had failed to satisfy his obligation to his employer to cooperate in stopping thievery from the plant.

In a reverse situation [53] the grievant refused to testify on the ground that his criminal trial was pending, and that the arbitration record could be subpoenaed for that proceeding. The arbitrator thought the refusal was justified in such a case, and ought not to be used against the grievant. In discussions of this case many other arbitrators have indicated that they agree with the ruling. It is, in a sense, inconsistent with the majority of the court cases which have held

---

[48] Los Angeles Daily News, 19 Lab. Arb. 39 (1952).
[49] Bethlehem Steel Co., 24 Lab. Arb. 852 (1955).
[50] Burt Mfg. Co., 21 Lab. Arb. 532 (1953).
[51] Republic Steel Corp., 28 Lab. Arb. 810 (1957).
[52] Wirtz, *supra* note 34, at 20.
[53] New York Times Co., 29 Lab. Arb. 442 (1957).

that a witness may not refuse to testify on the ground that his answers may subject him to prosecution in another forum.[54]

All of the above examples involve situations in which dual proceedings account for the difficulties in connection with the privilege against self-incrimination. Only rarely, arbitrators report, do they get a case in which a witness makes a direct issue of the privilege against self-incrimination where the problem is limited to the arbitration proceeding. One such case is an unreported one in which the employee was discharged for having advised other employees to violate a clear company rule. In the course of the arbitration hearing the dischargee refused to take the stand and testify on the question of whether he had given such advice. He justified his position on the basis of the privilege against self-incrimination. The arbitrator could not force the grievant to take the stand, but he did infer from the employee's failure to do so that he had probably given the advice. Of course, in arbitration, as in court cases, it is difficult to know how much weight to assign to the adverse inference. Usually the grievant defendant's greatest difficulty is not the inference arising out of refusal to testify, but the fact that there is other evidence in the record which remains uncontradicted because the defendant refuses to speak.

Many arbitrators feel that the privilege against self-incrimination has no place in the arbitration proceeding. Often they explain this on the ground that the arbitration is not a criminal proceeding. Since the courts have long held, as indicated previously, that the privilege extends beyond criminal proceedings, this may be an unsound ground for an otherwise correct conclusion. Would not the following rules adequately serve the purpose in dealing with the privilege against self-incrimination in arbitration proceedings?

1. Since the privilege against self-incrimination owes much of its existence to historical developments which have no relevancy to the field of arbitration, the privilege should have only a very limited application to arbitration.

2. When the grievant claims the privilege against self-incrimination for purposes of the arbitration proceeding, either without reference to another forum or on the ground that a criminal proceeding elsewhere is pending against him for the same offense, he should be

---

[54] McCORMICK, EVIDENCE § 135 (1954).

advised that a failure or refusal to testify may give rise to an inference against him.

3. An adverse inference arising out of failure or refusal to testify,
whether before the arbitrator or elsewhere, will rarely, if ever, be
sufficient by itself to sustain the penalty which has been imposed.

4. An adverse inference arising out of failure or refusal to testify
before the arbitrator or elsewhere may, when coupled with unrefuted
evidence against the grievant, be used to sustain the penalty.

5. Insofar as the privilege against self-incrimination has any
standing before an arbitration tribunal it should not apply to other
than testimonial compulsion.

In brief, these rules give a minimum scope in arbitration to the
privilege against self-incrimination. This, it is submitted, is desirable. Justice can, as Cardozo so eloquently pointed out, survive without the privilege.[55] Employment with a given employer is not a
right.[56] The importation into the field of arbitration of concepts having little relevance to the special problems before the tribunal would
be unfortunate.

SEARCH AND SEIZURE

There appear to be very few reported arbitration cases which
squarely face the question of whether evidence obtained by an illegal
search is admissible. Interestingly enough, one of the few was decided in 1946 by Joseph D. Lohman, who has recently been appointed
Dean of the School of Criminology at the University of California at
Berkeley. In that case,[57] a woman had been discharged for violation
of a company rule which prohibited possession by employees of a
dangerous knife on company premises. The evidence showed that a
guard had allegedly seen the knife in the woman's purse through
the open door of her locker. This information was conveyed to a
supervisor who then asked the grievant to report to the office on her
way off duty. The employee, without being told the reason for the
request, was then asked by the head guard to empty her purse. This
she did, with the result that the knife was revealed. A majority of
the arbitration board ruled that the evidence of possession of the
knife was inadmissible and that the discharge was unjustified. Although the whole incident took place on company property, the ma-

---

[55] Palko v. Connecticut, 302 U.S. 319, 325–26 (1937).

[56] U. S. Steel Corp. v. Nichols, 229 F.2d 396, 399 (6th Cir. 1956).

[57] Campbell Soup Co., 2 Lab. Arb. 27 (1946).

jority said that "the aggrieved's locker and purse continue inviolate as the private realm of the individual and are not to be searched or seized in an illegal fashion." [58] The opinion speaks of entrapment, self-incrimination, and illegal search and seizure. One gets the impression that the majority felt there were other, and better, ways in which the company could implement its undeniably valid rule. It is a little difficult to know just how much weight to assign to each of the respective factors relied upon by the arbitrators.

A 1957 decision,[59] involving an employee who was discharged for "writing numbers" on company property, furnishes an interesting comparison with the above case. In that case plant protection officers detained a cook at the company's canteen and asked him to go to the plant protection office. En route a numbers slip was found in a package of cigarettes carried by the employee. At the plant protection office the employee was told to empty his pockets, which he did. Several other slips were then discovered. This evidence was turned over to a city magistrate who tried the defendant and found him guilty. Subsequently the man was discharged. No point was apparently made of an alleged illegal seizure, and the discharge was sustained without referring to the question.

Most of the arbitrators who have been asked about illegal search and seizure cases indicate that they have never had such an issue. However, there are some unreported cases in which arbitrators say they have dealt with the following situations:

1. The company furnished lockers and padlocks to individual employees. Upon suspicion that an employee was stealing tools, the company opened his locker in his absence and without his permission and found some missing tools. The arbitrator admitted the evidence.

2. An employee had developed a gadget for his machine which would greatly speed up production. However, he used it covertly and refused to enter it in the company's suggestion system. Knowing of the gadget the company attempted, unsuccessfully, to take it out of his personal tool box. When the employee was discharged the arbitrator held that the company could not search the tool box.

3. An employee, X, was suspected by his fellow employees of stealing their tools. They broke into his locker (which belonged to

---

[58] *Id.* at 31.
[59] Jones & Laughlin Steel Corp., 29 Lab. Arb. 778 (1957).

the company but had on it his personal lock). While this was taking place the company guard came along and found that the locker contained tools belonging to the company. X was discharged and the arbitrator allowed the evidence to be entered on the theory that the company did not break into the locker.

4. An employee was suspected of stealing inventory. Company guards went to his home when he was not there, and were permitted by the man's wife to search his house. They found evidence which resulted in his discharge. The arbitrator permitted the evidence to be entered in the record.

5. An employee, X, was opposed to the contract which his union officers had negotiated with the company, and which was about to be offered to the local for ratification. X started making notes for a speech on the floor of the meeting in opposition to the proposed contract. The foreman found the notes and attempted to get them away from X. In the process the notes were torn. X refused to give up the balance of the notes and was fired. The arbitrator reinstated him on the ground that the notes were his personal property.

None of these cases deny the right of the company to impose, as a condition of employment, an inspection of the employee's clothes and packages on entering and leaving the plant.[60] Arbitrators know that industrial pilferage is a major problem, and there is no disposition to interfere with proper rules to control it.

At common law the admissibility of evidence was not affected by the illegality of the means through which it had been obtained.[61] However, in 1914 the Supreme Court ruled that illegally obtained evidence was inadmissible in the federal courts,[62] and in a very recent decision, *Mapp v. Ohio*,[63] has ruled that all evidence obtained by searches and seizures in violation of the Constitution is inadmissible even in state courts. Since the latter decision was placed squarely on constitutional grounds it may also wipe out the "standing" requirement, which had been imposed by the lower federal courts, and which considerably diluted the impact of the 1941 decision.[64] The effect of the "standing" requirement was to impose

---

[60] See Sunbeam Corp. reports in Bus. Week, Feb. 11, 1956, p. 148; *id.* March 31, 1956, p. 167.

[61] 8 WIGMORE, EVIDENCE § 2183, at 7 (McNaughton rev. ed. 1961).

[62] Weeks v. United States, 232 U.S. 383 (1914).

[63] 367 U.S. 643 (1961).

[64] See *Comment*, 55 MICH. L. REV. 567 (1957).

on one seeking to suppress illegally obtained evidence the necessity of showing a definite interest in either the premises searched, or the property seized, or both. Unless the defendant insisted that the property belonged to him he had no standing to challenge its admission. But if he claimed the property he waived his privilege against self-incrimination.

The constitutional protection which the *Mapp* case extends against illegally obtained evidence applies to governmental rather than private acts. Conceivably there are circumstances under which a private arbitration award could be considered governmental action for purposes of invoking the constitutional protections. The more important question is whether arbitrators ought to evolve a rule against the receipt of illegally obtained evidence simply because this would contribute to the fairness and integrity of the arbitration process. Here one suspects there is a great difference between the privilege against self-incrimination, for instance, and the use of illegally obtained evidence. The difference is both theoretical and practical. The historic influences which gave rise to the self-incrimination rule have little or no relevance to arbitration. On the other hand, the fact that the modern industrial age requires most individuals to work for another, rather than for themselves, should not necessarily deprive them of historic rights with respect to private property. And on the purely practical level, management can in fact establish rules and procedures which will adequately protect its business without resorting to illegal searches. The individual is entitled to know the rules under which he is working, and these normally preclude illegal searches and seizures.

Interrogation reveals that all arbitrators agree that a company may impose reasonable rules as to the search of one's person and property where such rules are made a condition of employment. Many arbitrators would permit companies to use evidence obtained without the knowledge or consent of the employee if it is obtained from company property (e.g., a locker), even though the property is momentarily under the control of the employee. Few, if any, arbitrators think that a company ought to be permitted to use evidence obtained by breaking and entering an employee's personal property, even though the property is located on the plant premises. There is a difference of opinion among arbitrators as to the use of evidence of this type when the employee's personal property is searched without his consent, but without the necessity for entering by force.

Since all arbitrators agree that a company can, as a condition of employment, impose reasonable rules as to search of one's person and property, why should there be any other guideline for what to do about illegally obtained evidence? In the absence of a rule known to the employee, if evidence is obtained without his consent and from property under his control (even though without a breaking and entering), should it not be barred? There is no apparent handicap to the company in such a rule, and it contributes to the employee's sense of dignity. Surely human values are not to be completely ignored in the industrial context.

WIRETAPPING

Wiretapping has apparently not constituted much of a problem before arbitrators. Only one reported case had been located, and in response to an inquiry no other cases were disclosed. Nevertheless, the subject is deserving of comment, if for no other reason than its early and largely disreputable history in the field of labor-management relations. There was a time when employers' associations, Pinkerton offices, and so-called "vigilante" committees, which were hostile to labor, made widespread use of wiretapping.[65] And there have been many unfair labor practice cases before the NLRB which involved employer use of tapped wires in connection with alleged anti-union activity.[66]

There is one reported arbitration case involving the warehousing operation of the Sun Drug Co. which deals with the problem of wiretapping.[67] In that case, outsiders had complained to the company that "numbers-writing" was being carried on within the warehouse. In the course of its investigation the company installed a microphone in the telephone booth and connected it to a recording machine. After gathering incontrovertible evidence against one of its employees the company turned the evidence over to the district attorney who then carried the investigation further. Three detectives apprehended the employee as he left the telephone booth following completion of a conversation to which they had listened on the recording machine. The employee admitted writing numbers,

---

[65] *Hearings on S. 266 Before a Subcommittee of the Senate Committee on Education and Labor*, 75th Cong., 1st Sess. 1585–88 (1937).

[66] Chesapeake & Potomac Tel. Co., 98 N.L.R.B. 1122 (1952); Mid-Continent Petroleum Corp., 54 N.L.R.B. 912 (1944).

[67] Sun Drug Co., 31 Lab. Arb. 191 (1958).

and both money and slips were confiscated from him. The employee was discharged and in arbitration the union contended that the company had entrapped the individual, that placing numbers bets was common knowledge to all employees in the warehouse, that the employee accrued no profit from this activity, and that his discharge really stemmed from his activity as a shop steward rather than from writing numbers. There was a Pennsylvania statute which made number writing illegal, but there was also a statute making it a misdemeanor to intercept a communication by telephone.[68] The latter act specifically stated: "Except as proof in a suit or prosecution for a violation of this act, no evidence obtained as a result of an unlawful interception shall be admissible in any such proceeding." [69] The opinion in *Sun Drug Co.* does not indicate whether the union argued that the wiretapping evidence was inadmissible, but it does say: "Suffice it to say that while the legality of the means by which information has been gathered is for other authorities to determine, it is sufficient for the purpose of arbitration, based upon the uncontroverted facts in the instant case, for the arbitrator to sustain the discharge."[70] Thus, for all practical purposes, the evidence was received.

Although the *Sun* case had not been decided at the time arbitrators were being asked what they would do with a wiretapping case, it turned out that the hypothetical example which was used in the interrogation almost exactly paralleled that case. Arbitrators were badly split in their responses. Many said that they would not admit evidence which had been illegally obtained; others said that they would follow the law of the particular state as to admissibility; and still others pointed out that illegal methods used in securing the evidence did not impair its truth or relevancy.

In view of the dearth of arbitration experience with wiretapping, it is likely that arbitrators will look to the law for guidance in dealing with the problem. If so, they may find less help than they had expected. More than thirty years ago the Supreme Court, despite an eloquent dissent by Mr. Justice Brandeis, settled on the rule that neither the unreasonable searches and seizures provision of the fourth amendment, nor the self-incrimination provisions of the fifth amendment, were violated by the introduction of evidence

---

[68] PA. STAT. ANN. tit. 15, § 2443 (1958).
[69] *Ibid.*
[70] 31 Lab. Arb. 191, 194 (1958).

obtained by tapping wires.[71] Subsequently Congress passed the Federal Communications Act, which included the provision that "no person not being authorized by the sender shall intercept any communication and divulge or publish the existence, contents, substance, purport, effect, or meaning of such intercepted communication to any person. . . ."[72] Supreme Court decisions then established that the act applied to federal officers and forbade the introduction in federal court of intercepted messages,[73] or evidence gained thereby;[74] that intra-state messages were protected from disclosure equally with interstate communications;[75] and that the consent of one party to the conversation, secured by confronting him with recording of the conversation and by promises of leniency, was not "authorization by the sender" within the meaning of the act.[76] On the other hand the Supreme Court also held that it was not a violation of the act to use a detectaphone to overhear the words of one party to the conversation, and if this was done without a trespass it was not a search or seizure;[77] that only the participants in the conversation may object to the use of intercepted conversations since they are the only ones whose privacy has been invaded;[78] that the Federal Communications Act does not require the exclusion of wiretap evidence in the state courts;[79] and that a conversation which is overheard on a regularly used telephone extension, with the consent of the person who is both the subscriber to the extension and a party to the conversation, is admissible because it is not an "intercepted" message within the meaning of the act.[80] All of this may have been complicated, however, by two decisions of the Supreme Court more recently. In *Mapp v. Ohio*[81] the Court held for the first time that evidence obtained by searches and seizures in violation of the Constitution were constitutionally inadmissible in state courts. But at the same time, in a per curiam opinion, it upheld a lower court

---

[71] Olmstead v. United States, 277 U.S. 438 (1928).
[72] Communications Act of 1934, 48 STAT. 1104 (1934), 47 U.S.C. § 605 (1958).
[73] Nardone v. United States, 302 U.S. 379 (1937).
[74] Nardone v. United States, 308 U.S. 338 (1939).
[75] Weiss v. United States, 308 U.S. 321 (1939).
[76] *Ibid.*
[77] Goldman v. United States, 316 U.S. 129 (1942).
[78] Goldstein v. United States, 316 U.S. 114 (1942).
[79] Schwartz v. Texas, 344 U.S. 199 (1952).
[80] Rathbun v. United States, 355 U.S. 107 (1957).
[81] 367 U.S. 643 (1961).

decision denying an injunction against the use of illegally obtained wiretap evidence in a state court.[82] In point of time, the *Mapp* case was the last decided. Does this foreshadow a change in the rule with respect to the admissibility of wiretap evidence in state courts?

Many states have wiretap statutes. They vary in type from the Pennsylvania statute, under which evidence obtained as the result of unlawful interception is inadmissible,[83] to the New York constitutional provision which permits wiretapping after obtaining a warrant in accordance with the state law.[84] Some states, like New Hampshire, have no statute and admit wiretap evidence.[85]

Unless and until the Supreme Court holds the introduction of wiretap evidence inadmissible in state courts — and this decision may not be far off — an easy rule for arbitrators to follow would be to abide by the law of the state in which the case is being heard. But such a rule would not be entirely satisfactory. Multiplant companies and unions would find themselves with different rules, depending on the state in which the incident took place. Moreover, such an automatic rule would give no consideration to the differences between an employer's use of wiretap evidence to maintain production and plant discipline, and police use of wiretap evidence in criminal cases. Clearly there are some differences. An employee is on company property, and perhaps on company time. The telephone which he is using may very well be the company's. Is this not different from tapping an individual's private phone at his home or business? At least one well-known arbitrator thought so, for he said in no uncertain terms that the problems of the public prosecutor in trying to use wiretap evidence in court in no way related to the in-plant problem.

In the last analysis, one must weigh in the balance the problem of the employer in maintaining production and discipline against the privacy of the individual — even though the latter is in an industrial plant. This calls for a value judgment on which there can be legitimate differences of opinion. The facts of the case might well influence the decision. Should an employer who is harassed with in-plant gambling be denied the right to introduce in an arbitra-

---

[82] Pugach v. Dollinger, 365 U.S. 458 (1961).
[83] PA. STAT. ANN. tit. 15, § 2443 (1958).
[84] N.Y. CONST. art. I, § 12.
[85] 8 WIGMORE, EVIDENCE § 2184(b), at 57 (McNaughton rev. ed. 1957).

tion hearing evidence obtained by tapping his own telephone during working hours? On the other hand, suppose the employer gets his evidence when the police, at the employer's suggestion, tap a public telephone across the street from the plant and during the noon hour?

Wiretapping is at best a dirty business.[86] Surely it has no place in the plant under any save extraordinary circumstances. Would it not be better for arbitrators generally to discourage the use of such evidence? And at the present time can any better rule be suggested?

THE LIE DETECTOR

Prior to 1959 only one reported arbitration case has been located which involved the question of the admissibility and weight of lie detector evidence.[87] Responses from arbitrators confirm the conclusion that there were, indeed, few such cases. However, there is reason to believe that the problem is going to become more important. There were at least five reported cases in 1959,[88] and since then there has been a steady sprinkling of cases.[89] Personnel literature suggests that the polygraph is very widely used in American industry for testing prospective or present employees of banks, department stores, chain stores, etc., for honesty in previous employment, honesty during current employment, or in connection with a particular theft.[90] Massachusetts has found this practice sufficiently distasteful to pass a law forbidding an employer, under penalty of a 200-dollar fine, to require or subject any employee to a lie detector test as a condition of employment or continued employment.[91] A similar bill was under consideration in New York in the spring of 1961. A major drug manufacturer urged its defeat on the ground that polygraph tests aided in the selection of trustworthy employees — a consideration which was particularly impor-

---

[86] See generally DASH, SCHWARTZ, & KNOWLTON, THE EAVESDROPPERS (1959).

[87] Allen Indus., Inc., 26 Lab. Arb. 363 (1956).

[88] Publishers' Ass'n of New York City, 32 Lab. Arb. 44 (1959); Marathon Elec. Mfg. Corp., 31 Lab. Arb. 1040 (1959); Coronet Phosphate Co., 31 Lab. Arb. 515 (1958).

[89] See, e.g., B. F. Goodrich Tire Co., 36 Lab. Arb. 552 (1961); Brass-Craft Mfg. Co., 36 Lab. Arb. 1177 (1961).

[90] Cf. McEvoy, *The Lie Detector Goes into Business*, Readers Digest, Feb., 1941, p. 69; *Lie Detectors for Employees*, Bus. Week, Sept. 16, 1939, p. 36.

[91] MASS. ANN. LAWS c. 149, § 19-B (Supp. 1961).

tant where narcotics were involved.[92] And a consultant who specialized in pre-employment examinations for bus drivers also opposed the bill on the ground that polygraph tests helped to detect potential child molesters, on-the-job drinkers, narcotics users, and accident-prone persons.[93]

A number of the arbitration cases involving lie detectors have been discharge cases. Interestingly enough, in some of the cases the company wanted the employee to take a lie detector test or have an inference of guilt drawn against him, while in other cases the employee wanted to take a lie detector test to establish his innocence. Generally, arbitrators have attached no significance to an employee's refusal to take a test,[94] but in one case the arbitrator appeared to give it considerable weight.[95] On the question of admissibility arbitrators have tended to rule against lie detector evidence whether offered for the purpose of proving innocence or guilt.[96]

Two other cases illustrate the limited significance which lie detector tests seem to have in arbitration. In one of them[97] false productions reports had been filed under circumstances which made it impossible to pin the blame on any individual or individuals. The company therefore deducted a proportionate amount of pay from the wages of all employees in the department. The union protested that this was unfair because it penalized innocent employees. The company then sought what amounted to a declaratory judgment from the arbitrator which would permit it to insist that all of the employees take a lie detector test. Those who refused, or failed to pass the test, would then have the amount of money which had been wrongfully paid deducted from their wages. Those who passed the test would not be so charged. The arbitrator held that the employer could not impose a lie detector test wholesale, when it lacked a basis for a formal accusation against any given employee. In the other case,[98] a company was losing spark plugs from its Chicago warehouse. By 1960 losses were running as high as

[92] N.Y. Times, March 15, 1961, p. 41, col. 1.

[93] *Ibid.*

[94] Publishers' Ass'n of New York City, 32 Lab. Arb. 44, 48 (1959).

[95] Allen Indus., Inc., 26 Lab. Arb. 363 (1956).

[96] Brass-Craft Mfg. Co., 36 Lab. Arb. 1177 (1961); Marathon Elec. Mfg. Corp., 31 Lab. Arb. 1040 (1959).

[97] General Am. Transp. Corp., 31 Lab. Arb. 355 (1958).

[98] B. F. Goodrich Tire Co., 36 Lab. Arb. 552 (1961).

$50,000, and no system of prevention seemed to work. Since everything pointed to an inside job the company gave lie detector tests to all warehouse employees. The employees agreed to submit to such tests and the first round showed that three employees were lying. Two of them refused to take any further tests, while the third took the test over and again failed. The company then suspended all three for failure to cooperate with the investigation. The arbitrator held that the suspensions were unjustified since no evidence connected any of the three employees with the thefts, and their consent should not operate as a waiver in view of the "implicit social threat" of refusing.

Although the reported cases would indicate that arbitrators are tending more and more to exclude lie detector evidence, inquiry among arbitrators suggests that there are unreported cases in which arbitrators have admitted lie detector evidence but given it little weight.

In excluding lie detector evidence arbitrators have tended to cite, in support of their position, the fact that courts typically do not admit it.[99] The constitutional question of whether an individual can be required to take a lie detector test is unlikely to arise, since the art of lie detection is not at the moment sufficiently well developed to make a reliable test possible upon a person who is unwilling to submit.[100]

No experienced arbitrator harbors the illusion that he can unerringly separate truth from falsehood in proceedings before him. There is evidence that the lie detector, in competent hands, is accurate about 80 per cent of the time.[101] This may well be substantially higher than the unaided judgment of the average arbitrator. But it does not follow that the lie detector will be a constructive addition to either the grievance procedure or the arbitration tribunal. Hardly a grievance arises which does not present some form of dispute as to what was said or done on a given occasion. Did the business agent privately agree in a telephone conversation with the personnel manager that the company could make a certain promotion without having it contested by the union? When an employee called in to report his absence did he say that

---

[99] See Brass-Craft Mfg. Co., 36 Lab. Arb. 1177 (1961).

[100] Trovillo, *Scientific Proof of Credibility*, 22 TENN. L. REV. 743 (1953).

[101] Cureton, *A Consensus as to the Validity of Polygraph Procedures*, 22 TENN. L. REV. 728 (1953).

he would be out for two days or only one? In the course of negotiations did the parties discuss clause X and agree that it was to be interpreted in the same way as clause Y in a companion contract? Is the foreman or the production worker telling the truth with respect to their altercation?

Can a union live with its members if, when a grievance arises on which there is a conflict of testimony, it accepts resolution of the grievance through the lie detector? Can a company maintain morale among its supervisors if, when their reports are contradicted by employees, the company uses the lie detector to discern the truth? Suppose the business agent did tell the personnel manager that the company could make a promotion without opposition from the union, and then found that his membership felt strongly to the contrary. Does the company really want to prove that the business agent is lying?

In summary, when arbitrators deny admission to lie detector evidence, and decline to draw an inference against the employee who refused to take such a test, is not their position sound? Sound not just in the court sense that such tests are still unreliable, but in the policy sense that the lie detector has little to contribute to the arbitration procedure. If there is to be any exception would it not be wise to limit it, as have the courts,[102] to those cases where the parties have entered into an agreement and stipulation as to the use of the results?

CONCLUSION

Arbitrators have, happily, largely dispensed with the exclusionary rules of evidence developed at common law for the jury trial system. One can say that this is a happy result because, in the colorful language of Judge Traynor, "just as no one will tell the emperor that he has no clothes, there are too few who will whisper that the law of evidence has too many."[103] Even so there are situations in which evidence which may be relevant and of probative value should be excluded. Sometimes this is for constitutional reasons, and other times it is simply for reasons of policy.

Since the arbitration tribunal is private it is not likely that a con-

---

[102] See INBAU & REID, LIE DETECTION AND CRIMINAL INTERROGATION 132–35 (3d ed. 1953).

[103] Traynor, *Law and Social Change in a Democratic Society*, 1956 U. ILL. L. FORUM 234.

stitutional question of due process will arise. But this could happen, at least in theory, in either of two ways. In a proceeding to enforce an award the claim might be made that there was a denial of due process before the arbitrator. There is clear precedent for a holding that even privately constituted tribunals must accord their constituents due process. Second, it is not beyond the realm of possibility that some future court will hold, under an expanded concept of what constitutes governmental action, that the labor arbitrator is an agent of the state and as such bound by the provisions of the fifth and fourteenth amendments.

Only a few of the issues here discussed are even remotely likely to raise a question of legal due process in the constitutional sense. More often it is policy which is involved — policy from the standpoint of the arbitrator and the parties in the sense that the arbitration process will have dignity, integrity, and fairness in every respect, and policy from the standpoint of the company and the union in that the methods which are used in processing and trying grievances will contribute to the harmonious and productive relationship of the parties.

Arbitral experience in certain areas of evidence is meager. When sensitive personal rights are involved the experience of the courts may be instructive, though not necessarily binding. The attempt here has been to analyze certain problems and suggest guidelines for the future. Experience and the perspective of time and events will no doubt suggest variations.

Chapter 8

SOME CONCLUDING OBSERVATIONS

In the foregoing chapters we have reviewed the growth and development of grievance arbitration and some of its current problems. From this review two conclusions clearly emerge. One is that significant criticisms of grievance arbitration are now appearing, and they must be taken into account if the institution is to retain its usefulness and popularity. The other is that grievance arbitration is a more complex and sophisticated process than is generally recognized, and there are a great many things about it which we need to study if our understanding is to be complete.

On the mechanical side, grievance arbitration is being criticized because it is said to be too costly, too legalistic, and too time-consuming. Collateral and related problems involve the availability of new and acceptable arbitrators, "due process" and its applicability to an area of private jurisprudence, tricky problems in the handling of evidence, and the difficult question of individual rights in the grievance process. A primary difficulty in meeting these criticisms is that arbitration practices vary greatly with the parties, and reforms are therefore heavily dependent on private initiative. Nevertheless, there is sufficient commonality to justify the appointing agencies (the Federal Mediation and Conciliation Service and the American Arbitration Association) and the National Academy of Arbitrators (the professional association to which most of the active arbitrators belong) in directing concerted attention to some of the problems. Perhaps this could best be done by borrowing from the courts the idea of the judicial conference.

The Judicial Conference of the United States is charged with the statutory duty of giving advice on the needs of the circuits and upon other matters concerning the administration of justice in the courts of the United States.[1] A recently added duty is the continuous study of the federal rules of procedure. The bulk of the work of the Conference is done through committees which are composed of judges, practicing lawyers, and scholars. Appointments to the

---

[1] 28 U.S.C. § 331 (1958).

committees are made by the Chief Justice of the Supreme Court of the United States.

In addition to the Judicial Conference of the United States, there are Judicial Conferences of the Circuits. These conferences also have a statutory origin and are called annually by the chief judge of the circuit. Under the statute, provision is made for representation and active participation in the conference by members of the bar. Committees, consisting of twenty to twenty-five persons, are set up ahead of time to prepare reports and recommendations on assigned topics. A sample of the subjects recently discussed in the judicial conferences of the circuits includes: law and religion;[2] "*McNaughten, Durham,* and Psychiatry";[3] problems in lengthy trials in criminal cases;[4] and discovery in criminal cases in the federal courts.[5]

The idea of the judicial conference has been applied to the administrative agencies, though it does not yet enjoy the same permanent status.[6] The proposal for an Administrative Conference came from a Judicial Conference Committee which was created in response to a congressional plea for suggestions as to ways in which delay, both in the courts and before administrative agencies, could be reduced. The need for a conference to provide continuing suggestions to the agencies had long been recognized by persons prominent in the field. Chief Justice Warren had this to say on the subject: "Today, it is generally recognized that far too many administrative proceedings in Federal agencies are also subject to excessive and unnecessary delay. Perhaps even more discouraging in the agency proceedings is the fact that meaningful information on the state of the backlog, and the extent of the delay, *is not even available.*"[7]

Since arbitration is private in character, it is appropriate that any

---

[2] EXCERPTS FROM THE PROCEEDINGS OF THE ANNUAL JUDICIAL CONFERENCE OF THE TENTH JUDICIAL CIRCUIT OF THE UNITED STATES, 34 F.R.D. 29 (1964).

[3] Rome, McNaughten, Durham *and Psychiatry*, 34 F.R.D. 93 (1964) (presentation to the Judicial Conference of the Eighth Circuit).

[4] *The Problems of Long Criminal Trials*, 34 F.R.D. 155 (1964) (panel discussion in the Judicial Conference of the Second Circuit).

[5] *Discovery in Federal Criminal Cases*, 33 F.R.D. 47 (1963) (symposium in the Judicial Conference of the District of Columbia Circuit).

[6] 5 U.S.C.A. § 1045 et seq. (1964 supp.).

[7] Warren, Speech to the Annual Convention of the Federal Bar Ass'n, Sept. 24, 1959, in Prettyman, *The Administrative Conference of the United States*, 28 ICC PRAC. J. 1195, 1199–1200 (1961).

Arbitration Conference, patterned on the judicial model, be voluntary rather than statutory in origin. The logical group to take the initiative in starting and directing such a conference is the National Academy of Arbitrators, for its members are the counterparts of the judges who direct the judicial conferences. The immediate aid and cooperation of the Federal Mediation and Conciliation Service and the American Arbitration Association should, however, be enlisted because they are the principal appointing agencies and they have both great interest and expertise in the field.

Through the device of a continuing Arbitration Conference some of the problems which now challenge grievance arbitration could be subjected to study. As with the Judicial Conference, most of the work would be done by committees which would be composed of arbitrators, officials from the appointing agencies, experienced lawyers representing labor and management, and knowledgeable laymen from the ranks of labor and management. Considerable care would be required in the appointment of committees, and members should be chosen for the contribution which they might make rather than for geographical or organizational reasons. Some central direction would be required, particularly in exercising the initial choice of topics for committee assignment and study. This could be handled by the creation of a small executive committee, probably chaired by the president of the National Academy of Arbitrators or his representative, and composed of representatives of the appointing agencies and labor and management.

Committee reports, prepared under the auspices of the proposed Arbitration Conference, should be published. They would serve to disseminate information which is not now generally available, but which would be gathered by the committees. Such reports would also familiarize the less experienced participants with the best practices of their more experienced colleagues. Additionally, reports prepared under broadly representative auspices might persuade the parties to experiment with new procedures which seem to hold the promise of meeting current problems. To cite but one example, it is entirely possible that arbitrators would be willing in many cases to render decisions at the conclusion of the hearing and that written opinions would then be unnecessary. Such a procedure would greatly decrease the present time-lag in getting decisions. The parties presently seem to have little enthusiasm for such an idea, but if they knew more about the experience of others with it, and if it came to them with the endorsement of a broadly representative study committee, they might show more interest.

There are doubtless other and perhaps better ways in which to improve the grievance arbitration process and keep it abreast of the times. The important thing is that the problem not be neglected. Growth and changing circumstances inevitably alter institutions, and grievance arbitration is no exception to the rule. Like the small community which has suddenly become urbanized, grievance arbitration has some new problems with which it must deal. There is no immutable law which insures that arbitration will remain either useful or viable. In this connection, one is reminded of the history of workmen's compensation. The bright hope of the early years that a simple administrative agency could provide an inexpensive, expeditious, and informal procedure for litigating work injury cases has now largely faded. Two of the closest students of that subject have said: "Social legislation requires continuous revision to keep it abreast of a changing environment, and it requires administrative arrangements adequate for its purposes. Lacking these, all the virtues attributable to the original intention will not prevent its distortion or decay."[8]

Few other institutions have enjoyed such widespread growth and popularity as has grievance arbitration. It is important to all those who believe that it makes a major contribution to peaceful and democratic industrial relations that the process remain healthy. That is why the arbitrators who make up the National Academy of Arbitrators should take the lead in subjecting the area to close and continuing scrutiny. Such a step would go a long way toward insuring that defects would be studied and constructive solutions proposed.

Our conclusion that there is growing criticism of arbitration which ought to be taken into account leads to our recommendation that an Arbitration Conference be established. Our other major conclusion, that there are still a great many things about the arbitration process which we do not sufficiently understand, remains to be discussed.

---

[8] H. A. & Anne Somers, *Workmen's Compensation: Unfulfilled Promise*, 7 IND. & LAB. REL. REV. 32 (1953).

SOME POSSIBILITIES FOR RESEARCH

On the surface, grievance arbitration seems to be a simple, rational way of resolving differences over the meaning and interpretation of a collective bargaining contract. The model is uncomplicated. When controversies arise, the parties first attempt, in the course of a three- or four-step grievance procedure, to settle their own disputes. If they fail, provision is made for third-party determination through arbitration.

The trouble with this explanation, like most other over-simplifications, is that it leaves out a good deal more than it tells. For one thing, the moment arbitration was institutionalized it began to change in character. For another, industrial strife is not entirely issue-oriented. The strike, for instance, is an over-manifestation of industrial strife. A contractual no-strike clause may be, as the Supreme Court once said, the *quid pro quo* for the arbitration clause. But a strike is more than a test of strength over a particular issue. It is also a release from the humdrum existence of everyday industrial life, a proving ground for union leaders, a moment of excitement, glory, and perhaps of disillusionment in a battle against an opponent who usually holds the upper hand, a sharing of hardship which may weld the union together, and a high-level poker game in which plays and counterplays are expected. A strike substitute, if it is to be a genuine substitute, must therefore do more than resolve the issue in dispute; it must also accommodate some of the social and psychological pressures which are associated with industrial strife. If one analyzes grievance arbitration with this in mind, it becomes much more understandable. It also becomes much more complex!

Before arbitration clauses were widely adopted, the parties sometimes made last-minute decisions to arbitrate particularly serious issues then pending. But the decisions were made at the summit and in the context of less desirable alternatives which were plainly visible. The machinery was not readily available, the parties were not familiar with its use, and the process was surrounded by unknowns. Once the contract provides for arbitration as the terminal point in the grievance procedure, this situation changes. Then the parties know from the outset that arbitration will be available to settle contractual disputes. They know what the procedure will be, and, after a bit, they are familiar with the strategic opportunities which are inherent in the process. In addition, they must find ways and means of transferring some of the sounds and symbols of industrial strife to the new arena. *In toto* grievance arbitration thus becomes much more than a device for the adjudication of disputes.

How the contractual arbitration machinery will be used depends a great deal, of course, on the nature of the existing relationship. If it has been very harmonious, the probability is that grievances which go to arbitration will be rare. If it has been characterized by a good deal of tension, there may be many grievances and many arbitrations. In the area in between the variations will be infinite. In any event, numerous decisions which labor and management representatives make with respect to whether or not to take a given grievance to arbitration have little or nothing to do with the merits of the grievance. Students of industrial relations know, for instance, that it is very common for grievances slated to go to arbitration to multiply about the time contract negotiations occur. In many cases this is because the union has made a studied decision to stir up grievances as part of the process of getting the membership aroused and interested in the terms of the new contract, and in order to take a militant stance before management. Sometimes the same phenomenon takes place when there is a fight for the leadership of the local union. The incumbents must show diligence in looking after the membership, and one way to do this is to file grievances without respect to their ultimate merits.

How carefully the union should screen grievances which go to arbitration is part of the same problem, but it also has other implications. There are inopportune moments in which to tell an active member that his grievance is without merit, and the period of a union election campaign is one of those times. An appointed business agent is likely to exercise more discretion in eliminating or settling grievances than is one who is elected and whose re-election is pending. Apart from the politics of the situation, sometimes the decision which must be made is simply distasteful, and the union officer prefers to let someone else shoulder the burden of delivering the bad news.

Other questions arise as to the appropriate prerequisites of office for union stewards and committeemen who serve on a day-to-day basis. There are ceremonial aspects of the arbitration machinery which may, in a sense, reward such officials for services rendered. A tight or lenient attitude toward the necessity for a visit on the part of the local committee to international headquarters may be taken. Many, or few, representatives may be present at the actual arbitration hearing (partly depending on whether the company or the union is paying for their lost wages). Arguably some non-meritorious grievances should be allowed to go to arbitration just to let the local committeemen gain some experience against the day when their participation in an important case will pay off.

In the actual hearing, the union representative has to decide how important it is to him that his constituents, who may be present, get the impression that the union will take no nonsense from the company. Some table-pounding may be in order so that the union's militancy cannot be mistaken. Gains in collective bargaining are not always the result of the application of sweet reason, and, if part of the function of arbitration is to release pressures inherent in collective bargaining, it may have to be accompanied by some of the same sounds and symbols.

Company officials are likewise faced with some new problems once arbitration is provided by contract. One strategy for dealing with an extremely militant union which seems to be bent on filing frivolous grievances is to allow most of them to go to arbitration on the theory that the company will win the great bulk of the cases and the expense will be more onerous for the union than for the company. If the relationship is very cordial, the company may go out of its way to settle grievances rather than run the risk that an outsider will award the union what the company has appeared unwilling to grant.

A sophisticated management knows that if arbitrations are at all frequent, as they may be in a large system, it cannot win all the cases and expect the system to remain acceptable to the union rank-and-file. It must therefore decide how carefully to screen the grievances which it allows to go to arbitration. To put it baldly, how many cases must it lose if the system is to remain viable, and to what extent can it choose the cases which it expects to lose? (One highly placed union official told us that in his experience management should win about 70 per cent of the cases. If it did not, there was something wrong with management. If it won more than that, the union might have difficulty in persuading the membership that the system was desirable. Thus one management counterpart called him to say that he had observed that the company was winning the bulk of their umpire decisions, and to ask if it would be helpful to the union if the company allowed some sure losers to go to the umpire. An affirmative answer was given to this question, though the union official said that he would not have called the company to ask that it do this.)

The availability of arbitration also has implications for management decision-making. Corporations are not completely monolithic, and there may be quite different views as to the best and most productive way to conduct the company's business. Sometimes this takes the form of a clash between the industrial relations people and the production people. From the standpoint of the former, the union view of a particular grievance may be not only understandable, but correct. To the production people such a view may seem outrageous. Depending on the influence which each group has within the corporation, the case may be allowed to go to arbitration to settle what is essentially a split within the management ranks. This kind of situation is often found in the area of work practices, where the production people are anxious to get rid of what they consider to be restrictive rules, and the industrial relations people are confident that this cannot be done successfully in arbitration.

Finally, there is evidence that both unions and companies are using some of the more stable umpire systems to help them over difficult areas in which the answers are unclear to both sides. Within limits, the umpire may come to know more about particular kinds of problems than do the parties, simply because he sees them repeatedly in different contexts. Thus the contract may be deliberately left vague with the idea that the umpire will have the problem of finding the most desirable route out of the difficulty. The parties' confidence in the judgment of the umpire is often very great. If the relationship between the parties is good, in such a situation they will be confident that they can negotiate out of a decision which seems wholly unworkable.

It is clear, then, that one who views arbitration as a mechanism which exists separate and apart from the balance of the labor-management relationship is in error. On the contrary, there is a constant interaction with collective bargaining, the internal needs of the union and management, and the strategies of ever-changing leaders on both sides who feel they must fit their conduct and attitudes toward arbitration into a bigger picture.

Much of the research on the subject of grievance arbitration has been done by economists and lawyers. This is not surprising since most of the academicians who are knowledgeable in the field come from those disciplines. Some of the problems will receive adequate treatment, however, only when the skills of the political scientist, the sociologist, and the psychologist are mobilized.

Perhaps it is worthwhile to enumerate some of the questions which could usefully be explored. The list does not pretend to be comprehensive, but is ranged widely over the area. Included are the following items:

1. *What accounts for the difference in the way in which grievances are screened, and what is the significance of this?*

Some of the considerations which might influence companies and unions in the screening of grievances have already been mentioned. There are many others. We know, for instance, that some international unions exercise a fairly strong central control over the processing of grievances, and others make almost no effort to influence the handling of local grievances. What are the philosophical and practical reasons for the difference, and what accompanying side effects are there?

One might logically anticipate that grievance screening would be issue-oriented. The consequences of discharge are so serious that a union might wish to arbitrate any discharge case in which there was the slightest chance of success. Two hours of work on a higher-rated job for which only the lower rate was paid might, on the other hand, not seem to be worth the cost of arbitration. If one examined the mass of grievances in any given company-union relationship, would the grievances which were taken to arbitration follow along predictable lines associated with the nature of the grievance, or would this turn out to be largely irrelevant?

We know very little about the way in which local unions decide which grievances they will take to arbitration. Membership meetings often authorize arbitration, but what does this mean in practice? When union leaders plan their strategy with respect to submitting the question of whether a given grievance shall go to arbitration to the membership, how does this fit into their varying concepts of leadership?

We know that bargaining strategy, internal union politics, personal animosities, and other extraneous factors often determine which issues unions will take to arbitration. What we don't know is the extent to which this influences the effectiveness of the arbitration machinery. Arguably any given arbitrator would be unlikely to serve frequently in a situation characterized by a large number of grievances submitted for reasons foreign to their merits.

There are sometimes strong feelings on the subject of the submission of single versus multiple grievances. Some companies and unions clearly think that arbitrators are prone to compromise and that multiple grievances give them an opportunity to do so. This might suggest to the parties that "good" and "bad" grievances be bracketed in order to give the arbitrator the anticipated opportunity to rule partly for each of the parties. How frequently do the parties try to do this, and with what success? Can both labor and management play the game at the same time?

We know that companies sometimes use the arbitration machinery for extraneous reasons, but we know little about how often this is done, or to what extent it proves useful in resolving collateral problems. Some companies believe that it is better to back a supervisor who is probably wrong in his decision than to reverse him and undermine his authority with the workers. Others follow exactly the opposite strategy. Is it possible to document the validity of either of those approaches? More broadly, what is the impact of the reversal of a managerial decision in arbitration, and how is it handled by different companies? Multiplant corporate executives are sometimes known to believe that there is educational and strategic value in letting local plant officials be reversed in arbitration rather than by their corporate superiors. Is there any firm basis for such a conclusion, or does it simply represent the judgment of occasional executives? Are there occasions on which there is prestige value in getting an arbitrator's decision in support of company action, and, if this is so, what accounts for the existence of the prestige? Is it based on knowledge, or is it something about the psychology of nonpartisan decision-making?

Within umpire systems, company executives charged with arbitration responsibilities are often acutely aware of the box-score problem, i.e., the number of cases being won by the union. If the union is winning too many, it reflects on either the management personnel who are preparing and arguing the cases, or on the executive who is insisting that the cases be submitted to outside decision. If the union is winning too few the system may be in jeopardy. Very little is known about the nature of internal management discussions of this subject, or about the kinds of remedial action which may be taken. Insofar as the remedy may be to allow selected cases to go to arbitration which are "certain" to be lost, it would be interesting to know the outcome of such cases, whether they are readily identified by the union, and whether they do in fact serve the purpose.

2. *How do the parties go about choosing arbitrators?*

If cost factors are really relevant in grievance arbitration, local arbitrators ought to be more attractive than those who come from a distance. And if local attitudes are important to the decision, it might be better to have a local arbitrator who would be familiar with the problem. Lack of confidence in any local arbitrator might result in preference for someone else even at greater expense. Obviously the parties may weigh various considerations in making their choice. Are there general rules which may be said to govern the choice which will be made, and if so what are they? Is the cost factor really as important as some of the criticisms would suggest, or is the cost problem accentuated because the parties are unwilling to utilize local arbitrators?

Experienced arbitrators come from many disciplines, and most, but not all, have other jobs. On the face of it certain issues might more logically be resolved by a man trained as an economist than by a lawyer or an engineer. Is there any disposition on the part of labor and management to follow this line of reasoning in choosing an arbitrator? If the arbitrator comes from the academic world, are the parties much concerned with his affiliation within the university, i.e., does it make any difference that he is affiliated with a business school or a labor education program?

There are relatively few full-time arbitrators, while there are a great many part-time arbitrators. Those who arbitrate full-time will almost certainly be more experienced but it can also be argued that they have a greater stake in continued acceptance, and may therefore be more inclined to compromise. Is the part-time versus full-time dimension a significant factor in the choice of arbitrators or is it largely irrelevant?

In politics we know that more industry support is likely to be found behind the Republican than the Democratic party, and that the reverse is true of labor. Sometimes the political affiliation of an arbitrator is fairly well known, while in other instances it is not public information. In either event is this ever a factor involved in the choice of an arbitrator, and if so, why?

Arbitrators from the academic world often write on the subject the arbitration. Is this a factor of any importance in influencing the judgment of the parties? There is some evidence that counsel peruse published decisions before choosing arbitrators and that they sometimes make choices based on decisions in other cases. The effect of other writings could be simply to increase the reputation of the author and make him better known to the parties, or it could be to expose his views in a particular kind of case. It could also be that the parties are almost entirely unaware of what, if anything, he has written.

Some international unions give advice to locals on the choice of arbitrators, and on the management side manufacturers' associations, chambers of commerce, and private organizations often furnish information about arbitrators. The simplest criterion consists of a box-score which shows how many cases the arbitrator decided for the union and how many he decided for the company. Almost any experienced observer could agree that this is a wholly unrealistic way to provide a meaningful analysis. The more sophisticated analysts must go further. How do they attempt to do this, and what can one say about the judgments or expressions of preference which result? Are there certain key issues, such as the management prerogative, which are used in rating arbitrators? If so, would a more thorough analysis of that particular arbitrator's views bear out the conclusions advanced as to his capabilities?

Where the parties rely on lawyers to represent them in arbitrations, are the lawyers playing a decisive role in the choice of arbitrators, or do they prefer not to be involved on the ground that a loss before an arbitrator whom they had helped to choose would impair their standing with the client? When lawyers do influence the choice of an arbitrator, on what factors do they rely in making a judgment? Are they more likely to judge solely on the basis of published decisions, or do they also subscribe to services which purport to rate arbitrators?

The parties are notoriously reluctant to use new and inexperienced arbitrators despite the growing case load. It would be interesting to know to what extent this represents normal human reluctance to utilize new and unknown as against old and familiar faces. Some of our experiments suggest that routine cases will be decided the same way by either experienced or inexperienced arbitrators. Is it possible not only to identify reasons which the parties give for their unwillingness to try new arbitrators, but to test the rationality of these reasons?

3. *To what extent do the parties believe that the outcome of cases is predictable?*

Factors other than merit admittedly influence both companies and unions in deciding whether to take certain grievances to arbitration, but it is fair to assume that in the majority of cases the probable outcome is an important consideration in making that decision. On the union side, officers could base rationalizations for different decisions on whether to undertake the expense of an arbitration on the importance of the issues. A discharge might, for instance, always be worthy of arbitration provided there was the slightest chance of victory. Holiday pay for a single individual in a factual context which seemed to be without precedential value might not be worth the cost of arbitration even though the odds on winning were high. In any such situations there is an implicit assumption that the union can, with some degree of accuracy, predict the outcome of a case. Nevertheless, we know very little about the assumptions on which such judgments rest. Is predictability closely related to the use of a particular arbitrator, or is the issue more important? Similar questions could be asked with respect to companies.

If both companies and unions feel that the outcome of most cases is reasonably predictable, is this conclusion based on the fact that there is an identifiable body of "common law" which now guides decisions, or are other reasons more important?

Many arbitrators say that by the end of the hearing they have reached a tentative conclusion as to the probable outcome of the case, and that the record and briefs tend more to corroborate than change this view. Does the hearing have a similar effect on the parties so that they too have a fairly firm feeling by the end of the hearing as to the outcome of the case? If so, is this because hearing the other side's presentation has clarified the issue, because questions from the arbitrator have suggested his line of thinking, or because the hearing simply tended to confirm what was already known? If the arbitrator's questions do reveal his line of thinking, is this helpful in preparing parties for the ultimate decision?

If the parties often believe, as do arbitrators, that the decision is fairly clear by the conclusion of the hearing, what reservations do they have to "bench" decisions rendered without further study of the case? Would the image of arbitration be impaired if immediate decisions were rendered? Is it important that the parties, though reasonably aware of the probable decision, have some time to adjust to it before the award is actually announced?

4. *To what extent do management personnel and employees understand the arbitration process, and of what significance is this?*

A relatively specialized group of people from management and the unions deal directly with the arbitration process. Among the general public, terms like "arbitration," "conciliation," and "mediation" are often used interchangeably; therefore, it would be logical to suppose that this same thing might be true within the plant unless companies and unions make special efforts to educate their members. Do they do this, or is it true that most management people and most of the employees are not well informed on the real nature of arbitration? How important is it to the specialists on either side that their colleagues understand the arbitration process and all that it implies? If it is important, how do they insure that there is some degree of understanding of their work?

If one constructed an attitude survey on the subject of arbitration, and administered it to such diverse management groups as accountants, production personnel, sales people, and personnel executives, what would the results be? Are those removed from immediate contact with it more or less cynical toward third-party decision-making? In any event, what is the source of information which shapes the view of management people who have no immediate contact with their own labor relations problems?

Production supervisors and executives usually feel the most direct impact of contractual restrictions imposed by the collective bargaining agreement. What determines whether they view the grievance procedure and arbitration as a form of harassment or a chance to explain their views and to gain support for them? Is the possibility of reversal a source of serious concern to the supervisor, and if so, how does he hedge against it?

Since most arbitrators are professional people it would not be surprising if employees regarded them as either management-oriented, or in any event unfamiliar with the problems of workers. Is this a typical view, and if not, what has occasioned a different outlook? Do workers understand that it is the function of the arbitrator to interpret the contract, or do they believe it is his duty to reach a "just" solution, perhaps based upon hardship or inequity?

There are many reasons why arbitration might appeal to company and union specialists though it would not have a similar appeal to their constituents. Is this true, or does the widespread contractual acceptance of arbitration reflect a broad consensus, even among those who are removed from it, on the value of the process? Is it of any real importance whether this is true or not?

5. *To what extent have decisions from the United States Supreme Court expanding the role of arbitrators influenced the view of labor and management toward grievance arbitration?*

Many surveys on this subject have been made, and at least one is reported at some length.[9] Nevertheless, court decisions continue to expand the arbitrator's role, and as one result, a bill has been introduced in Congress to change the court's decision as to the respective roles of courts and arbitrators with respect to arbitrability.[10]

How widely are the court's decisions known, let alone understood, among labor and management people? Is this a debate among lawyers who represent them? Preliminary surveys suggest that contractual efforts to circumvent the decisions are minor. Does this continue to be the case, or is experience with arbitrators' decisions bringing about a change in view? Is there a correlation between management and labor's view of the decisions and their own utilization of an *ad hoc* or umpire system of arbitration?

Carey v. Westinghouse Elec. Corp. opened the door to arbitration of disputes involving a single union and the employer even when a second union might be affected by the decision.[11] At least one arbitrator has developed the interpleader device to involve the second union so that a final decision can be reached.[12] What is happening in other similar cases? Is the interpleader becoming established, or are other ways being found to resolve the problem?

In view of *Atkinson v. Sinclair Refining Co.*,[13] will the Supreme

---

[9] Smith, *The Question of "Arbitrability" — The Roles of the Arbitrator, the Court, and the Parties*, 16 Sw. L.J. 1 (1962).

[10] H.R. 12127, 88th Cong., 2d Sess. (1964).

[11] 375 U.S. 261 (1964).

[12] E. Jones, *An Arbitral Answer to a Judicial Dilemma: The Carey Decision and Trilateral Arbitration of Jurisdictional Disputes*, 11 U.C.L.A.L. REV. 327 (1964); E. Jones, *Autobiography of a Decision: The Function of Innovation in Labor Arbitration, and the* National Steel *Orders of Joinder and Interpleader*, 10 U.C.L.A.L. REV. 987 (1963).

[13] 370 U.S. 238 (1962).

Court tolerate the enforcement of arbitral awards against the violation of no-strike clauses? If so, will unions be more reluctant to include such clauses in contracts and will this, in turn, affect management's attitude toward arbitration? Do union members, who often have bitter reactions to the use of court injunctions, react similarly to what amounts to the same thing at the hands of arbitrators?

6. *Can a solution be found to the difficult problem of individual rights in arbitration?*

There is a possibility that the National Labor Relations Board will shortly hold that it is unfair labor practice for a union to refuse unfairly to process a grievance through arbitration. Will the possibility of such a ruling encourage unions to take more cases to arbitration in order to avoid any claim of unfairness? If so, will union losses in arbitration increase, and will this cause disenchantment with resort to arbitration?

There are collective bargaining contracts which authorize individual grievances in arbitration. Little is known about the experience under such contracts. It might, if studied, reveal that most of the fears about the number of grievances which would go to arbitration are groundless. It would also throw light on the mechanics of such a system, i.e., the choice of an arbitrator, allocations of costs, and other problems. We do not now know whether the fact that such contract clauses are not widespread is due to disinterest, knowledge of adverse experience where they have been used, opposition in principle, fear of disruptive consequences, or indifference.

Court remedies for the individual are continually being tested. One of the supposed problems in utilizing the courts is that the cost factor is a deterrent to the individual. There is little documentation for this point, and it may be that cost is not as important a factor as one might suppose.

Many of the Western European labor courts provide a means whereby the individual may test his claim in court. This suggests the possibility that even in the absence of labor courts a similar right before the civil courts could be developed in this country without impairing the collective relationship. Would it help to know more about the foreign experience in this connection?

The composition of the American labor force is changing. If unions are to maintain their strength they must successfully organize white-collar workers. The latter may, because of educational qualifications and a traditional reluctance to adopt completely the collective tactics of the union, prefer greater individual rights in the grievance procedure. Is there anything in the experience of present white-collar unions which is instructive in this connection?

There are obvious reasons why both the company and the union may prefer a grievance system which gives the union power to settle individual grievances. The incentives which might persuade them that it is desirable to permit individuals to carry complaints to arbitration are not so obvious. If one assumes that such a policy is desirable, how can attractive incentives be developed?

7. *Why is the arbitration of production standards so controversial?*

In industries like clothing and shoes, production standards are commonly arbitrated. In the auto industry they are not. During contract negotiations in the late summer of 1964 the Ford Motor Company stated that it had lost 7½ million man-hours in ten strikes over production standards, health and safety issues, and new job rates, which the union had the legal right to conduct under the 1961 contract. Yet Ford did not wish to deprive the union of the right to strike over these issues.[14] Why? Do clothing and shoe manufacturers readily submit to arbitration of production standards because it is easy for them to avoid an onerous rate by changing styles and patterns? Or is it because they have a different attitude toward the capabilities of arbitrators in such a sensitive area?

Among unions, some are quite willing to arbitrate production standards while others are vigorously opposed. Can this difference in attitude be attributed in any sense to a conclusion on the part of some unions that it is desirable to maintain a legal outlet for tensions which might otherwise cause illegal strikes? In this connection, is it true, as management sometimes charges, that legal strikes are in fact often motivated by disputes over other issues which are subject to arbitration, but which the union is unwilling to submit to a third-party decision?

It is a well-known fact that many arbitrators do not like to handle cases involving production standards. It is not nearly so clear whether this is because they feel incompetent in the face of technical problems, whether they believe the parties fail to present adequate infor-

---

[14] BNA REPORT No. 500, WHAT'S NEW IN COLLECTIVE BARGAINING NEGOTIATIONS AND CONTRACTS 4 (July 31, 1964).

mation on which a judgment can be based, or whether they reject the alleged scientific base for such systems. It would be interesting to know to what extent the reasoning behind the reluctance of arbitrators to handle production standard cases parallels the reasoning used by the union and management people in withholding such cases.

Tripartite arbitration boards, which include partisan members, can be useful in technical cases to insure that the neutral member reaches a viable conclusion. Theoretically, such boards should be especially useful in production standards cases. Does experience prove this to be true, or do those companies and unions which are willing to arbitrate production standards find that results are just as satisfactory where a single neutral arbitrator is used? If tripartite boards are more effective is this because solutions are actually bargained within the board, or because the advice of the partisan members is particularly helpful?

8. *What functions do arbitration opinions serve, other than to decide the case, and how widely are they communicated within the ranks of the company and the union?*

There is no doubt that company disciplinary practices are affected by past awards, or that both companies and unions seek to utilize lines of reasoning suggested by arbitrators in previous decisions. Little is known, however, about how companies and unions go about briefing their own people on the results of decisions. Management is better organized for the purpose, but it has many choices as to how best to make the content of decisions known to its own people and how widely to disseminate the information within the company. Do companies find it valuable to reproduce the opinion and distribute it widely, do they prepare a synopsis with or without an explanation, do they hold briefing sessions, do they comment on the award as it is distributed, or do they do little or nothing about it? Is what they do a function of the size and past experience of the company? As the result of certain decisions do management executives sometimes set up test cases to resolve an ambiguity in a past decision?

Unions are not as well organized to distribute arbitral opinions as are companies, nor do they have the initial responsibility for seeing that the intent of an award is respected in the future. Once an award is received it could be read at the next membership meeting (which would probably be poorly attended), copies could be made available to stewards, or the result simply communicated by word of mouth. How important do union officers believe it is for the membership to know the line of an arbitrator's reasoning? Does the grievant himself even want to read the award in the normal case, or does he just want to know the outcome? Is the opinion much more valuable to the company than the union because it is the company which must take the initiative in administering the contract?

There are services which publish arbitration awards, but some companies and unions do not permit their awards to be published. One wonders whether there is any consistent reason why companies and unions take this position. Is it because they do not wish internal plant business made public, is it because they believe (rightly or wrongly) that the precedent value of the award is reduced if it is not published, is it because they believe published opinions do not serve a useful purpose, or is it for some other reason?

9. *What happens in the course of implementing arbitration decisions?*

As a result of arbitration decisions discharged employees are reinstated, overlooked senior employees are promoted, unions are enjoined from striking, the company's right to subcontract is restricted, and a host of other changes are made. Once the decision is transmitted to the parties the arbitrator rarely knows what happens. There have been a few studies of reinstated employees, industrial discipline, and seniority cases,[15] but the information on what happens after decisions are rendered is still meager. Occasional situations come to light in which the parties have, by mutual agreement, rejected the award and negotiated a more satisfactory solution, or even resubmitted the issue to another arbitrator!

Subcontracting cases would be particularly useful to follow up. If a decision restricts the company's right to subcontract, how does it attempt to minimize the effect of the decision? In subsequent negotiations is the contract changed? Are ways found to reduce costs within the existing framework? Does the company move the plant, or a part of it? How often, in other words, does an adverse decision simply mean that the company seeks another way to accomplish the same end? If the purpose of the subcontracting is cost reduction,

---

[15] D. JONES, ARBITRATION AND INDUSTRIAL DISCIPLINE (1961); Ross, *The Arbitration of Discharge Cases: What Happens After Reinstatement,* in CRITICAL ISSUES IN LABOR ARBITRATION, PROCEEDINGS OF THE 10TH ANNUAL MEETING OF THE NATIONAL ACADEMY OF ARBITRATORS 21 (McKelvey ed. 1957).

unions might, under continuing pressure, change their views. Does this happen in some of the cases? Strikes could easily result at the time of contract negotiations in an attempt to change the result of an arbitrator's decision on subcontracting. Or the company's right to subcontract might be reinforced by a new contract provision. Does this in fact happen in many cases? The new Alcoa and Reynolds Aluminum contracts reject the U.S. Steel pattern of submitting sub-contracting disputes to arbitration and make it a strike issue.[16] By the end of the present contract periods which method will prove to be the more satisfactory to the companies and the unions?

Apart from the subcontracting cases, there are unquestionably cases in which management finds it possible to circumvent the decision by changing a method of operation or using some new method. With what frequency does this occur? There are also said to be occasional cases in which a company simply declines to put an award into effect and the union makes no effort to get court enforcement. Is this a rare and unusual occurrence of no general interest?

Many arbitration decisions involve matters of interest to the parties, but do not touch especially sensitive nerves. Would it be fair to say that most decisions are not critical, and that the tolerance of the parties for *any* decision is rather high? Is this especially true where the parties do not make a serious effort to settle grievances short of arbitration, or is exactly the reverse true?

Back pay is often awarded in discharge cases. Unemployment compensation may have been paid to the individual in question. Different states take different attitudes toward reclaiming unemployment compensation in this situation. What is the going practice among labor and management people, insofar as their attitude toward the deduction of unemployment compensation is concerned? Where back pay is onerous do the parties sometimes negotiate a different solution?

10. *Why do the parties often delay so long in bringing cases to arbitration, and what effect does this have on the value of the process?*

Despite frequent complaints about delays in getting arbitration decisions, the statistics show that the parties bear a major share of the responsibility for the lapse of time in bringing the case to arbitration. Is this because there is not as much interest in expeditious

---

[16] BNA REPORT No. 475, WHAT'S NEW IN COLLECTIVE BARGAINING NEGOTIATIONS AND CONTRACTS 4 (Aug. 16, 1963).

decisions as the sound and fury would indicate? Is it because the internal machinery of the company and/or the union has become overburdened or creaky? Do the parties think that delay will wash out difficult cases? Are more delicate issues arising about which the parties are sensitive and for which they hope to find solutions short of arbitration?

Delay in bringing cases to arbitration accentuates the back pay issue. It also suggests that arbitrators may demonstrate little consistency in the amount of back pay which is allowed in connection with reinstatements for various kinds of offenses. How important is the issue of back pay to the parties in scheduling cases?

If arbitration reduces industrial strife, it ought to follow that machinery which is continually clogged or long delayed would lose some of its effectiveness. Does this happen, or do workers become accustomed to the delay?

Can the suspicion that there is an increased use of lawyers be documented, and if so does this have anything to do with delay — either because their schedules must be accommodated, or because they are resorting to delaying tactics?

When unions rely upon personnel from central union headquarters to handle arbitration cases for them, hearings are often delayed until a date can be found on which such a person can be present. Some efforts have been made to devise educational programs which would prepare local officers to handle their own cases. Can anything be said about the success or failure of such programs, and if they have failed could better programs be devised?

11. *What are the conditions of survival for a "permanent" umpire?*

Certain companies and unions utilize so-called "permanent" umpires to handle all their arbitration cases. In some cases an individual serves indefinitely, while in others he is likely to last not more than a year. What accounts for the difference in tenure? Is permanence at all associated with the kind of cases an arbitrator must hear, e.g., is it easier for an auto umpire, who does not have to hear production standards cases, to survive than for his counterpart in the clothing industry? Are certain industries tension-prone, while others are inherently stable? Does the role which the arbitrator is expected to play, i.e., pure adjudicator or adjudicator-mediator, have anything to do with his longevity?

Company and union specialists in arbitration are close to the scene and may therefore have great appreciation of the difficulties which the umpire faces. Does this mean that they are likely to be more sympathetic to him than are their colleagues who are more removed from the scene?

In a multiplant system single umpires often serve all the plants and central personnel argue all cases. Does this widen the gap which may already exist between central and local officials within the union and the company, or does it narrow it? Do local plant managers feel as well satisfied with the umpire system as do the central personnel who work closely with it? Would substantial differences in attitude toward the system be found among local and central people on both sides?

Almost inevitably permanent umpires get to know the representatives of the parties fairly well over a period of time. Informal hints or casual advice outside the framework of the hearing could play an important role in influencing pending decisions. Does this happen, and if so, does it contribute to the permanence of the umpire or to his quick departure?

A militant union which forces a large number of issues to arbitration could end up losing a disproportionate share of them. Does this mean that umpires rarely survive long in such surroundings? Or are there other factors, e.g., the presence of volatile ethnic groups in the work force, which are more influential in determining the stability of the system?

12. *To what extent do the parties rate arbitrators on the basis of factors other than the outcome of cases brought before them?*

As we mentioned earlier, a survey of lawyers' clients recently showed that success or failure in pleading the case was not always particularly important in determining the client's view of his lawyers.[17] Could the same be said of arbitrators? How important are such factors as personal warmth, perceptive questions at the hearing, apparent sympathy and understanding for the problem of the parties, personal dignity, the ability to write clear decisions, integrity, a well-known name, and knowledge of industrial relations issues? Is it possible that negative factors, such as arrogance, lack of consideration for the parties, inept conduct of the hearing, cupidity, social views outside the labor-management area, and the imposition of unduly restrictive rules, are more important than positive factors?

13. *What constitutes good decision-writing in arbitration cases?*

---

[17] Richter, *What the Layman Thinks of Lawyers: A Survey Report,* 9 STUDENT LAW. J. 8 (1964).

Individual arbitrators will naturally write decisions differently. Nevertheless, one would suppose that there might be hallmarks of good decisions. This could depend on the use which the parties make of the decisions. If the decisions become a part of the common law of the plant, a premium must be placed on clarity.

The criticisms which are most often heard of opinions revolve around the inclusion of gratuitous advice, the resort to a line of reasoning which the parties have not argued, and reliance upon implied clauses which one or both parties may feel was not intended.

The format of some arbitrators' decisions includes an outline of the arguments of the parties, while other arbitrators omit such arguments completely. It is arguable that to outline the arguments runs the risk of misstating a position, while to ignore them is to leave the parties in doubt as to what was influential.

Latin phrases have a way of creeping into the awards of lawyer-arbitrators. Does this cause any reaction, favorable or unfavorable, among company and union people? Is it best to use the simplest possible language, or is one writing for the experts anyway?

When the complaint is made that arbitrators' decisions are too long, is this because they include irrelevant material, and, if so, what is irrelevant material? Is there such a thing as too brief a decision? Are there times when it is better for an arbitrator to decide a case without giving any reasons? In what sort of situation would this be true?

14. *Under what circumstances are tripartite arbitration boards effective?*

Many agreements call for the use of tripartite boards of arbitration. Typically, the labor and management representatives on the board do not purport to be unbiased. In Europe the tradition is to the contrary. Labor and management appointees commonly sit on labor courts, but they are expected to view the issue impartially. How is it that these completely different traditions have developed? Would an effort in the United States to change the prevailing view be of use? Is the only purpose of a tripartite board to give the neutral member guidance so that he does not come up with an impossible solution?

When tripartite boards are used, a common procedure is for the neutral member to draft a decision and then meet with his colleagues for discussion of the award. This tends to put the arbitrator on the defensive in the discussions and to make it less likely that a result different from his first conclusions will ensue than if the board met for a free-wheeling discussion in the absence of a draft opinion. What are the respective merits, in the eyes of the parties, of the two different methods of procedure?

If the only purpose of partisan board members is to guard against careless language or reasoning on the part of the neutral member, would it be better to nominate advisors from each of the parties who would look over decisions in advance?

Among arbitrators is there any sentiment in favor of tripartite boards, and if so, in what kinds of cases?

15. *In view of the need for more arbitrators who are acceptable to the parties, is it possible to identify individuals who will make good arbitrators?*

As the case load grows there is a need for more arbitrators who will be acceptable to the parties. There is not necessarily any lack of individuals who would be willing to arbitrate, for in academic and professional circles there are many individuals who would be happy to render such a service. Experience shows, however, that some individuals never do become successful arbitrators while others, who lack any common background or training to identify them, succeed. Aptitudes in other areas are increasingly evaluated. Is it possible to tell which individuals will make successful arbitrators, and, if so, what are the dominant characteristics which can be identified? Is there such a thing as a "judicial temperament" and, if there is, how does one identify it? Is intelligence a key factor? The ability to reason logically? Or must one conclude that trial and error, based on common-sense selectivity, is still the best basis for predicting success?

A collateral inquiry, almost wholly unexplored to date, is the difference in self-image which the successful arbitrator may have as opposed to the reasons which his clients give for his success.

CONCLUSIONS

The strength of the grievance arbitration process is that it provides an extremely flexible and democratic system for resolving disputes over the meaning and interpretation of the collective bargaining agreement. But it must function in a rapidly changing social order, and it is unlikely to remain viable unless careful attention is given to the resolution of emerging problems. Some of these problems have been examined in earlier chapters of this book. Others will come to the fore in the days ahead. What is needed is a mechanism which will enable labor, management, and professional arbitrators to examine existing practices jointly and make proposals for improvement. It is here suggested that the way to do this is to establish an Arbitration Conference, patterned after the Judicial Conferences of the federal courts. Tripartite participation in such a conference would give any studies which it might make a greater air of reality, and would also make subsequent reports more acceptable.

On the research side, there are still many facets of the arbitration process which are not well understood. Grievance arbitration is not, and cannot be, a simple adjudicative system, isolated from the collective bargaining postures and attitudes of the parties. Some of the areas in which fruitful research might be undertaken are suggested herein. Others readily suggest themselves. Research inquiries, sometimes undertaken at the instance of or in conjunction with the Arbitration Conference, can contribute immeasurably to the continued success of an institution which must surely go down in history as one of democracy's most successful experiments in private self-government.

Index of Cases

Index